Congreve, the Drama, and the Printed Word

𝕮𝖔𝖓𝖌𝖗𝖊𝖛𝖊,
the Drama, and the
Printed Word

Julie Stone Peters

STANFORD UNIVERSITY PRESS
Stanford, California 1990

Stanford University Press
Stanford, California
© 1990 by the Board of Trustees of the
Leland Stanford Junior University
Printed in the United States of America

CIP data appear at the end of the book

For M.A.P. and M.B.P.

Acknowledgments

There have been innumerable people who offered support for this project, but I would like to thank, in particular, Margaret Anne Doody and Earl Miner, who guided me through the early stages of this project. Alvin Kernan, Michael Seidel, James Shapiro, and Edward Tayler offered patient readings of various chapter drafts. I am especially grateful to James A. Winn, whose extraordinary Dryden lectures first brought me to the late seventeenth century, and who has given me invaluable advice and encouragement ever since. I would like to thank Kamyar Atabai, Cristina Caruso, and Janet Meyer for library work and typing. Helen Tartar and Karen Brown Davison have been most helpful and sympathetic editors.

The first chapter is a revised version of an article that originally appeared in *Publishing History* (Chadwyck-Healey, Spring 1986). Part of Chapter 6 is a revised version of an article that originally appeared in *English Studies* (April 1987). I am obliged to them for permission to publish. The photographs have been reproduced by permission of the British Library, the Trustees of the British Museum, and the Folger Shakespeare Library. I am grateful to the Fulbright Foundation for a grant that enabled me to spend a year in Oxford and London, and to the staffs of the Bodleian, British Library, Public Records Offices (London and Kew), Princeton and Columbia University libraries, Folger Shakespeare Library, and Bibliothèque Nationale (Paris).

I would like to thank my family for its supportiveness. Finally, for encouragement, and suggestions on everything from Greek recitation to eighteenth-century time to modern metaphors of inscription, even more for all the conversations, I am grateful to Kerry Christensen, Jacob Meskin, Rachel Rue, and Stuart Sherman, and to Paul Holdengräber for his ceaseless memory for the right books, his inspiration, his accompaniment of the project from its beginnings.

J.S.P.

Contents

Illustrations

Note to the Reader

Quotations from Congreve's poems are from *The Complete Works of William Congreve*, ed. Montague Summers, 4 vols. (London: Nonesuch Press, 1923). In-text citations to this edition bear the abbreviation "S," as in (S: p. 29), and all refer to volume 4. Unless otherwise specified, quotations from *Incognita* are from *Incognita or Love and Duty Reconcil'd*, ed. H. F. B. Brett-Smith (Oxford: Basil Blackwell, 1922). In-text citations to this edition bear the abbreviation *I*, as in (*I*: p. 52).

The following abbreviations serve as occasional identification of Congreve's plays:

DD	*The Double-Dealer*
LL	*Love for Love*
MB	*The Mourning Bride*
OB	*The Old Batchelour*
WW	*The Way of the World*

Unless otherwise specified, quotations from the plays and their prefaces are from *The Complete Plays of William Congreve*, ed. Herbert Davis (Chicago: University of Chicago Press, 1967). Some citations are simply to page number, but where appropriate, the citations include the act and scene number, as in (V.i., p. 62).

A complete edition of Congreve's works, which Oxford University Press was kind enough to permit me to examine and which will supplant Davis and Summers, is currently being prepared by D. F. McKenzie.

Congreve, the Drama, and the Printed Word

Introduction

In the late seventeenth century, theater and print began the history of their tense relations and imperfect alliance. Plays, of course, had been printed in England for more than a century: *Everyman*, *Fulgens and Lucrece*, *Magnyfycence* had all seen their way into print, but they were not the work of living playwrights and had little connection to a live theater. Shakespeare quartos were printed during his lifetime, but most were haphazardly reconstructed from the memory of others.[1] Jonson was frustrated by the transitory nature of the masque (which could not be duplicated in print) and carefully watched over the publication of his plays, but he was mocked by contemporaries for including an inferior genre under the lofty heading *Works*. It was not until the late seventeenth century, not until Tonson began to produce fine editions of English playwrights like Dryden, that dramatists began to worry over the details of both performance and print, regularly seeing to the publication of their own works and thus confirming the connection between print and the stage. The theater was joining itself to the page, defining itself against the printed word. It would never again entirely free itself from this strange relation. Congreve's struggles to integrate print and performance, his sensitivity to the problems of the book trade, and his irritation with the swelling masses of cheaply printed material are at the heart of this relation. His contact with the physical and material world of print shows the

foundations of his more subtle responses; the objects and institutions with which he surrounded himself, in turn, suggest
something of theatrical and print culture as a whole. A printed
work's story is not only that which unfolds in the words imprinted on its pages, but its own physical life, the way it was
made, the reasons for its making, the place it inhabits on the
shelf, the hands through which it has passed. Congreve's books
are not only those he wrote, but those he read, those he owned,
those sold beside his, those that others claimed he wrote, those
that told him what he was permitted to write and in what way.
The books printed by his publishers and the presses that pirated
his works, the books neatly arranged in the catalog of his library
shelves, and the books he never would have seen constitute a part
of the history of seventeenth-century relations between the
press and the stage.

Congreve's life, which mingles work in the theater with varied experiences with publishing and the book trade (as a playwright, poet, editor, translator, and scholar), serves as an
interval in which to investigate both the material and the
ideological relations between print and the stage. From the
publication of his novel, *Incognita*, to the appearance of *The Way
of the World*, he stressed his commitment to the world of the
theater. He was, above all, a dramatist, one who still believed
in performance as the supreme locus of poetry. But he worked
closely with the world of print, editing his own works and Dryden's, and keeping a detailed catalog of his meticulously chosen
personal library, which represented the best in English and Continental printing.[2] His life is not necessarily representative; his
writings are certainly not an accurate image of his life in any
literal sense and do not cover a very broad span of time. But the
most active phase of Congreve's career, stretching from the first
draft of *The Old Batchelour* in 1689 to the publication of the
three-volume *Works of Mr. William Congreve* in 1710, is a tense
and important juncture in the history of print: it encompasses
both the lapse of the Licensing Act in 1695 and the inaugura-

tion of the Copyright Act in 1710; in a few decades, the book trade swelled into a great and intricate financial organization.[3]

The material products of this organization wrought profound physical changes on the urban landscape in the form not only of books, newspapers, and pamphlets, but also of printed posters, theater bills and programs, printed handbills, bill headings, labels, tickets, printed forms, legal documents, receipts.[4] But the transformations in consciousness caused by print were even greater than the physical changes. The real story of the relation between print and performance lies in the interstices, in the less conscious gestures of a man of the stage whose theatrical productions have been shaped, to a large extent, by print. Congreve's five plays, poems, novel, and translations speak implicitly not only of the physical text itself, but also of the ways in which the physical text had altered experience, the experience of the stage in particular. My explorations in this study of the impact of print and the book (as physical object and sociocultural text) on Congreve and the late-seventeenth-century stage show the points of contact between the physical and cultural changes. Historical circumstances serve as the foundation for the broader connections I trace between material and literary culture, between the printed text and its place in dramatic consciousness, and for the distinctions I make between orality, print, and theater.

These three descriptive constructs, on which I rely throughout my work, have many variations and subdivisions.[5] Orality includes not only conscious invocation of the oral ("oral effects")—deliberate attempts to preserve it and its values—but also unconscious expressions of its values and qualities ("oral residue").[6] It includes the search for an appropriate oral expression in a print world, for instance in the praise of nonliterate song or the value of oral testimony; and it includes the retention of orality in literary conventions, for instance in the explicit imitation of epic models, in the value placed on aural formulas or the use of traditional themes as a species of cultural memory.

Print includes not only conscious use of print and its effects (for instance, in imagery derived from the book or the press) or further dissemination of religious, scientific, occult, and historical ideas spread by the press. It also includes both deliberate promotion of print values (such as standardization and categorization) and the unconscious assimilation of values and qualities on which a print culture places particular emphasis (for instance, originality, fancy, conciseness). Similarly, theater includes not only work in the physical theater itself, or explicit claims for the theater as a living art (as opposed to drama as a textual literature)—claims for the live voice, the presence of the actor, and the motion of gesture. It also includes a less-conscious devotion to the qualities of the live theater (for instance, presence, gesture, visible motion, change, and atemporality).[7]

By the late seventeenth century, the distinction between orality and literacy is greatly complicated by the expansion of print: preliterate residue mixes with and is often indistinguishable from reactions of opposition to the supposedly excessive literacy of print culture.[8] There is no direct and necessary set of equivalencies between orality and the live theater, and literacy and the printed drama. It is thus impossible to make two neatly divided lists that would detail a perfect dichotomy. Some of the more interesting elements of Congreve's relation to orality, literacy, print, the live theater, and the published dramatic text defy all categorization and qualify substantially the more generalized conclusions at which I have arrived. In consequence, I have tried to qualify all such generalized conclusions (and the generalized distinctions necessary to historical description); I have preferred not to blur contradictory details, even where they seemed to threaten consistency of argument.

I start with the presupposition that Congreve's works have a fundamental connection with oral culture and that their orality comes from several realms or sources, although there are not always rigid distinctions among these.[9] The most obvious and persistent kind of orality is that of everyday speech and communication (the orality that is the basis of a living, spoken language), which includes the studied orality of the witty elite. More subtle but equally strong for Congreve is the orality of classical oratory and Latin (which includes both the residual orality of preliterate Greece carried in the literary tradition and the active orality of seventeenth-century educational recitation, disputation, and oratory). The orality of the theater is inherent in the theater's form, especially insofar as it incorporates a formulaic, nontextual drama. It includes the other two forms of the oral (conversation and oratory) and is partially defined by them, but is more formulaic than conversation, more vernacular than oratory.[10] The strongly oral nature of late-seventeenth-century theater in particular appears partly in its repetition of themes and situations and in its rhetorical and formulaic nature (although, as I show, the subtle play and extraordinary variation within formulas suggest a movement away from the predominantly oral).[11] With the presupposition that Congreve is writing and thinking in an oral context, I explore the effect of print on these versions of orality.

In the first chapter, I look back at the theater during the four decades that followed the Restoration and trace how the published dramatic text changed the oral status of the theater, both in material and in ideological and rhetorical terms. Then, in Chapter 2, I turn to Congreve's material environment, the print institutions and forms that physically surrounded him. His publishers and his library began to dominate his notions of the live theater and the status of the dramatic poet. The ways in which he reconciled the interests of the stage with them show that he grew to imagine his own writing more in terms of Tonson's printing house and the catalog of his own library than in terms of the stage. In Chapter 3, I explore how Congreve's more generalized notions of orality were circumscribed by literacy, a literacy increasingly identified with print. Looking particularly closely at Congreve's poems, I identify the hold of print on the ostensibly oral realm of the ancients, of pastoral song and Homeric recitation. Chapter 4 extends this argument, examining

notions of scholarship, satire of pedantry, and Congreve's "theatrical" novel, *Incognita*, to identify the particular relation of the
tension between orality and print to the dichotomy between the
ancients and the moderns, and its effect on ideas of truth, time,
and inheritance.

In the next two chapters, I focus more on issues of specific
concern to the theater. I explore the ways that print, in particular, and the verbal, in general, put pressure on such theatrical
modes of expression as the visual image (in Chapter 5) and the
gestural sign and material object (in Chapter 6). In the last
chapter, I examine the ways that Congreve's resolution of the
old dichotomy between nature and art, in a fusion of the theatrical mask and novelistic naturalism, suggests a paradigm for
understanding his retreat from the theater into the library, into
the private spaces of the mind. The Conclusion tracks some of
the paths that the later theater will follow in trying to understand its particular relation to the world of print.

After the invention of printing in the mid-fifteenth century,
the effects of the print revolution were not fully interiorized (by
the theater or by the culture as a whole) until the mid-
seventeenth century. In Congreve, one can trace the discreet
marks of print's cultural assimilation taking place throughout
Europe; only after this assimilation had occurred was there, in
the 1730's and 1740's, a large-scale and animated discussion of
print (and its relation to the stage) in reaction to the culture's
recognition, finally, of the effects of an invention that had existed for three centuries.[12] My argument does not suggest that
print eliminates orality and the theatrical, either in Congreve
or elsewhere, but only identifies the ways in which print (as a
physical phenomenon and as a state of consciousness) has a more
profound impact than might be expected during this period,
which is at least thirty years before violent and explicit resistance to print becomes a literary and dramatic topos (in Pope
and Fielding, in particular, who are then echoed throughout the
eighteenth century). Neither do I wish to imply, with a naive
assertion of causal historicism, that literary fascination with is-

sues I examine (for instance, novelty, gossip, masks) is *caused* primarily by print. Print does influence the birth or (more often) rebirth of certain intellectual issues and literary gestures, especially as they arise in certain combinations and conjunctions; it influences those qualities the period chooses to identify in earlier models as worthy of imitation. But clearly many of the concerns I explore in relation to print arose with literacy, many reflect the early effects of the press during the Renaissance, and many are simply eternal human and literary concerns, although print has shifted their frequency and forms.

I am more interested in interaction than in genesis; I am more interested in the ways that print distorts the forms of older concerns than in the novelty (or lack of it) of such concerns. Nonetheless, if I am not making a purely causal historical argument, my argument is necessarily a historical one, although limited in its historicism.[13] Believing strongly that "God is in the details," as Blake wrote, that we can understand historical change only by standing still for a moment, I have chosen to identify only one phase (as seen in one man) of a larger transformation. That transformation does not indicate a steady progression from one step to another, but a cultural consciousness in constant flux, a consciousness that turns toward the light certain sides of itself at certain times. Nonetheless, I am able to trace some larger cultural reverberations in Congreve's life and works; these manifestations, exemplary for his period, point toward even greater changes in the eighteenth century. In brief, if Congreve's theater was still very much part of the oral past, whose forms it reiterated, Congreve strove to unify the physically manifested forms of print and the theatrical. This effort was strengthened by the fact that cultural consciousness of the oral and the theatrical was already circumscribed, more than he recognized, by print and the dramatic text. I have deliberately chosen to examine central problems (such as classicism, the concept of *ut pictura poesis*, the distinction between words and things, the investigation of the relation between nature and art), nearly clichés, both for the period and for the scholars who have investigated these problems repeatedly. I have chosen to examine the automatic and repetitive rhetorical gestures and thematic concerns of Congreve and other dramatists during the period, because a period's repetitions, its stylistic tics, its "organized network of obsessions" say more about it than do its brief, spluttering (if glorious) eccentricities.[14] To show the ways in which the shapes of such gestures are altered by print is to rediscover them through the lens of orality, print, and theater.

Drama and Print:
Toward an Alliance,
1660-1700

Minerva walks upon the Stage before us, and we are
more assured of the real presence of Wit when it
is delivered *viva voce*.

I have gratified the Bookseller. . . . the other two
Persons concern'd are the Reader and my self.

—Congreve, *Incognita*

$\mathfrak{I}$n the *Phaedrus*, Plato suggests
that writing can never capture the essential nature of the oral
language, which is flexible and which can explain, defend, and
modulate itself. The oral responds; the written takes the attitude of life but is silent.[1] When the printing press began to
spread throughout Europe in the late fifteenth century, the written word became a much more powerful medium than the oral
for disseminating information, entertainment, and argument.
By the end of the seventeenth century, when the press had at
last spread to the English provinces and appeared to many to
dominate London culture, the oral arts (poetry and rhetoric)
seemed in danger of dying out altogether. But even after print
became the dominant cultural force in England, the old oral and ·

rhetorical tradition preserved itself both actively, through the teaching of rhetoric and disputation, and more passively, in the consciousness of literary productions modeled on oral forms. The relation between learned Latin and oral culture is a good example of the complex interactions of form, literary technology, and consciousness. Latin, the basis of oral disputation and the stronghold of oratory, was spoken only by those who could write it: those who taught Latin did so with the aid of printed books, and its teaching encouraged a reverence for the written word.[2] A similarly paradoxical relation existed for several other forms of communication: there were both oral and printed versions of debates in Parliament, sermons, teaching, and, above all, plays. Although the stage remained alien in its essential nature to the fixed realm of writing and print, and remained the locus of movement and gesture, of the continually fleeting and the continually reborn, it had partly emerged from an early union of the oral and literate.[3] After print, the stage became increasingly dependent on the written word, increasingly involved an idea of text, increasingly encouraged the prestige of the written and the preserved through its reappropriation of the classical theater.

Print had been in England for almost two hundred years at the time of the Restoration. But until the great pamphlet wars of the Interregnum, it had shown its force very little as a medium for popular discourse, and the amount of printed matter circulated had been limited by the Star Chamber and controlled by the Stationers' Company. Like the manuscript, the book was still sacred, the prerogative of the clergy or the plaything of the aristocracy. Although Ben Jonson, always a step ahead, revealed a good deal of antagonism toward the news sheets in his 1626 *The Staple of News* (the first sign of direct warfare between the press and the stage),[4] his attention was directed to a fairly limited press, and he was the only playwright of the time to pay much attention to print. The early theater was quite sure of its place and function. But with the abolition of the Star Chamber in 1641 and the closing of the theaters in 1642, the stage neither could be nor was needed to be the locus of popular discourse and entertainment. The press was given an opportunity to take over many functions that the stage had once performed. Pushed aside by journalism, the stage ceased to be the center of news, the source of public information, and the focus of debate.[5]

When the theaters were reopened by Charles II in 1660, and two years later a Licensing Act was passed in response to a request by the Stationers' Company for control of the printers, the balance was temporarily readjusted. The trade was weakened by the power struggle between the printers and publishers.[6] Sir William Davenant's and Thomas Killigrew's patent acting companies began encouraging new playwrights (despite the fact that in the first few years of the Restoration revivals took up most of the season). In 1662, the new Licensing Act restricted printing to London, Oxford, Cambridge, and York, and the number of legal presses in London dropped from 60 to 20. In 1663, Roger L'Estrange, who was given sole right of printing news, began to enact severe measures against offending printers, publishers, and booksellers. (John Twyn, a London printer, was hanged, drawn, and quartered for seditious publishing in the year of L'Estrange's appointment.)[7] Many authors turned to the stage.

Piracy, nonetheless, had increased, not decreased, and in any case the readjustment did not last long. The plague and the great fire of 1665–66—which resulted in the deaths of many involved in printing, publishing, and bookselling, and which destroyed great numbers of books, including those preserved in St. Paul's Churchyard—paradoxically helped the trade regain some of the strength it had lost in 1662, for a need was felt to replace the lost printed matter. John Evelyn, in fact, complained to Lord Clarendon in 1666 of the haste of the booksellers to issue books, especially the classics, which had been destroyed in the fire:

Our booksellers follow their own judgment in printing the ancient authors, according to such text as they found extant, when first they entered their copy; whereas, out of the MSS. collated by the industry of later critics, those authors are exceedingly improved. . . . The printer taking up any smatterer in the tongues, to be the less loser; an exactness in this no ways importing the stipulation; by which means errors repeat and multiply in every edition, and that most notoriously in some most necessary school-books of value, which they obtrude upon the buyer, unless men will be at unreasonable rates for foreign editions.[8]

L'Estrange's activities were much moderated, new presses arose, and Henry Muddiman challenged L'Estrange's sole right to print news with his *Oxford Gazette* (1665), which became the *London Gazette* after the plague had retreated.[9] London printing rapidly expanded, and the Act of 1662 never regained its original strength. The Licensing Act was renewed in 1679 and reintroduced in 1684, and in 1685 L'Estrange was knighted and given a warrant to enforce printing regulations with all severity. Yet London publishing continued to expand. With the crowning of William, who deprived L'Estrange of his license and sent him to prison, a new flood of newspapers and pamphlets appeared. When the Licensing Act was not renewed in 1695, there was no longer a limit of twenty presses, and London publishing burgeoned.

Thus, for the first time in England, an abundant publishing world and two lively, competitive theaters were attempting to live side by side. The uneasy alliance that (as I will argue) did eventually develop between publishing and the theater grew only gradually during the thirty or forty years following the Restoration. It did not even achieve full and conscious form until the first decades of the eighteenth century, when the idea of the perfected library edition of the dramatic text was more fully established. These editions were protected by the Copyright Act of 1710, which guaranteed authors the rights to their own works.[10] The stage and print did eventually form a bond, although it was never to be an untroubled one. The earlier alliance that might have been expected to develop soon after the advent of printed plays, since play texts were often printed within a year after the first performance, did not take place in any significant way. Not only do Renaissance and early Restoration dramatic texts reflect little of the actual performance (aside from the usual dramatis personae), giving little stage direction and in fact often disguising the nature of relations among characters and scene groupings,[11] but the plays themselves, in their subject matter and frame of reference, barely acknowledge the existence of a print culture. The acted play still predominated over the printed.[12]

One might posit a theoretical reason for this lack of initial fellowship between text and stage: that orality is inherently alien to print, which does not permit spontaneous change and refuses language the power of response, is surely significant in the theater's initial resistance to print. But this theoretical reason was probably a less important factor than the more practical reasons. Throughout the seventeenth century, printed plays were of little monetary value to publishers (compared, for example, with dictionaries, classical texts, or religious writings) and were of even less monetary value to playwrights.[13] Because printed play texts were not used as scripts for actors, as performance aids (like our theater programs), or as re-creations of the theatrical experience at home after the performance, there was little correlation between stage success and publication success: Dryden's *Spanish Fryar* (1681), for instance, had enormous success on stage but was a publishing failure.[14] Thus, even the most successful play might bring the author little money from sale to a publisher. Other forms might be equally unprofitable. Translation, for instance, was usually paid only in copies.[15] Performance, on the other hand, could be quite lucrative: in addition to the initial sale to a theater at between £6 and £20, there were the author benefits, in which all proceeds from the third performance went to the dramatist, which, for a successful and prolific playwright, could provide a comfortable living.

Printing a play could, in fact, be a definite disadvantage for playwrights and theater managers. Even during the days of more stringent licensing, theft was common, especially by Irish and Scottish printers, who smuggled cheap editions back into

England. Although play piracy was less common than other forms of piracy, after the lapse of the Licensing Act in 1695, theft was no longer punishable, and the less scrupulous booksellers began to hire copyists expressly for that purpose.[16] The bookseller John Dunton wrote of the hacks employed by pirating booksellers: "These Gormandizers will eat you the very life out of a copy so soon as ever it appears; for, as the times go, *Original* and *Abridgement* are almost reckoned as necessary as Man and Wife; so that I am really afraid that a *Bookseller* and a *good conscience* will shortly grow some strange thing in the earth."[17] It is hardly surprising, then, that playwrights who earned nearly nothing from the printing of their own plays felt hostility toward this host of literary copyists (impoverished as they themselves may have been) and, by association, toward all involved in the expanding book market, which seemed to threaten all the older relations between patron and writer, stage and audience. The hostility was not yet as clearly defined as it was to become in the eighteenth century (in Swift, Pope, and Fielding, in particular), when the alliance of the physical forms of stage and print was stronger, perhaps because the market was in the process of experimenting. What were to become the stable arrangements among writers, booksellers, publishers, and printers were only beginning to develop.

But the radical expansion of bookselling, printing, and reading was real enough to have replaced the sense of the book as sacred manuscript with the sense of the book as all-too-secular trade production. It was real enough to have replaced the grand old trope of the Book of Nature with the literal forms of printed matter: the scribblings of hacks and the dirty sheets of the news press. Through most of classical, medieval, and Renaissance literature, writing and the book seem to fuse with the natural world: quills are ploughs or the finger of God, paper is fields or the expanse of the heavens, ink the seed or the wash of death. Writing and the book were also often imagined as representing abstract qualities, such as the human heart, intellectual processes, or physical urges (in both metaphors that compared these with writing and metaphors that compared writing with them). Shakespeare's Duke can still find "tongues in trees, books in the running brooks, / Sermons in stones" in *As You Like It* (1600).[18] Bacon, in *The Advancement of Learning* (1602), recommends "laying before us two books or volumes to study, if we will be secured from error; first the Scriptures, revealing the will of God, and then the creatures expressing his power," trying to speak to the memory of a world unmediated by the accumulation of material books.[19] Milton's blindness cuts him off from what he still imagines, in *Paradise Lost* (1667), as the "Book of knowledge fair," which to him is "Presented with a Universal blanc."[20] "Print" as metaphor in the Renaissance is incorporated into the divine-book topos. In 1623, George Wither, worried about the danger of "little prints," can write of "that Wisdome, Power, and Loue, Which is imprinted on the Heav'ns aboue In larger volumes, for their eies to see That in such little prints behold not thee."[21]

But over the course of the seventeenth century, the natural description that was once figured in writing and books is often most powerfully associated with secular print and the social or literal form of the book. The metaphoric forms of the book, writing, and literacy become strongly identified with print. For Suckling in *Aglaura* (1637), print can wittily serve as metonymy for perception: "Well, I'le away first, for the print's too big / If we be seen together."[22] In his *Sculptura* (1662), Evelyn insists on the link between the modern art of printed engraving, which he is promoting, and the biblical "graven image," at once literal and figural: print is the descendant of "the Tables of stone, engraven by the Finger of God himself."[23] The earlier denotation of "print" as general impression or indentation begins to mingle with its denotation as typographic copy: in Thomas Carew's erotic "Rapture" (1640), he makes "a tract for lovers on the printed snow" of his lover's body.[24] In Congreve's "Pindaric Ode" (1706) to the Earl of Godolphin, he imagines an Olympian horse race, in which the horses are "Th' Ætherial Authors of their Race" who "print the Plain" (S: pp. 135–36).[25]

Even more often, print serves as a metaphor for social situations: Molière's Trissotin and Vadius in *Les Femmes savantes* fight their battle for supremacy "chez Barbin" the bookseller.[26] Swift's battle between the ancients and moderns, several years later, will take the form of a struggle among printed books in St. James's library. For Wycherley's Harcourt in *The Country Wife*, "mistresses are like books. If you pore upon them too much, they doze you."[27] Jeremy's "Spirit of Famine" in *Love for Love* appears as a "bilk'd Bookseller" (I.i, p. 219). Bellmour in *The Old Batchelour* reads plays on a rainy day to get "into a fair Lady's Books" (I.i, p. 44). By the eighteenth century, the word *print*, even in metaphor, has a hard time disrobing itself of its identification with typography: Thomas Hearne threatens, "There may be danger they may print upon you, unless you print more Copies."[28] Pope's lisping numbers lead inevitably, in desperation at the inundations of the dunces, to the press:

> In Durance, Exile, Bedlam, or the Mint,
> Like *Lee* or *Budgell*, I will Rhyme and Print.[29]

Congreve does use the "book of time" figure as one of the ordering metaphors in his panegyric on William III, "The Birth of the Muse" (1697). There, in imitation of the Renaissance trope, "Nature" is written in the book:

> Abroad the bulky Volume [God] displays,
> And present views the Deeds of future Days.
> A beauteous Prospect paints the foremost Page,
> Where Nature's Bloom presents the Golden Age. (S: p. 55)

But in the plays, books are almost always literal books and are always social. They are "Play-books" and "Prayer-books" (or salacious novels under the cover of prayer books). They are "musty Books" of philosophy and "Folio Books." They are books of miscellany poems and books on poetic theory. Books less and less frequently make up the metaphoric texture of literature and increasingly appear in their literal forms, more particularly in the forms most widely disseminated by print. They are no longer the fields and the heavens but immutable materializations of the artifice of human machines.

Out of this sense of a world overflowing with the productions of the press come the period's stylized and conventional forms of complaint against the excesses of writing made possible by print. For Congreve, each season produces "Crops of Coxcombs" and "Flouds of Fools."[30] He refers self-mockingly to his *Old Batchelour* as "the first Offence I have committed in . . . Poetry" (p. 29). In *Love for Love*, the servant Jeremy may eventually "learn to make Couplets, to tag the ends of Acts" and even "get the Maids to Crambo in an Evening, and learn the knack of Rhiming" (I.i, p. 218). And in *The Way of the World*, Petulant no longer speaks few words, but *"Volumes, Folio's, in less than Decimo Sexto"* (IV.i, p. 453).

The expansion of the trade both resulted from and caused the increase in literacy, which by the late seventeenth century was a norm, at least among upper-middle-class city dwellers.[31] By the Restoration, every "person of breeding" had easy access to books, if not a complete and well-documented library, and the rapid growth of book auctions, after the first one in 1676, encouraged reading in the provinces, which spread with the founding of provincial printing and publishing after 1695.[32] Illiteracy becomes the exception rather than the rule. Even the illiterate Petulant (tormented by Witwoud for his illiteracy) can write his name. *Illiterate* becomes a common adjective and epithet, reflecting the cultural importance of literacy. For instance, Congreve (in the epilogue to *The Double-Dealer*) taunts his potential critics for their figurative illiteracy:

> But tho' he [Congreve] cannot Write, let him be freed
> At least from their Contempt, who cannot Read. (p. 204)

One response to the expansion of literacy and the press was the increasingly clamorous demand for a stricter regulation of the press, particularly after 1695. Examples include Francis Gregory's *A Modest Plea for the Due Regulation of the Press* (1699) or the anonymous *A Letter to a Member of Parliament, shewing the*

Necessity of Regulating the Press (1699). In 1701–2, an advertiser in *The Post Man* suggests: "That whereas the Shop-keepers throughout this Kingdom have received great prejudice by the Hawkers, Pedlers and Petty Chapmen, it is proposed that all Shop-keepers of the said Cities, Towns and Corporations, do represent their Grievances to their Representatives, that so some good Bill may pass the House of Commons, that this clandestine way of Trade may be prevented."[33] Surreptitious publishing employed numerous hawkers and "Mercury-Women" to distribute the literature that had evaded licensing, and the established booksellers complained of "Market Higlers and Pedlars in the Country" who destroyed trade.[34] But these only added to the already growing numbers of regular book runners for the lighter presses and the bookselling establishments of the members of the lawful press.

Booksellers' shops began to spread throughout London, and certain locations became renowned for their specialties. Publishing was also developing new kinds of material. Bibliography and bibliographical history were appearing increasingly: in 1668, Robert Clavell and John Starkey began to publish their periodical register of books, *Mercurius Librarius*, which was superseded in 1670 by the Term Catalogues; in 1673, Thomas Basset published the first English catalog of law books. After 1695, the increase in printing was even more substantial and included an exceptionally large number of new plays, in addition to new newspapers, broadsides, pamphlets, and other printed ephemera. Even the paper and pamphlet duties of 1696 did not slow the increase of printed matter in London but merely encouraged foreign printers, who glutted the English market with their more cheaply printed surreptitious books.[35] If there was a decrease in quality with an increase in output, as Evelyn asserted and as such examples as the Bible (with no fewer than 6,000 errors) seemed to prove,[36] this may have been due to the increasing complexity of the trade, as it tried to adjust itself to greater specialization and as the market, rather than the Stationers' Company, became the regulating body. The power of the Stationers' Company had been on the decline throughout the Interregnum, and the new office created for L'Estrange, Surveyor of the Press, effectively took over the duties that had formerly belonged to the stationers.[37] Although the Stationers' Company attempted to regain old privileges (among them, searching for unlicensed books and controlling those stationers who tried to make their own rules), L'Estrange's *Considerations and Proposals in Order to the Regulation of the Press* (1663), addressed to Charles II, which denounced the Stationers' Company, seemed to be winning the battle for a time. Even after the 1688 Revolution, when L'Estrange lost his power, the Stationers' Company remained weakened and never regained its sway.

Different combinations of the matrix of printer, publisher, and bookseller occurred during the 40 years following the Restoration, but slowly the independent publisher-bookseller began to predominate. The bookseller would acquire the manuscript from the author (whether by sale or by another arrangement), sometimes edit the manuscript, hire an outside printer, and then sell the finished sheets or books.[38] (After the 1710 Copyright Act, the three functions diverged even further.) Such specialization left the publisher-bookseller freer to perform certain functions, such as increased editing and proofreading and prepublication binding. It also meant greater economic complexity for the trade and thus greater economic importance. Further, it led to more diversified ways of selling old stock, such as auctions and trade-sale dinners, where members of the trade would begin drinking and eating early in the morning, start the sale with the midday meal, and finish in the evening (an old practice, but on the increase during the late seventeenth century).[39] Another previously little-tried way of selling stock was subscription publishing. This had first been attempted as early as 1617 but became a reliable technique for assuring sales only with the publication of Tonson's edition of *Paradise Lost* in 1688. In the same year, the Licensing Act expired, and new techniques were needed to handle the vastly increased competition.

By 1700, when Congreve was associating closely with Tonson, who had published his last four plays and several of his
poems, the trade had changed. Tonson's achievements were
both the culmination of several decades of trade experimentation and the beginning of an era in publishing. Although there
are no direct causes and effects, the physical and legal changes
I have outlined helped bring about a number of other important
changes. For instance, the rise of the powerful independent
publisher-bookseller with a distinctive vision encouraged pressure toward the stabilization of copyright to protect such publishers. The benefits that accrued to authors as a result, including author-held copyright after 1710, gave a new power to the
author-celebrity, which in turn encouraged the modern conception of individual authorship and other notions of authorial individualism.

These conjunctions of circumstance mark the true beginning
of alliance between publishing and the theater, both the technical alliance (which takes place in the physical text) and the
alliance of consciousness (which expresses itself in the theater's
absorption and reformulation of print values). The former can
be quite clearly traced in the decades that preceded the
Congreve-Tonson partnership. It is not mere coincidence that,
during this period for the first time, living playwrights were
treated as celebrities and that editions of their works were at
least planned, if not produced, during their lifetimes. (Jonson
had appeared ridiculous to his contemporaries, in 1616, for
calling his own edition *The Works*.) Dryden and Congreve were
the most notable of these new playwrights, and as Dryden noticed, Congreve was the first playwright to have his name
printed in the playbills, a mark of the new status of the
dramatist.[40] The condition of authorship had changed, and with
it the price of literature had risen, at least for some publishers.
In 1667, Milton had received £5 for *Paradise Lost*, with a promise of £5 more for each new edition; a decade earlier, Dryden
may have been doing hackwork for the publisher, Henry Herringman, in exchange for room and board.[41] The 250 guineas

that Tonson paid for Dryden's *Fables* in 1698–99 shows the radical nature of the change.[42]

A strong association between playwright and publisher, such as that between Dryden or Congreve and Tonson, was possible only now that many publishers were functioning as independent agents. It was possible only now that playwrights in need of money (as opposed to courtier-playwrights like Sedley and Buckingham) felt they had some grounds for both an artistic and a financial claim. Other factors also affected the change in the relationship between playwright and publisher: the old patronage system had been showing signs of overload for some time, as the expanding press had disseminated increasingly fulsome dedications. After the death of Charles II and the flight of James, the court no longer had as much impact on the kind of theater performed, and despite Mary's interest, plays were not written primarily for the court. Under William and Mary, commerce was given much more serious attention, and gentlemen could more legitimately involve themselves with it. Printing itself—the dissemination and standardization of certain kinds of writing—had as much cultural impact as changes in attitudes toward commerce. Dictionaries and grammars influenced ideas about correctness in language and printing, and the French interest in both language and design was carried to England by beautiful editions of the French classical stage, later by books such as the translation of Simon Gribelin's engraving guide, *Book of Several Ornaments Invented and Engraved* (1687), and Jean de la Caille's *Histoire de l'imprimerie* (1689). The achievements of the French Academy suggested to the English that they ought to have one of their own. Dryden, for instance, in his 1664 preface to *The Rival Ladies*, wrote: "I am Sorry, that (Speaking so noble a Language as we do) we have not a more certain Measure of it, as they have in *France*, where they have an Academy erected for that purpose."[43]

Under these conditions, Congreve was not the only playwright to become increasingly involved in the publication of his own works; playwrights and their publishers grew less care-

less about the accidentals of printing. This meant greater experimentation with, and greater standardization of, such elements as arrangement of the text on the page, spelling, and
punctuation, in addition to more careful proofreading and the
reediting of subsequent editions. Reediting, in turn, meant
that texts began to reflect more of the reader's taste. Playwrights
also discovered certain advantages in publishing their plays:
they could offer to their public segments that had been left out
in performance, as was the case with many productions (including Dryden's *Don Sebastian* in 1689, Congreve's *Double-
Dealer* in 1694, Granville's *Heroick Love* in 1698, and Rowe's
Ambitious Stepmother in 1700). They could also defend themselves from attack (by means of critical commentary) in their
prefaces and dedications, asserting their authorship against the
more communal authority of the company or the often tyrannic
authority of the manager.[44] It is hard to see a direct, clear, and
simultaneous increase in all these factors: Jonson had given his
printed masques "those briefe touches, which may leave behind
some shadow of what it was"; proofreading had been on the increase throughout the century, even for the illegal presses; modern spelling was not much used until the first years of the eighteenth century.[45] But there was a general development that cul-
minated in the work of publishers such as Tonson.

As a result, the later playwrights showed less of an unequiv-
ocally rejecting attitude toward the publishing world than the
playwrights under Charles II had shown. Those interested in
the actual publication of their texts, in the standardization of
the written and printed language, or in the great critical debates
about the stage (debates that had spawned a storm of pamphlet
criticism) could not simply pretend that they had nothing to do
with the print world and that publication was an event involv-
ing only the publisher and a few readers, necessary only to prevent miscopying. They had an active share in the interests and
business of publishing, and their plays show a greater assimilation of print-world values, although explicit references to the
print world continue to be, at their mildest, self-consciously

ironic or, more usually, harshly satiric. Such a development could be proved only with numerous examples, and there are also admittedly many counterexamples: the drama of the late seventeenth century is too varied to hold up to any rigid descriptions of development.[46] But drama throughout the period incorporates ideas that could emerge only from a prolific press, while it mocks images of the same ideas because of their connections with the world of print. For instance, it is true that the concern for a "more certain measure" of language, the obsession with the distinctions between false and true wit, and the satiric indignation over the misuse of words (which includes not only misapplication and mispronunciation but also jargon and regional accents) are all repeatedly expressed on the stage throughout the later seventeenth century. There are, however, a change of tone and an increasing consciousness on the part of the playwrights that they are situated in a print world, in and against which they must define themselves. This crisis in the theater's assimilation of print, which would grow more powerful during the eighteenth century, begins to express itself clearly during the decade in which Congreve is writing.

Many of the wit-sex-and-money comedies so popular during the 1670's fight the hardening of rules into orthodoxy, celebrate the flexibility that language has of inverting its own intentions, insist upon the refusal of language to bow to dictionary definitions. These plays seem to reject the rigidity of a printed language: the word *honour* gets distorted until it ceases to have a determinate meaning; both heroes and heroines use wit to defend themselves against the larger confinement that a rigidly referential language represents, liberating language from context in order to liberate themselves. The late 1670's and the 1680's were uneven years for the theater: a spate of political plays was followed by a period in which few new plays were performed, but finally, in the last few years, the kinds of plays that would dominate the 1690's began to appear. It is difficult to see a sharp discontinuity for the theater in any of the major events of the period (the Popish Plot, the end of the King's Company,

the death of Charles II, and the 1688 revolution). But the fact
that the issue of important differences between the plays of the
1670's and the plays of the 1690's has been so insistently debated by critics suggests that something happened, and the
plays of the 1690's do reflect a significant change.[47] The more
humane wit-contract-and-sympathy comedies that came after
the 1688 revolution are as concerned with language as those of
the 1670's had been, but even those that deliberately imitate
the "harder" comedy of the 1670's still incorporate highly stylized language and reject more firmly the mad flow of wit's implied and semicoherent connections to meaning. The witty
cuckolding heroes (Horners and Dorimants) become the witty
ladies' tea-table coxcombs (Tattles and Witwouds); the heroines
ponder their choices more closely; the heroes talk less wit and
more judgment, in more balanced clauses, more like a printed
page.

The opposition of Dorimant's quicksilver patter (in Etherege's *The Man of Mode*) to the sound sentences of Mirabell (in
The Way of the World) illustrates the difference. When Mirabell
has been begging a word with Millamant, and she finally gives
him leave to say what he would, he can only exclaim, "I say that
a Man may as soon make a Friend by his Wit, or a Fortune by
his Honesty, as win a Woman with plain Dealing and Sincerity." Her response begins an exchange that emphasizes the contrast between his "Sincerity" and her refusal to offer a similar
sincerity during their courtship:

MILLAMANT   Sententious *Mirabell*! Prithee don't look with that vi-
    olent and inflexible wise Face, like *Solomon* at the dividing of
    the Child in an old Tapestry-hanging.

MIRABELL   You are merry, Madam, but I wou'd perswade you for
    one Moment to be serious.

MILLAMANT   What, with that Face? No, if you keep your Coun-
    tenance, 'tis impossible I shou'd hold mine . . . Think of me.
                                                            Exit.

MIRABELL   I have something more—Gone—Think of you! To
    think of a Whirlwind, tho' 'twere in a Whirlwind, were a Case

of more steady Contemplation; a very tranquility of Mind and Mansion. A Fellow that lives in a Windmill, has not a more whimsical Dwelling than the Heart of a Man that is lodg'd in a Woman. There is no Point of the Compass to which they cannot turn, and by which they are not turn'd; and by one as well as another; for Motion not Method is their Occupation. To know this, and yet continue to be in Love, is to be made wise from the Dictates of Reason, and yet persevere to play the Fool by the force of Instinct. (II.i, pp. 422–23)

The symmetrical phrases of "sententious *Mirabell*" have both the carefulness and the inflexibility of the printed page. His mind is not framed for an easy acceptance of Millamant's constant motion, her unceasing flickerings and regenerations, her theatrical state.[48] It is primarily his assertions, not hers (in the famous "proviso" scene), that are labeled "Item," "Article," "Imprimis"; his is the language of legal contract. Whirlwind Millamant, the woman of performance, is in a sense defeated in the end; she is brought into the contract that he insists they share and is won into a society that can trust only the inflexibly written. When Mirabell closes the last seeming loophole of a play without loopholes, a play as tightly structured as a legal document, he does so by producing a legal document (Mrs. Fainall's deed of conveyance) in order to get a legal document (a marriage contract that would include all of Millamant's fortune). Mirabell's well-edited speeches and his contractual, print-world mind are the promise of the future for them, whether or not Millamant remains "sole Empress" of her tea table.

If print freezes motion, it also allows leisure for characters to engage more in complex thought and to put themselves through elaborate self-examination: a theater audience can follow only large gesture and simple plot; the reader, on the other hand, can turn back pages, put down the book, and in novels and other prose fiction, follow a character's inner experience without the artificial intrusion of asides and soliloquies. The distinction between the externally focused oral theater and the internally focused literate theater can be seen in the transition from early-

Greek to late-Roman theater. Greek theater, insistently verbal as it may be, is less interested in private thought than in the use of aurally effective rhetoric for the narration of event. Seneca's use of the private internal passions in his closet drama shows one difference between the notion of appropriate subject matter held by the dominantly oral drama and that held by a drama already strongly literate. In drawing so heavily on Seneca (rather than, say, Sophocles) for treatment of character, the Renaissance instinctively understood the importance of private thought on stage for an audience that had known the silent reading of prose narrative. The abundant use of asides and soliloquies was one way of filling this need to expose private thought in the midst of public action; the particular gift of Shakespeare, for instance, for this revelation of internal complexity, was another way of answering this need more than adequately.[49] Still, neither Seneca nor Shakespeare would have imagined his plays being read in the silent solitude of a private room, even if the works might be read aloud rather than performed. Shakespeare's growing reputation during the eighteenth century is partly due to that gift for the revelation of internal experience, which filled a need that grew more powerful as print literacy became increasingly dominant. The eighteenth and nineteenth centuries canonized particular Renaissance soliloquies precisely because of their affinity with the internal complexity of novelistic experience. Although Shakespeare could make Hamlet ask whether it was better to be or not to be, it was only a more print-formed era that could define this internal incertitude, this "inability to *act*" (as the twentieth century would have it) as the highest moment of the theater.

By the last decade of the seventeenth century, the sense that the drama was not only theatrical action but also private and solitary reading had already increased the need for the revelation of internal experience, which asides and soliloquies could offer. But it had led at the same time to an expectation for naturalism (which prose narrative seemed to be able to provide), and asides and soliloquies interfered with that naturalism. Audiences were beginning to feel uncomfortable with the oral expression of silent thought. It was unnatural, after all, to speak private thoughts aloud, the "critics" complained. In defending the use of soliloquies in the theater in his dedication to *The Double-Dealer*, Congreve was protecting the theater from what seemed to him the inappropriate application of one genre's naturalism on another genre:

When a man in Soliloquy reasons with himself, and *Pro's* and *Con's*, and weighs all his Designs: We ought not to imagine that this Man either talks to us, or to himself; he is only thinking, and thinking such Matter, as were inexcusable Folly in him to speak. But because we are conceal'd Spectators of the Plot in agitation, and the Poet finds it necessary to let us know the whole Mystery of his Contrivance he is willing to inform us of this Person's Thoughts; and to that end is forced to make use of the expedient of Speech, no other better way being yet invented for the Communication of Thought. (p. 120)

Against the evidence that writing is in fact quite an effective tool for communicating thought silently, Congreve here attempts to claim that live speech is still the best means for communicating thought. The theater must be defended from the infiltration of prose fiction, which (unpleasant to admit as it may be) can offer the communication of thought without forcing characters into the folly of speaking aloud what ought to be private. But even while he defends the prerogatives of the live voice, Congreve asserts the primacy of the print-culture value for character complexity. He defends the very quality that contributes to the reading (rather than performance) value of the plays and that partially replaces the performance qualities not reproducible in print. The plot may be in agitation (live and in the process of being performed), but the viewers, like readers, are "conceal'd Spectators," hidden recipients of the "Mystery" of the poet's "Contrivance."

Other playwrights responded similarly. The secret histories, novels, criminal "biographies," fictitious letters, and other forms that poured from the press during the 1690's encouraged playwrights to try to reproduce the inward struggle on stage.

Hamlet echoes were at the height of fashion, even in comedies—for instance in *Love for Love*, in which Valentine's mad
scenes parody Hamlet's. Vanbrugh's *The Provoked Wife* (1697)
offers a typical example of the inward struggle articulated, in
Lady Brute's self-examination on what to do about her brutish
husband:

> I thought I had charms enough to govern him, and that where
> there was an estate a woman must needs be happy; so my vanity
> has deceived me and my ambition has made me uneasy. But
> some comfort still. . . . I never loved him, yet I have been ever
> true to him, and that in spite of all the attacks of art and nature
> upon a poor weak woman's heart in favor of a tempting lover.
> Methinks so noble a defense as I have made should be rewarded
> with a better usage. Or who can tell? Perhaps a good part of
> what I suffer from my husband may be a judgement upon me
> for my cruelty to my lover. Lord, with what pleasure could I
> indulge that thought, were there but a possibility of finding
> arguments to make it good. And how do I know but there may?
> Let me see. What opposes?[50]

From this follows a lengthy philosophical debate from which
she emerges with the conclusion, "Lord, what fine notions of
virtue do we women take up upon the credit of old foolish philosophers."

In the tragedies, the ethical assumptions based on "foolish"
ancients were similarly replaced by pensive, pathos-ridden
moderns, although these characters often retained the heroism
and heroic diction of the tragedies of the 1660's and 1670's.
During the 1670's, spectacular tragedy, full of horror and fancy
machines, reigned alongside (and sometimes in conjunction
with) continuations of the heroic mode and attempts at more
classical tragedy. Few of these plays were intended for reading;
many relied so heavily on effects that they would have had little
impact on the closet reader. The late 1670's and the early 1680's
brought political plays, but soon after, serious theater almost
entirely disappeared. Tragedy reemerged after the revolution,
and characters began soliloquizing less to explain plot and more

to reveal their thoughts and passions: as in the comedies, the psychology of prose fiction began to appear on the stage. A few brief examples demonstrate the mode. In Southerne's *Fatal Marriage* (1694), Isabella has remarried, and her long-lost husband, Biron, bewails his tragic circumstances:

> O, any Curse but this might be remov'd!
> But 'twas the rancorous Malignity
> Of all ill Stars combin'd, of Heaven and Fate,
> To put it quite out of their Mercies reach,
> To speak Peace to us if; [*sic*] they cou'd repent,
> They cannot help us now. Alas! I rave:
> Why do I tax the Stars, or Heaven, or Fate?
> They are all innocent of driving us
> Into despair; they have not urg'd my Doom.[51]

Such pathos changes to melancholy passion when a villainous heroine, like Homais in Delarivière Manley's *Royal Mischief* (1696), soliloquizes:

> Strickt silence fills the lodgings, the Musick's placed,
> The Banquet's ready, and I more so than all,
> Will he not come, 'tis a long Parly:
> Methinks on such a Summons, he shou'd grow
> Fond of a Surrender; but hence be gone
> These Melancholy Doubts that loads [*sic*] my Thoughts,
> And turns them into Fears; the Fantoms
> Cannot stand, the day break off my Eyes.
> Ay, see they fly before this Lovely Face,
> My Hopes glow in my Cheeks and speak my Joy,
> My Eyes take fire at their own Luster, and
> All my Charms receive addition from themselves,
> Pleas'd at their own Perfection.[52]

This soliloquy is colored by the psychological intimacy that a sense of echoing solitude can achieve. The emptiness of the social apparatus and the prepared music and banquet so far unheard and untasted only emphasize Homais's solitude. She addresses her "Doubts" as sentient forces and seems to people her world with the "Fantoms" of these personified doubts, thoughts, and fears, just as Richard II in the prison "people[s] this little world" with his thoughts.[53] But Homais goes even farther, for this act of generation twists itself into a narcissistic solipsism in which other humans seem to be redundant. Her eyes become mirrors that see into themselves; her "Charms" find all the sensual pleasure they need in "their own Perfection." For a moment, only her consciousness of her self, the union of her passions and body, is important.

If the pathetic soliloquies and the (particularly female) passionate self-observation of the later tragedies were not the soliloquies of the neoclassical drama, it did not mean that the tragedians were any less interested in following the standards set out by the critics, as long as they could do so without destroying the entertainment value of their productions or contradicting "history." In the plays, they increasingly attempt to assert their own critical standards, defending themselves (in their prefaces and dedications) from critical objections that had been made after the productions. "The principal Objection made against this Tragedy is the warmth of it," wrote Manley in the preface to *The Royal Mischief*, but "all wou'd have condemn'd me if venturing on another [passion than love] I had fail'd, when gentle love stood ready to afford an easy Victory, I did not believe it possible to pursue him too far, or that my Lawrel shou'd seem less graceful for having made an entire Conquest." Passion and pathos are important features in the defenses. "Some have objected, that it is unnatural for a Hero to Swoon," wrote George Granville in the preface to his *Heroick Love* (1698), but "Indeed in some Cases where the Passion must be presum'd so Violent or so Tender, that words can but faintly represent it, it is then a Beauty to express it in this manner, and by far more Pathetick, than any Speech thô never so Rhetorical."[54] Rhetoric is here opposed to passion; the critic, who belongs to the rhetorical world of oral disputation, is opposed to the playwright, who needs the printed preface to buttress his use of gesture.

Strangely enough, print had been responsible for much of the prestige of the oral-rhetorical criticism that so many playwrights opposed in the 1690's. Plays written after the Restoration had been the first in England to show much response to literary criticism and to develop to any extent a native criticism based only partly on the ancients. Increased publishing had permitted greater access to and wider dissemination of not only classical texts but also the criticism that had emerged from the French stage and (eventually) contemporary English criticism. It had also given rise, through its impulse toward standardization, to a concept of criticism as absolute knowledge: if all have access to the same information (as they do in a widespread print culture), then surely all who think rightly will have the same ideas.

This is the unstated assumption of Buckingham's satire of rhymed heroic tragedy, *The Rehearsal* (1671), in which Buckingham's attitudes are reflected (in reverse) in the voice of the poet Bayes.[55] The prologue claims that *The Rehearsal* promotes the "Rules" by showing the abuse of them:

> For (changing Rules of late as if men writ
> In spite of Reason, Nature, Art and Wit)
> Poets make us laugh at Tragœdy,
> And with their Comedies they make us cry.[56]

As might be expected, Bayes does not much like the tyrannic critics who make such rules, critics who, insisting on a Jonsonian neoclassicism, object to Bayes's failure to observe the unities, his verbal excesses, and his lack of proper characterization (all shown in scenes from Bayes's play):

BAYES   Let a man write never so well, there are, now-a-days, a sort of persons they call Critiques, that, I'gad, have no more wit in 'em than so many Hobby-horses; but they'l laugh you, Sir, and find fault, and censure things that, A gad, I'm sure they are not able to do themselves. A sort of envious persons, that emulate the glories of persons of parts, and think to build their fame, by calumniating of persons that, I gad, to my knowledge, of all persons in the world are, in nature, the persons that do as much despise all that.[57]

If these worthy critics (in Buckingham's view) troubled poets like Bayes, the critic was in turn faced with a problem, one that Bayes identified: in a culture in which all (theoretically) had access to the same literature, then the right to write and to comment, the right to assert critical judgment, no longer belonged only to the privileged. When all have access, it was felt, too many can claim expertise.[58] Rymer, in his 1674 preface to a translation of Rapin's *Reflections on Aristotle's Treatise of Poesie*, complained:

Till of late years *England* was as free from Criticks, as it is from *Wolves*, that a harmless well-meaning Book might pass without any danger. But now this priviledge, whatever extraordinary Talent it requires, is usurped by the most ignorant: and they who are least acquainted with the game, are aptest to bark at every thing that comes in their way. Our fortune is, *Aristotle*, on whom our Author makes these *Reflections*, came to this great work better accomplished.[59]

This complaint, and the satire that emerged from it, grew increasingly clamorous, as each work of written criticism generated even more comment. Interestingly enough, it was the spoken criticism, not the written, that the playwrights grew to resent toward the last decade of the century. The word *critick* came to connote less and less the learned writer of treatises on Aristotle. Increasingly, the word was identified with such sleazy figures as the critic picking the mercenary poet's pocket in the *Love for Love* "portraits" (I.i, p. 233). Critics were, increasingly, ignorant playgoers, typified by Calista in the anonymous *Female Wits* (first performed in 1696). According to the dramatis personae, Calista is "a Lady that pretends to the learned Languages, and assumes to her self the Name of a Critick."[60] Or they were simply members of the audience toward whom the poet might have reason to feel hostile (as in the preface to *The Female Wits*).

Most of those playwrights who complained were established, had written some criticism themselves, and were complaining about each other very little, if at all. They were instead referring primarily to those who, as Bayes had said, censure what they themselves cannot do. Some of the "criticks" were aristocrats (wealthy and less than wealthy), but many were young lawyers, second sons, or others who wished to compensate for their meager means with a form of literary nobility. And many were women, increasingly a vocal group, as the prologues that plead with "the ladies" attest. They were those critics in the boxes, pit, and coffeehouses who could threaten playwrights' livelihoods by damaging the reputations of their plays, or those outsiders (women, for instance) who threatened the right of established playwrights to control the literary market. Those playwrights who complained were defending themselves (successful published playwrights, increasingly a professional group)[61] from two other sectors: one was made up of the older style of learned gentleman "critick," who disdained the vulgarity of print and who would have no need for the money generated from it; the other was made up of the impoverished outsider, the female playwright, for instance, or the wit at Will's Coffeehouse, where "the spirit of Famine appears" (*LL*, I.i, p. 218) to haunt those trying unsuccessfully to publish. The professionally successful could afford to take an old-style gentlemanly stance in declining the need for patronage or publishing income from their works, even when they belonged to a new and distinctly ungentlemanly class. Bayes, a man of the print world, disdains those who write for money: "For what care I for money? I gad, I write for Fame and Reputation."[62] John Oldmixon (as a later, living incarnation of Bayes), in his dedication to *The Grove* (1700), describes more gently the class of hungry playwrights who write only for money: "Fame is not the Mistress they Court: To talk of a future Reputation when a present Supply is to be rais'd wou'd to them seem Silly and Extravagant. Indeed I think they are very much to be excus'd; for a man must have little Stomach to hear of an Immortal Name, when his own puts him in mind of Mortality."[63] But Oldmixon quite clearly distinguishes himself from them. Calista of *The Female Wits*, on the other hand, can represent both kinds of threat at once to Oldmixon-style professionalism: she is forever marginal, economically and socially; but she has leisure for pretending (like Molière's *femmes savantes*) to be part of the older nobility of learning:

CALISTA   Madam, I have read all your excellent Works, and I dare say, by the regular Correction, you are a Latinist, tho' *Marsilia* laughs at it.

MRS. WELLFED   *Marsilia* shows her Folly, in laughing at what she don't understand. Faith, Madam, I must own my ignorance, I can go no further than the eight Parts of Speech.

CALISTA   Then I cannot but take the Freedom to say, you, or whoever writes, imposes upon the Town. . . . I'll maintain it with my Life; Learning is absolutely necessary to all who pretend to Poetry.[64]

The Female Wits was "written in imitation of the Rehearsal," according to the preface, and the imitation is close in many respects. But one thing it chooses not to follow is Buckingham's satire of Bayes's worship of innovation. Such satire belongs to a theater hostile to the print world, not to a theater essentially tied to print, for innovation is largely a postprint value. In a culture in which it is difficult to accumulate and preserve knowledge—a preprint culture—the preservation of the old remains the most important concern. But in a culture in which accumulation and preservation become easier, the old loses some of its value through excess supply, and originality increases in demand.[65] If print produces numerous tangible versions of accumulated and repeated history, if pirates in a print culture can flood markets with reprocessed classics and plagiarized pages, the whole notion of piracy and plagiarism can emerge only from a print culture that encourages novelty, originality, and the ownership of words.

Print, then, produces both reduplications and a value for novelty. Bayes, as a man of print, embodies the paradox. His "Rule of Transversion," which amounts to theft and then compilation of scraps snatched from assorted books, has results all too similar to the kinds of things pirates had been producing for decades. At the same time, his value for the new approximates what an active news press had taught the public to crave: only the most recent, the most fresh, the most hot-off-the-press, the most original.[66] Bayes will do nothing onstage "that ever was done before." In defense of his play, he offers the poetics of his plot (the dual reign of the kings of Brentford):

> Why? because it's new; and that's it I aim at. I despise your Johnson, and Beaumont, that borrow'd all they writ from Nature: I am for fetching it purely out of my own fancie, I.[67]

Bayes's interest in "fancie," his insistence on "elevation and surprise," his joy in mystery and obfuscation are similarly part of values that can be promoted only by those who have the leisure of a print culture, in which clarity and direct knowledge are too easily accessible.[68] Thus, "instead of beginning with a Scene that discovers something of the Plot," Bayes begins "with a whisper,"[69] and when one of the observers complains that the sense of Bayes's song is "not very plain," Bayes answers:

> Plain? why, did you ever hear any people in Clouds speak plain? They must be all for flight of fancie, at its full range, without the least check or controul upon it. When once you tie up spirits, and people in Clouds to speak plain, you spoil all.[70]

It is easy to see the debate of the ancients and moderns suggested in these issues, to see it accelerating during this period, even in literature that does not label itself part of the debate. The insistence on the primacy of "fancie," the value for novelty, the rejection of the older criticism—all these were typical modern stances (at least on the nonscientific side of the argument); all these accorded with print-culture values. The playwrights, then, who found themselves engaged in such a culture and yet who continued to align themselves with the ancients, were increasingly developing an idea of two kinds of theater. One was the classic, including not only ancient drama, but also Jonson, Beaumont, and Fletcher (although they were replaced by Shakespeare toward the end of the century). The other was the kind

produced by most modern playwrights, by hacks and penniless
poets, the refuse of print. This double view of the theater—the
veneration of it, on the one hand, as the site where poetry had
been born in Greece, and the disdain for it as the locus of popular spectacle—was not new. Sir Thomas Bodley suggested such
a double view when he recommended that his keepers include
all classical drama in his library, but that they exclude "Such
Books as Almanacks, Plays, and an infinite Number, that are
daily Printed, of very unworthy matters and handling such, as
methinks, both the Keeper and Underkeeper should Disdain to
seek out, to deliver to any Man. . . . Haply some Plays may be
worthy the Keeping: But hardly one in Forty."[71]

The double view, however, became more pronounced during
the second half of the seventeenth century, as the ranks of penniless playwrights swelled, and as the increase in print led to a
wider dissemination of writings that heightened the prestige of
the stage. The increased circulation of the ancients had fur-
thered the classical view of the stage, and native criticism had
led many playwrights (most notably Dryden) to try to determine their position in the larger history of classical and Continental theater. Such attempts were inspired not only by criticism but also by the growing matrix of bibliography and theater history emerging from the presses (which itself had grown
from the compilation of sources provided by an active press).
Besides Clavell and Starkey's 1668 *Mercurius Librarius*, a host of
periodicals devoted to books and plays appeared by the 1690's
(the *Athenian Mercury*, the *Works of the Learned*, the *Compleat Library or News of the Ingenious*).[72] In addition, there were, for the
first time, substantial attempts to document theater history
(Langbaine's *Momus Triumphans* in 1687 and his expanded version in 1691; James Wright's *Historia Histrionica* in 1699). In
works as different as Dryden's *Essay of Dramatic Poesie* (1668)
and Collier's *Short View* (1698), there is a powerful attempt to
estimate English theater in terms of its preservation of the best
(or the worst, according to Collier) of the old and to evaluate
its innovations.[73]

Dryden, in his poem on *The Double-Dealer* (1694), slyly included himself in his version of the great tradition (Shakespeare, Jonson, and Fletcher) by offering his laurel to Congreve; but his praise was generous, and Congreve must have been honored by the lines:

> Heav'n that but once was Prodigal before,
> To *Shakespeare* gave as much; she could not give him more.[74]

For Congreve had always felt that "all Traditions must indisputably give place to the *Drama*," as he wrote in the preface to *Incognita* (1692). It was the allied force of the prestige that print could give drama and its oral nature (its part in the flexible preprint tradition) that gave it its superiority. Drama "brings forth alive the Conceptions of the Brain," he wrote. "*Minerva* walks upon the Stage before us, and we are more assured of the real presence of Wit when it is delivered *viva voce*."[75] But Congreve's acceptance of the stage's double nature and his disdain for the postprint playwright are clear, even if Scandal (in his character as plain dealer) somewhat overstates the case when he tells Valentine, in *Love for Love*:

> No, turn Pimp, Flatterer, Quack, Lawyer, Parson, be Chaplain to an Atheist, or Stallion to an Old Woman, any thing but Poet; a Modern Poet is worse, more servile, timorous, and fawning, than any I have nam'd. (I.i, p. 220)

Nonetheless, there is an "unless" clause in Scandal's speech that changes everything, for he tells Valentine not to become a poet *unless* "you could retrieve the Ancient Honours of the Name, recall the Stage of *Athens*, and be allow'd the force of open honest Satire."

Congreve was attempting to do just that, to tip the balance toward an honorable theater, and his few critical writings (particularly the "Essay Concerning Humour in Comedy") show that he took his role as a retriever of ancient honors seriously. It is one of the paradoxes of print that some of the writers most distressed by the invasion of an overabundant print culture—

by its value for novelty, its presumptuousness, its commercialism and pecuniary nature—came to feel that the only way they
could redeem the literature of their day was by becoming part
of that culture. Congreve and Pope, attending to the minute
details of editing and printing, are the most powerful examples,
but nearly all joined the pamphlet wars in some form or another.
Congreve may have finally felt that the modern stage was beyond retrieval (as his failure to write for it after 1700 suggests),
that it was forever tainted by a world that could neither value
the old oral culture nor preserve the appropriate values of print,
a world that could communicate only through "marginal
Notes" and "asterisms."[76] He may have felt that a new drama
was needed that would marry the two cultures more closely and
that he was not capable of such a drama. In either case, he contributed to an alliance between print and the theater that print
would increasingly dominate in the centuries to come.

CHAPTER TWO

Publishers, Pirates, and the Library Text: The Creation of the "Dramatick Poet"

If I were not a king, and . . . if it were so that I must be a prisoner, . . . I would desire to have no other prison than a library, and to be chained together with so many good authors *et mortuis magistris*. —King James I

'Slife, Sir, what do you mean, to mew your self up here with Three or Four musty Books, in commendation of Starving and Poverty? —Congreve, *Love for Love*

That hate Books (such as come daily out / By Publick License to the Reading Rout)," wrote Congreve in a commendatory epistle, "here assert, if any thing's amiss, / It can be only the Compiler's Fault."[1] In a habitual gesture, Congreve condemns the "Reading Rout" and, by association, the erring "compiler," or editor. He condemns both consumer and producer of the quotidian book market, publicly "licensed" (after the 1695 lapse of the government's Licensing Act) and so unlicensed, licentious, both symptom and cause of things amiss at century's end. By 1699, he had probably had sufficient experience with sloppy typesetters and somnolent proofreaders for many of the mysteries of publishing to have resolved themselves, in his mind, into the most irritating of certainties about the carelessness of printers and publishers in the last years of the seventeenth century. If he dissociated himself from the literary license of the masses and their faulty publishers, their world was nonetheless a world through which he had passed. Just a decade earlier, when he was a nineteen-year-old who had lived principally among the bookshops of Kilkenny and Dublin, among the shelves of school and family libraries, he must have thought of the London presses, even those of the "Reading Rout," with more reverence. Having left Ireland at the revolution, Congreve arrived as a student at the Middle Temple in London, the city of Dryden and Wycherley, the city of money and the machine.[2] He must have been aware of the great tradition of barrister wits and the possibilities of fitting himself and his pen to the urban stage and to the world of London publishing.

There is, unfortunately, little evidence from which it is possible to gather an understanding of Congreve's arrival in London in 1689 or 1690 or of his first entry into the literary and publishing world. No letter of his survives from before 1692, when he had already been long settled in London, and he offers no lengthy, self-explanatory, convoluted prefaces in the manner of Dryden, no revealing autobiographical poems in the manner of Pope. We have a few comments about problems with publishers, a series of friendly letters to Tonson, a small neat body of critical prefaces, and Congreve's library catalog, but nothing of the young Congreve's responses to London literary institutions. Furthermore, evidence about his work with publishers is sparse and confusing. Despite these difficulties, however—the ephemerality of William Congreve himself, his disappearing booksellers—it is nonetheless possible to understand something about his early London experience and the careers of three publishers with whom he defined his own career: Peter Buck, who published Congreve's first works; Jacob Tonson, with whom he had a long collaboration and friendship; and Henry Hills, who successfully pirated his plays. These three very different careers reveal much about the problems of the trade in the late seventeenth and early eighteenth centuries and about the significance of the two most important changes in publishing law of the period: the 1695 lapse of the Licensing Act and the 1710 enactment of the Copyright Act. The careers of these three men offer insight into the problems of the developing publishing profession, into the relations among government regulation, human art, and technology, and into the period's notions of the writer's place in society, which helped form Congreve's public persona.

As the press became a more precise and efficient tool, and as book publication became more a profession (rather than a trade), authors increasingly adopted a dual stance: they had to be, at once, clever careerists handling the competing financial interests around them, and artists who countered the machine with the voice of the muses. For playwrights who believed (as Congreve did) that the live voice of the stage was more powerful and important than any printed word could be, and for the lettered gentry who perceived the encroaching commercialism of the life of letters, the tension between financial professionalism and a "poetic" stance was even more complicated. This tension becomes especially evident in the shifting tonalities of Congreve's correspondence. In most of the public anecdotes about him and in his surviving letters to such close friends as Joseph Keally, Congreve presents himself as the gentleman who insisted (according to Voltaire) that Voltaire "should visit him upon no other Foot than that of a Gentleman, who led a life of Plainness and Simplicity."[3] In his letters to Tonson and in his involvement in the publishing contracts between Dryden and Tonson, Congreve is highly attentive to the details of business. In his personal letters, Congreve is the man of the theater, present among the actors and singers to comment on the spectacle. And in his formal epistles, he is the dramatic poet, reshaping a poetics conveyed by those who preceded him. As long as Congreve continued to write, he continued to play his various roles: gentleman, wily businessman, man of the theater, and dramatic poet. His works themselves express these tensions with greater subtlety and approach a resolution of them in a notion of the "dramatist" that was to dominate, if not the reality of the eighteenth-century stage, at least its form in the public imagination.

Little is known about Peter Buck, Congreve's first publisher, but the few scraps from official records and imprints offer a sketchy outline of his life in the trade. Buck was born in Cobham, Kent, the son of John Buck, a clergyman.[4] John Buck had died before Peter's apprenticeship began, and he probably gave young Peter sufficient education to suit him for a trade that required some understanding of letters. Peter Buck went to London and was apprenticed to William Churchill, a stationer and bookseller, for a seven-year term on October 6, 1684. He was probably between fourteen and seventeen years old.[5] (During the same year, the fourteen-year-old Congreve was a student at Kilkenny College in Ireland.) A little over a year later, Buck was turned over to Christopher Wilkinson, not an unusual practice: the skilled unpaid labor that a partially trained apprentice could offer was valuable, and many stationers bought apprentices from their colleagues. One apprentice had run away from Wilkinson's service in 1679–80, and Wilkinson was fined for receiving another without the proper formalities at Stationers' Hall (thus avoiding fees and getting around the limitations on the number of apprentices allowed); otherwise, Wilkinson's career was impeccable. At Wilkinson's active shop in Fleet Street, Buck shared his apprenticeship with the slightly older Abel Roper, whose career was to be far less reputable (if more colorful) than Buck's and who would later marry Wilkinson's widow.[6] There is insufficient evidence about the actual life of an apprentice, but it is likely that Buck and Roper mixed freely with Wilkinson's family and, while learning about the trade, were occupied with menial domestic chores such as cleaning and sweeping, making deliveries and collections, and packing books for shipment. Buck was freed from apprenticeship on November 2, 1691, after the usual seven years; a month and a half later, on

December 22, 1691, Congreve's novel, *Incognita*, was licensed in his name.

It is impossible to know how Congreve and Buck met each other, but one can easily imagine a chance conversation between two young men, both hoping to establish themselves in their respective metiers. Buck's shop, "at the Sign of the Temple, near Temple Bar in Fleet-street" (as his books proclaimed it), was close to the Middle Temple, where Congreve was a law student; although Buck was not related to the fine publishers of Cambridge (Thomas and John Buck), Congreve might have been attracted to the shop by the name, which he would have seen on a number of fine editions of the classics from the 1630's, 1640's, and 1650's.[7] Neither had much to lose: Congreve had been in London for over two years, and although he had almost certainly by this time written a draft of *The Old Batchelour*, *Incognita*, and perhaps some poems, he had seen none of his work performed or printed.[8] He must have received this opportunity for an entry into the literary world eagerly, tentative as it was, "trifling" as he (ostensibly) considered the novel, which, as a precaution, he chose to publish under the pseudonym "Cleophil."[9] Buck, too, just out of his apprenticeship, having produced nothing, and recognizing that he would have to support his shop if he were to keep it, was probably pleased to find a clever, short, and well-written novel, which would be almost sure to sell. (Perhaps Congreve even wrote the novel during the fortnight preceding its licensing for the express purpose of publishing it with Buck.) There is a cheerful note suggesting an interest in critical commentary on Buck's part, in Congreve's assertion that "I have gratified the Bookseller in pretending an occasion for a Preface,"[10] although such a defense against accusations of presumption was common enough. It is tempting to think of Buck as something of a scholar (as his later publications suggest) and to imagine this as another bond between the two men. Perhaps Buck also heard something in Congreve's witty conversation (on which Swift, Lady Mary Wortley Montagu, and Dryden were all to comment later)[11] or in Congreve's critical powers, which convinced him that the poet would make sufficient impression on the wits to be taken under their banner. Congreve surely benefited, too, from his Irish literary connections: with Swift, who had preceded him at Kilkenny and Trinity College, and who was now working with Temple; or with Southerne, who had preceded him at Trinity and the Middle Temple, and for whose *Wives' Excuse* Dryden had recently written a commendatory poem.

Incognita was published in February 1692, and it may have led to the sudden recognition of Congreve's gifts that followed the novel's publication. Charles Gildon, also new to the literary world, probably saw the novel. When he gathered a miscellany of poems and published them with Buck sometime later in 1692, he included Congreve's five poems alongside those of Buckingham and Cowley.[12] The exact chronology of the important events in Congreve's life at this period is difficult to sort out. But by 1692 he had met Dryden, perhaps through friends (Gildon, Swift, or more probably Southerne) or perhaps on his own at Will's Coffeehouse, and he had offered Dryden a translation of Juvenal's eleventh satire for Dryden's forthcoming edition of *Juvenal and Persius*, which was ready in August 1692 and published by Tonson that year with 1693 on the title page.[13] Congreve volunteered a laudatory epistle, "To Mr. Dryden on his Translation of Persius," which Dryden liked so much that he used it as the only poem to head the Persius volume, where its enormous signature, "Will. Congreve," seems almost paired with Dryden's name on the title page. While *Juvenal and Persius* was in preparation, Dryden read *The Old Batchelour* and offered his influence in getting it produced, claiming that he "never saw such a first play in his life" and that "it wanted only the fashionable cutt of the town." He, Southerne, and Arthur Maynwaring would revise it.[14] When Congreve translated a fragment of Homer for Dryden's miscellany, *Examen Poeticum*, published in July 1693, Dryden wrote in the dedication that he could not mention Congreve "without the Honour which is due to his Excellent Parts, and that entire Affection which I bear him," and

T O
Mr. DRYDEN,

ON HIS

TRANSLATION

OF

PERSIUS.

AS when of Old Heroïque Story tells
  Of Knights Imprison'd long by Magick Spells;
  Till future Time, the destin'd Hero send,
By whom, the dire Enchantment is to end:
Such seems this Work, and so reserv'd for thee,
Thou great Revealer of dark Poesie.
 Those sullen Clouds, which have for Ages past,
O're Persius's too-long-suffring Muse been cast,
Disperse, and flie before thy Sacred Pen,
And, in their room, bright tracks of light are seen.
Sure Phœbus self, thy swelling Breast inspires,
The God of Musick, and Poetique Fires:
Else, whence proceeds this great Surprise of Light!
How dawns this day, forth from the Womb of Night!
 Our Wonder, now, does our past Folly show,
Vainly Contemning what we did not know:
So, Unbelievers impiously despise
The Sacred Oracles, in Mysteries.

          Persius

Congreve's dedicatory poem to Dryden's 1692–93 edition of the
Satires of Juvenal and Persius, published by Jacob Tonson (continues on
p. 46). (By permission of the British Library.)

To Mr. Dryden.

Perſius, *before, in ſmall Eſteem was had,*
Unleſs, what to Antiquity is paid;
But like Apocrypha, with Scruple read,
(So far, our Ignorance, our Faith miſled)
'Till you, Apollo's darling Prieſt thought fit
To place it, in the Poet's Sacred Writ.

  As Coin, which bears ſome awful Monarchs Face,
For more than its Intrinſick Worth will paſs:
So your bright Image, which we here behold,
Adds Worth to Worth, and dignifies the Gold.
To you, we, all this following Treaſure owe,
This Hippocrene, *which from a Rock did flow.*

  Old Stoick *Virtue, clad in rugged lines,*
Poliſh'd by you, in Modern Brillant ſhines:
And as before, for Perſius *our Eſteem,*
To his Antiquity was paid, not him:
So now, whatever Praiſe, from us is due,
Belongs not to Old Perſius, *but the New.*
For ſtill Obſcure, to us no Light he gives;
Dead in himſelf, in you alone he lives.

  So, ſtubborn Flints, their inward heat conceal,
'Till Art and Force, th' unwilling Sparks reveal;
But through your Skill, from thoſe ſmall Seeds of Fire,
Bright Flames ariſe, which never can Expire.

Will. Congreve.

THE

referred to him as "more capable than any Man I know" of translating Homer.[15]

The greatest living poet had taken Congreve under his wing,
was making sure that his comedy would be performed, and had
introduced him, through *Juvenal and Persius*, to Jacob Tonson,
already the most powerful and influential literary publisher in
England. The introduction quickly developed into friendship,
or at least a deep professional connection that touched the personal lives of both men. Congreve moved to Tonson's lodgings
in Fleet Street by 1695 (and perhaps as early as 1693, only a few
months after the first performance of *The Old Batchelour*).[16] Although he probably lodged with Tonson only briefly, the two
maintained an intimate connection from that time forward,
sending each other domestic items such as linen and wine from
their various voyages and traveling together to the Continent in
1700. When, in 1691, Congreve had made arrangements for
the publication of *Incognita*, perhaps he had promised *The Old
Batchelour* to Buck, either with a contract or simply with a
gentleman's agreement; for although Congreve already knew
Tonson, the new play was published with Buck's imprint at the
sign of the Temple in March 1693 almost immediately after its
first performance at the Theatre Royal in Drury Lane. But with
Dryden and Tonson supporting his new literary career, Congreve never went back to Buck.

There are many possible reasons for Congreve's defection, not
the least of which is the obvious motive of Tonson's prestige.[17]
Buck was probably able to offer Congreve very little, perhaps
nothing, for the rights to publish *Incognita* and *The Old
Batchelour*.[18] Although works still had to be licensed, unless a
publisher had a strong position in the Stationers' Company or
other forms of influence, there was little value in owning a work
that could easily be pirated without much chance of prosecu-
tion. Even the Stationers' Company had almost no power
against London publishers and printers pirating popular works,
still less against provincial pirates, and none at all against foreign presses. If Tonson was able to pay more than most pub-

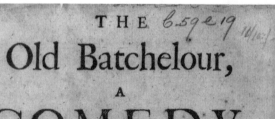

THE
Old Batchelour,
A
COMEDY.

As it is ACTED at the

Theatre Royal,

BY

Their MAJESTIES Servants.

Written by Mr. *Congreve.*

Quem tulit ad Scenam ventofo gloria Curru,
Exanimat lentus Spectator ; fedulus inflat.
Sic leve, fic parvum eft, animum quod laudis avarum
Subruit, aut reficit——

Horat. Epift. I. Lib. II.

LONDON,
Printed for *Peter Buck,* at the Sign of the *Temple*
near the *Temple-gate* in *Fleet-ftreet,* 1693.

Title page, 1693 quarto of *The Old Batchelour,* published by Peter Buck. (By permission of the British Library.)

lishers to his authors, it was because he had seen the advantage of forging a powerful reputation for himself, of gathering about his name the past and future great, of making his imprint a mark of canonization, even when he could not know whether an act would be passed that would protect his or his authors' rights to these works, despite the demand for such an act. Although none of the contracts between Tonson and Congreve have survived, it is clear from the contracts between Tonson and Dryden (for several of which Congreve served as witness) that Tonson was able to treat his authors as professionals to be paid accordingly for their work and that he could also guarantee them the highest quality printing.[19] It is unlikely that Buck could have afforded this luxury, especially with an unknown author who was testing himself in public (although perhaps, through the use of the pseudonym "Cleophil," Buck and Congreve had hoped to encourage speculation that *Incognita* had been written by an author with an established reputation or by an aristocrat in the style of Sidney).

One need only compare Buck's edition of Gildon's *Miscellany* with Tonson's edition of Dryden's *Juvenal and Persius* to discover another reason for Congreve's change of publisher. Buck and the unidentified printer either chose to do a modest job or were not accustomed to the beautiful folios created for much of late-seventeenth-century poetry. The *Miscellany* by Buck and Gildon is in octavo, spaciously enough printed, but with jagged lines; black letter mingles with italic, which mingles with roman. The poems have neither natural ordering nor tonal variation but seem to appear with a randomness that would have displeased Congreve's already developing sense of order, juxtaposition, and timing. Tonson's printers may not have been the appropriate partners for the publisher in the 1690's (before the period of his collaboration with the printer John Watts), and Dryden may have complained that Tonson's printer was "a beast" and "understands nothing I can say to him of correcting the press,"[20] but the printing of *Juvenal and Persius* is immaculate in comparison with the Buck *Miscellany*. Tonson's two folio volumes are neatly set, large lettered, and spacious without the exaggeration of space that seems a contrivance of grandeur; they are also well padded with scholarly notes, discreetly placed commentary at the end of each satire, not marginal "asterisms" (which Congreve refers to with disdain in *The Double-Dealer* [III.i, p. 165]). There is only one item in the errata section, and that is clearly not a printer's error: Congreve (or perhaps Dryden) has changed the word *ill* to *unpleasant*, thus regularizing the meter of the line into a smooth pentameter.[21]

What happened to Buck after Congreve began publishing with Tonson? *Incognita* went into a second edition in 1700 under the imprint of Richard Wellington, one of Buck's partners, who must have bought the copy for several of Buck's publications.[22] This edition and the various advertisements for the earlier edition at the back of Buck-Wellington publications throughout the 1690's were almost all anonymous, although after 1693 Congreve's name would have made sufficient impact to ensure higher sales. One can only speculate that Congreve had requested that the novel (which he never included in the various editions of his collected works) remain anonymous and that Buck agreed, not wanting to create rancor between himself and Congreve. He had reason to feel goodwill toward Congreve. The works by Congreve that Buck published proved two of his most successful acquisitions. With *Incognita*'s two editions and *The Old Batchelour*'s six editions under Buck (although some may have been simply new impressions or even continuations of a simultaneous impression) and with little investment either in the author or in the paper and printing, Buck is likely to have made some profit from the works. Only two of his other acquisitions went into second editions, and none went into third editions until they had passed into the hands of other, more adroit, publishers. Although the physical appearance of his books improved after *Incognita* and *The Old Batchelour*, and although he published several plays that were great successes in performance, most of Buck's authors published only one or two works with him.[23]

Buck did have some successes. In 1694 he published William Wotton's learned and influential *Reflections Upon Ancient and Modern Learning*, an octavo beautifully printed by John Leake on fine paper, a work including an elaborate (but simply designed) apparatus of marginal notes, dedication, preface, advertisement to the reader, and table of contents. The second edition was published, again printed by Leake, "with Large Additions," and with Bentley's "Dissertation Upon the Epistles of Phalaris." The postscript added to the second edition, dated April 30, 1697, offers an insight, however small, into Buck's work as a publisher. Wotton writes that the discourses added to the second edition have also been printed separately for the sake of those who have already bought the first edition and "have no curiosity to compare that with the second" (which only a rampant bibliographer, he suggests, would be patient enough to do). He has not reprinted the small additions, which are woven into the body of the book, because they would "appear only like a parcel of loose Scraps" and because "Something was to be done in compliance with the Bookseller, who, (having once more, at a time when Printing labours under so great Discouragements, adventured to publish so large a Book which so few People will care to read) desired that this Second Edition might be made as Valuable to him as well it cou'd."[24]

This portrait of Buck, in which Buck becomes a martyr for the sake of ancient and modern learning, suggests that Buck was only one of the reliable and serious publishers who suffered from the "time when Printing labours under so great Discouragements." That is, Buck was one of the typical victims of the 1695 lapse of the Licensing Act and the imposition in 1696 of paper and pamphlet duties. With piracy and failure to license no longer clearly punishable, law-abiding printers were all the more vulnerable to theft by surreptitious printers who could sell their works far more cheaply by evading the inconvenient expenses of paying an author and using fine quality paper. Buck's few publications were nearly all by living authors, and after his first few productions and aside from play quartos (always miserably printed, even by such great publishers as Tonson), almost all Buck's publications followed high standards. But his imprints show Buck struggling, as Wotton suggests, with the effects of the Licensing Act's lapse and the duties that followed. After 1695, one finds him more often publishing collectively with at least one other publisher, usually Wellington or Parker, but often with more. He is by no means alone in turning to these congers, which many other scrupulous publishers continued to use even after the Copyright Act of 1710. But he did not form any steady group on which he could rely, as for instance James Knapton, George Strahan, and Bernard Lintott did in the first years of the eighteenth century.

The frequent shifts in Buck's imprint during this period also suggest that he may have been struggling to attract customers: his shop is sometimes referred to as being near the Inner-Temple Gate, sometimes near the Middle-Temple Gate, sometimes just at the Temple-Gate, sometimes in Fleet Street, sometimes near Temple-Bar. These unstable designations suggest not that he moved his shop, but that he may have been concerned that the description of his location was hindering business. He even changed his sign from the Temple, which it had been throughout his career, to the "Roe Buck" in 1702, but by then it was probably too late. His last published works appeared in 1701. In 1702 John Rea's *Flora* was "sold by" Buck; in March of that year *The Post Man* advertised "The Comical History of Franchion," which it claimed "is now in the Press, and will be speedily published. . . . Printed for Peter Buck, at the sign of the Roe Buck, between the two Temple Gates in Fleet-street."[25] Although this suggests a possible revival of business, an apprentice he had bound in 1694 had never taken up his freedom, sometimes the sign of a master who was in trouble and unable to support or find enough work for an apprentice. On May 4, 1702, a few months after the advertisement for the "History of Franchion," he bound Robert Hurst as an apprentice, perhaps in a final attempt to save his business. But Hurst was turned over to Phillip Barrett on November 2, 1702. Buck's name does not appear again.

Perhaps Buck died in November 1702. Perhaps he merely retired to the country, not an uncommon choice, even for tradesmen, as one can see from the various announcements of stock sales in the newspapers during those years. Perhaps he returned to Cobham. Perhaps he changed trades (also quite common), but his recent binding of Hurst as an apprentice suggests otherwise.[26] Perhaps he continued as a bookseller but was unable to involve himself in any publishing ventures or to subscribe to a sufficient stock of books to have his name listed in an imprint as "sold by."[27] At any rate, it seems probable that he was unable to survive financially for many years after the lapse of the Licensing Act. Perhaps he would have become at least moderately successful if he had stayed in business until the Copyright Act of 1710, when many people began to identify finely printed books with a wider readership. But he did not have the business cleverness of Tonson, or even of some of the lesser but nonetheless successful publishers like Sam Briscoe or James Knapton. Congreve, legally and financially practical, may have sensed early that Buck was not a bookseller equal to him; Congreve did not have the patience (unlike Pope with Lintott) to make Buck into a publisher proper to a great poet, and he must have known that it was time to advance himself professionally. Unsupported by popular writers, and faced by competition from pirates, numerous small publishers like Buck were forced out of business.[28]

One of the most successful of the pirates who might be held responsible for the failure of such scrupulous publishers as Buck was Henry Hills, who produced an inexpensive edition of Congreve's plays, all five of which he also issued individually. Hills's father, Henry Hills Sr., had been active throughout the seventeenth century as the publisher for a number of conflicting enterprises. According to an anonymous broadside attack on him, "A view of . . . the many *Traiterous* . . . *Actions* of H. H. Senior" (1684), he was printer "to *Cromwell*, to the *Commonwealth*, to the *Anabaptist* Congregations, to *Cromwell*'s Army, Committee of Safety, Parliament," and, later, to Charles II and James. He was successful in all these posts until the 1688 revolution, when the Catholicism he had adopted at the accession of James caused his printing house to be sacked by an antipapist mob; Hills Sr. died only a few months later.[29] Henry Hills Jr. had been freed in July 1679 by patrimony from his apprenticeship to his father and began a prolific printing practice between 1683 and 1688, printing, among other things, numerous strongly Protestant tracts. The will of Hills Sr. showed the religious conflict between father and son. Hills Sr., when he died in 1689, left "unto my welbeloved son Henry Hills the summe of Twenty pounds as a Legacy to the said Henry Hills haveing been by me advanced already."[30] He left the rest of his estate to Gilham, Henry's full brother, and to Hills Sr.'s two sons by his second wife, Elizabeth, who shared Hills Sr.'s Catholic leanings. Hills Jr. petitioned the Crown numerous times to give him his patrimony, arguing that his loyalty to the true Church of England had been the only reason for his deprivation. But nothing came of these petitions except the right to act as a government spy in turning over unlicensed printing, which he did with a certain degree of ardor.

Perhaps he learned more than he ought to have learned from this position, for in the first decade of the eighteenth century, after the expiration of the Licensing Act and before passage of the Copyright Act, he began pirating vast numbers of successful plays, poems, and sermons, among them works by Atterbury, Tillotson, Swift, and Dryden. There is no solid evidence to suggest that, with the birth of his sixth child in 1695 (there would be more to come), he was finding it difficult to survive.[31] Neither is there strong evidence to suggest that he felt his business threatened by the other pirates on the increase during those years, but both may have been contributing elements to an advantageous situation that had simply presented itself. Presumably, had he not turned to piracy, Hills would have faced some of the same difficulties that Buck faced. But after 1695, with no authors to pay, with cheap paper (despite taxes) and cheap equipment, with no apprentices after 1690 (when Henry Hills III was nine years old and could probably do some of the work of an apprentice), with the enormous turnover of stock that his low prices probably permitted, Hills was probably able to survive quite well.[32] He almost certainly made a substantial profit even on the numerous one-penny sermons and other works "printed for the benefit of the poor." He may have made it possible for those who could not afford Tonson's thick tomes to own the works of the finest poets. But in choosing to print editions of Congreve, Swift, Tillotson, and others, he printed them so badly that some authors, already angry about the loss of payment, complained bitterly about the mangling of their work.

Congreve makes a typical complaint in his preface to Tonson's 1710 edition of the *Works*, when he says that his plays had undergone a "spurious Impression" and had been "very faultily, as well as very indirectly Published."[33] Hills's edition, *Five Plays written by Mr. Congreve*, had thin crumbling paper, bleeding ink, and wobbly and broken letters, and it was also full of errors (and naturally incorporated none of Congreve's post-quarto revisions). Where Congreve wrote "ungenerous Spirit," for instance, Hills's edition had "ungenerous Spight"; where Congreve wrote "And while with Clapping, we are just to you," Hills's edition had "And while our Clapping does you Justice do," to mention just two of the more obvious examples.[34] On April 10, 1710, the new Copyright Act went into effect, and Hills stopped publishing piracies. Perhaps Hills found that he could not survive without such production, or at least that his business was by then constructed for such production. In any case, he died soon after and his business was dismantled. On November 12, 1713, an advertisement in the *Evening Post* advertised the sale of the stock of the "late Henry Hills, printer in Blackfriars" and notified the public that "There

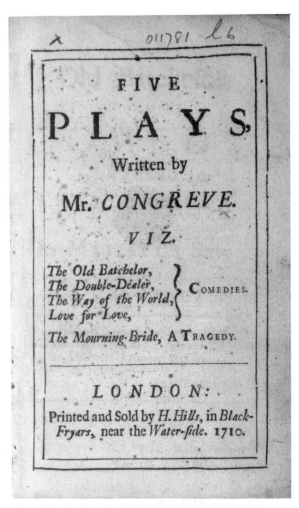

FIVE
PLAYS,

Written by

Mr. CONGREVE.

V I Z.

The Old Batchelor,	
The Double-Dealer,	COMEDIES.
The Way of the World,	
Love for Love,	

The Mourning-Bride, A TRAGEDY.

LONDON:

Printed and Sold by *H. Hills*, in *Black-
Fryars*, near the *Water-side*. 1710.

Title page, 1710 edition of Congreve's *Five Plays*, published by Henry Hills Jr. (By permission of the British Library.)

can never be any of the same, or any in the like manner, reprinted after these are gone, there being an Act of Parliament
to the contrary."[35]

Whereas small, inexperienced legitimate publishers like
Buck found it impossible to survive for long after the lapse of
the Licensing Act in 1695, and highly successful pirates like
Hills could not continue with their former practices after the
Copyright Act of 1710, well-connected, careful legitimate
publishers like Tonson and his nephew found in the Copyright
Act the reward for patience and hard work. It signaled both full
independence from the Stationers' Company and the security of
legal protection, even if such legal protection seemed directed
toward authors rather than publishers. To compete with publishers like Hills before 1710, it was impossible to spend great
amounts of money on book design and fine printing. The Copyright Act not only permitted such attention but also encouraged
it with a clause requiring publishers to present a fine paper copy
of every work to the public libraries. An anonymous set of lines
to Bernard Lintott in his 1712 *Miscellaneous Poems* celebrates the
victory of fine printing over the work of such printers as Hills:

> While neat old Elzevir is reckon'd better
> Than Pirate Hills' brown sheets and scurvy letter,
> While Print admirers careful Aldus chuse
> Before John Morphew, or the Weekly News.
> So long shall live thy Praise in Books of Fame,
> And *Tonson* yield to *Lintott*'s lofty Name.[36]

Tonson never yielded to Lintott, but he was a worthy model, as
his care with Congreve's works shows. Tonson, of course, had
done better (from a purely aesthetic point of view) than most
publishers in his very mixed production during the 1690's. The
Dryden-Tonson edition of *Juvenal and Persius*, in which Congreve's translation had been included, showed Tonson's capacity
for creating a sophisticated and clean volume. Tonson's play
quartos—*The Double-Dealer, Love for Love, The Mourning Bride,*
and *The Way of the World*—were haphazard productions, but

they were no worse than the usual quartos of the period, printed on cheap paper, badly inked, full of errors.[37] If the quartos were badly printed, many of the poems made up for this carelessness. For example, Tonson's edition of Congreve's "The Birth of the Muse" (1697), a panegyric on William III, is a simply lettered folio with large margins, large type, and no tilting or misplaced letters.

When, in 1703, there was a threatened piracy of Congreve's "Tears of Amaryllis for Amyntas," a pastoral elegy on the death of the Marquis of Blandford, Congreve and Tonson printed the poem themselves and successfully prevented the piracy. As Congreve wrote to Tonson, who was on a business trip in Amsterdam, "Your Nephew told me of Copies that were dispersed of the Pastoral and likely to be printed so we have thought it fit to prevent them and print it our selves."[38] This was not only a financial precaution for Tonson but also an aesthetic consideration for Congreve: the text might be faulty in a pirated edition, and the poem probably would not look right on the page. In an address "To the Reader" in the printed version of the pastoral, Congreve explains his justification for printing:

These Verses had been Printed soon after they were written if they had not been design'd rather privately to Condole, than publickly to Lament. . . . But, by some Accident, many Copies of 'em have been dispersed, and one, I was informed, had been shewn to a Bookseller. So that it was high time for me to prevent their appearing with more Faults than their own, which might probably have met with Encrease, if not from the Malice or Ignorance, at least from the Carelessness of an under-hand Publisher. (S: p. 67)

Congreve can publish, he reminds his readers, when he wishes. But a gentleman of letters has no need to publish those things intended for an intimate circle, for "private" condolence in this case. The implied publisher of the first sentence is contrasted with the "under-hand Publisher" of the last; Tonson is implicitly contrasted with Hills. The excuses Congreve makes for the "under-hand Publisher" (careless, rather than ignorant or full of malice) become ironic accusation in the lines that follow:

I have particularly Reason at this time to apprehend the disingenuous Proceeding of some such Person, having lately seen some Verses Printed, and Intitled *A Satyr against Love, Revised and Corrected by Mr.* Congreve; who does assure the Reader he never saw or heard of any such Verses before they were so Printed, viz. without either the Name of the Author, Bookseller or Printer, being Publish'd after the Manner of a Libel.

What disturbs Congreve here is not merely the "disingenuous Proceeding" of the publisher ("some such Person"), who steals Congreve's work for his private gain, but the theft of Congreve's name, so detached not only from his person but also from his work. The advantage of private condolence, of manuscript elegy, is that one's name cannot be so readily detached from one's person and attached elsewhere. The complaint by the celebrated that their names could be attached to works in which they had no part was a common one, no less common than the typical aristocratic complaint about the anonymous printer or hack who seemed increasingly to dominate the life of letters at the turn of the century. In fact, the anonymity of Congreve's disingenuous "Author, Bookseller or Printer" is linked with the abuse of Congreve's name: the more complex the publishing trade grew, the more detached letters could grow from the circle of familiar figures, recognized by each other in the street, the coffeehouse, the theater.

By contrast, the disingenuous proceedings of the anonymous could serve a purpose for those who had an inclination to publish without identifying themselves with those who did wish to publish.[39] The threat of piracy could "force" the unwilling gentleman of letters to give the public the "true" copy it deserved. The claim (sometimes genuine, sometimes not) to have published as a precaution against piracy was already a convention by the time Congreve published the pastoral.[40] But the necessity for the gentleman poet to distinguish himself from the hack seemed all the more pressing after the lapse of the Licensing Act. Even the kind of publishers to whom Congreve objects seemed to wish to distance themselves from those who labored under them, as the "Printer" of *Sot's Paradise* (attributed to Edward Ward) suggests in offering up to his readers an account of his relation with his author, who tells him:

> "Each Sentence should have *Gaul* and *Venom* in't
> Which you, to recompence your Drubs, shall Print . . ."
> He prest the Copy forward, I seem'd shye,
> Till by these words he brought me to comply.[41]

Congreve's particular effort to distinguish himself in his relationship with his publishers from such figures as the desperate writer of *Sot's Paradise*, and his concern for a careful and beautiful text, show in the editing he did for Tonson of Dryden's *Dramatick Works* in 1717–18, but he had already learned much from editing, with Tonson, his own plays and poems. By the time of Hills's pirated edition of the plays, and by the time Congreve and Tonson had begun compiling Congreve's collected works—which would first appear in 1710, eight months after the enactment of the Copyright Act[42]—the ideas of both men about the construction of a text and the layout of a page had fully developed. Although Congreve had written nearly nothing for ten years, he collaborated actively with Tonson on the preparation of the manuscript, making significant changes in the texts of his plays.[43] He eliminated or softened curses and sexual innuendos (partly to suit the taste of the time, partly to suit his own sense of the dignity of his work). He broke the acts according to the French style of scene division, basing scenes on character groupings. (This was probably always the way in which he had conceived of the scene divisions, although the quartos had nonetheless followed English conventions.) He incorporated what had once been stage directions into dialogue. The three volumes, of which there were two editions during Congreve's lifetime (and a third in two volumes), fully evoke the decorous gentleman playwright and poet that Congreve and Tonson wanted to bring forth between the bindings. Not only are the octavos carefully printed, but each play has a separate title page and holds its own shape within the volume. The de-

Will Hammond

THE
FIRST VOLUME
OF THE
WORKS
OF
Mr. *William Congreve*;

CONTAINING,

The OLD BATCHELOR.	Comedy.
The DOUBLE DEALER.	Comedy.
LOVE *for* LOVE.	Comedy.

LONDON:

Printed for *Jacob Tonfon*, at *Shakefpear*'s Head over-againſt
Catherine Street in the *Strand.* MDCCX.

Title page, first volume of the 1710 edition of Congreve's *Works*, published by Jacob Tonson. (By permission of the Folger Shakespeare Library.)

vices at the head of the preface and some of the plays are beautifully rendered, but not so domineering as to distract from the text. There are few errata. The early comedies make up the first volume; the second volume contains the four pieces that show the diversity of Congreve's production: *The Mourning Bride, The Way of the World, The Judgement of Paris,* and *Semele*—tragedy, comedy, masque, opera. The third and crowning volume contains Congreve's "Poems on Several Occasions." There are no advertisements, only the names of the dramatist and his publisher, an emblem of the growing alliance between the two professions.

The three-volume *Works* that Congreve and Tonson so carefully compiled gave Congreve a place both in the "imaginary library" of literature preserved and in the real and tangible libraries that had been expanding throughout the seventeenth century.[44] Such editions had to find their places on increasingly crowded library shelves, which, by the eighteenth century, began to seem overcrowded. The library had been the proper subject of panegyric for most of the seventeenth century. For Milton, as he wrote to the librarian of the Bodleian, it was "the delightful groves of the Muses and . . . the divine home of Phoebus . . . where the insolent noise of the crowd never shall enter and the vulgar mob of readers shall forever be excluded."[45] For Bacon, libraries were "the shrines wherein all the relics of the ancient saints full of true virtue are preserved."[46] For Cowley, the Bodleian was a

> Majestick Monument and Pyramide,
> Where still the shapes of parted Souls abide
> Embalm'd in verse, exalted souls which now
> Enjoy those Arts they woo'd so well below,
>   Which now all wonders plainly see,
> That have been, are, or are to be,
> In the mysterious Library.[47]

Although much of the poetic praise was directed at the Bodleian, the seventeenth century marked a high point for private libraries. But by the 1720's, attitudes had changed. Pope saw them principally as the nurturing ground for plagiarists like Cibber:

> Next, o'er his Books his eyes began to roll,
> In pleasing memory of all he stole,
> How here he sipp'd, how there he plunder'd snug
> And suck'd all o'er, like an industrious Bug.[48]

Congreve can be thought of as somewhere between the seventeenth-century panegyrists and Pope. More accurately, he understood the library as both the proper showcase for his and Tonson's beautiful edition and the crypt for those books "in commendation of Starving and Poverty" (as Jeremy puts it in *Love for Love* [I.i, p. 216]), pushed aside by the productions of the unlicensed press. His affection for the honorable gentleman's library, however, surpassed his anxiety about the place of the book in a world of unlicensed print. His three volumes needed a home. Congreve himself had a catalog made in the 1720's of the fairly large library he had collected at his lodgings in Surrey Street, a catalog that reflects many of the confusions and reformulations of the era. The catalog lists not only titles, authors, and editions, but also shelf numbers indicating the location of each of the 659 books on one of 33 shelves.[49] The library, cataloged, aristocratic, and restrained, served as a stay against the dangers of bibliographic bloatedness. Just as the Tonsons of the world were the cure for the Hillses of the world, Congreve's orderly library in Surrey Street was a cure for the overfilled courtyard of St. Paul's.

Congreve's library, "genteel & wel chosen," according to Tonson,[50] is characteristic of the late-seventeenth- and early-eighteenth-century mixture of the personal and the general, neither coldly schematic nor "singular" in a manner that the eighteenth century would have found unpleasant. The list and the shelving arrangements accord with an ideal of polite taste. While they avoid arcaneness and specialization, idiosyncrasy to the point of eccentricity, they also avoid formal completeness, the encyclopedic taxonomy that could serve as a machine for public understanding. They reject both the work of the old-style virtuoso, searching in vain for such obscure knowledge as the location of the fountain of life, and the work of the new-style academician (or Royal Society Fellow), seeking to catalog systematically all knowledge.[51] Congreve's shelves hint at general categories while retaining discreet and personal commentary through juxtapositions. For instance, shelf 14, in a subtle private gesture, is given to theater and theology equally, as if to counter the antitheatrical reformers or to suggest that a theater too can be a church, if rightly recognized.[52] Congreve's library has more than the requisite number of classical authors and essays on dramatic criticism and other philosophical subjects. But there are also books on jockeyship, herbal cures, and coinage, in addition to numerous histories and adventures. Many of the books seem to be part of the library of a conscious collector. Some editions were very valuable even then, such as Shakespeare's first folio, a 1561 Chaucer, and numerous fine editions of the classics from the 1690's and 1710's. But there are also clusters of cheap quartos and romances, "Tales of Mother Shipton" or "Hist. of Dorastus & Fawnia," mostly bound together, too voluminous for the catalog to ignore.

Both the shelf arrangements and the catalog reflect the shifting of principles during the late seventeenth century. With the great increase in bibliographic material, the keeper of a library was faced, more than ever, with problems of categorization and order. The catalog is alphabetical largely by author (by first letter of the surname only), listing author, short title, size (folio, quarto, etc.), sometimes the publisher, place of publication, date, and shelf number. But even the first entries do not follow the rule, and few entries follow with any regularity the ideas of standardization to which the twentieth-century eye is accustomed and which the late eighteenth century, in its encyclopedias and bibliographies, would achieve. If alphabetization succeeds only by first letter, and the element alphabetized (whether author, translator, subject, or title) is never constant, the cross-referencing serves partially to supply this deficiency. Cross-references, at first used only by those who, like Bodley, recognized the dangers of changing catalog practices, became more common over the course of the century.

Nonetheless, Congreve's cross-referencing is not consistent enough to suggest an interest in labels that would serve "public" identification, like those of late-eighteenth-century bibliography. The catalog fails to cross-reference many identifications that might be confusing and often lists things twice without cross-referencing them. The equally inconsistent shelving is formed partly on categories in distress: medicine mixed with cartography; voyages with Descartes and Horace for contrast; dictionaries and rhetorics with Virgil and the only Bible in the catalog. These groupings—medicine, voyages, reference— with their surprising inclusions, suggest the extent to which the burgeoning book trade generated classificatory confusion.

Despite their surprising contrasts, both Congreve's shelves and his catalog rely more on shared cultural groupings than is immediately apparent. The catalog offers consecutive lists for Dacier, Fénelon, and Scarron; grouped histories, from the history of the invasion of Spain to the history of infamous imposters; and title lists, from the *Amours de Psiché et de Cupidon* to the *Amours des dames illustres*, by a miscellaneous group of French writers.[53] Rhetoric and mathematics find themselves together, as do poetry and oratory, suggesting a recollection of the close bond between logic and rhetoric, and the original orality of poetry. Theology, law, and medicine are grouped with some consistency. Music and poetry find a place together on shelf 21, again identifying poetry with the aural. The most coherent and largest categories, however, seem to be the most modern ones: history, in the modern and restricted sense of the events of nations (although with *Don Quixote* and Pope's *Odyssey* as recollections of the older, more inclusive category); exotic tales; and contemporary poetry. The modern desire to divide the true from the false, the old from the new, has touched Congreve's shelving.

Similarly, the catalog relies on modern notions of bibliography. The generosity of bibliographical information in the list suggests the recognition of the physical book itself as an object to be classed in a bibliographical world, a world in which bibliography forms a secondary discourse of books on books.[54] In the catalog, most of the items published by Tonson, the Elzevirs (the Dutch family of publishers known especially for their beautifully designed and learned books), and Christophe Plantin (the French-born sixteenth-century publisher) mention the publisher, as if to acknowledge his equal prestige. Other details of the physical form of the book are also often given: some entries note large paper, "cuts" and "fig." for illustrations, or "foliis deauratis" for "gilded leaves"; entries often mention the edition. The shelving confirms this respect for the book as bibliographical production. Beautifully bound and very rare books are often shelved together, as on shelf 5, nearly half of which is made up of books published by the Elzevirs. Shelf 17 is devoted entirely to Tonson publications, with the single exception of Pope's *Iliad* (published by Lintott), which succeeds in gaining a place beside Tonson's Horace, Lucretius, Virgil, Milton, and others. The bibliographic becomes as essential a principle of order as author alphabetization and author grouping are.

Two figures, then, gain precedence in the catalog and shelving arrangements: the distinguished publisher and the elevated and individualized author, the kind of poet created by such editions as the 1710 edition of Congreve's *Works* and protected by the Copyright Act. In the catalog, Congreve is consciously crafting his oeuvre, making himself the author he would like to be. The catalog does not list *Incognita*, any of his quartos, or any of his folio poems or broadsides. (Perhaps he did not even own copies of these, although this seems unlikely.) The poems and translations fall under appropriate headings: the Juvenal under Dryden (a tribute to the master translator), the Ovid with the rest of the Ovid editions, the poetic miscellanies with the other miscellanies. Congreve is even so discreet (or so embarrassed by his early work) as to list Gildon's 1692 miscellany, published by Buck, as "Miscellaneous Poems by ye D. of Bucks Cowley &c." He does, however, list two of the three different editions of his collected works: the 1710 and the 1719 editions, both in the finest versions available (large and fine paper). A copy of the 1710 edition in small paper is listed, but then crossed out, either because he gave it to the Duchess of Marlborough or because he did not want to include it because such an inclusion would be redundant.[55] The only other work included next to the editions of his collected works is his critique of Jeremy Collier, listed as "Congreve's Amendments of Mr Collier's False & imperfect Citations from ye Old Batchelour &c Large Paper," one of the longest listings in the catalog. Perhaps he included it there only because Collier followed him in the list of C's, but more probably because it was his only piece of dramatic criticism published individually, and he wished to emphasize his status as a dramatist, as one who thinks about the art of the drama, not just as a playmaker.

This stress on the critical and serious nature of his dramatic works only reemphasizes the idea of drama that he was creating for himself in the collected works. By including Tonson among the three prestigious publishers who claim a place in the catalog listings, Congreve gives Tonson the authority to include Congreve's own work in Tonson's canon of authors worthy of being preserved. Congreve thus locates himself as one of those crowned by the living version of Plantin and the Elzevirs: he serves Tonson partly to serve his own immortality. Shelf 22, on which Congreve placed the two editions he owned of his collected works, holds a chronology of the drama and dramatic theory that begins with the central ancients and moderns: Horace (the *Art of Poetry*), Shakespeare, d'Aubignac (the *Art of the Stage*), Buckingham, Otway. It culminates with writers with whom he was personally acquainted: Dryden (several volumes), Congreve himself, Charles Hopkins (with whom Congreve may have roomed before he stayed with Tonson),[56] and a miscellany of Swift and Pope, just for company. The only other apt addition is Cowley, whose presence recalls Congreve's essay on the

Pindaric ode and his own efforts in the genre, serious productions that add weight and prestige to his dramatic works. For Congreve, the drama is an art with two conjoined natures: its oral nature and its print nature. This shelf is an attempt to unify fully these two natures into a form that absorbs theory, classical texts, and plays (like Hopkins's). Dryden presides, in seven volumes, a link between two worlds. He is both a member of the dramatists of the past, enshrined in library bindings, and a member of the community of playwrights of the present, allied to preserve themselves as the audiences of their printed works grow increasingly remote. He is both the playwright who assisted, with revisions and commentaries, in the first live productions of Congreve's plays, and the playwright who helped place Congreve in Tonson's canon.

It was not only Tonson but the vastness of the print trade itself that made possible the literary fame that Tonson offered Dryden and Congreve. With the growing network of booksellers, celebrity could be more widespread, and skilled publishers could more successfully promote glorified writers, distant from readers and so larger than life. The spread of literary fame and the expansion of the reading public and of literary material eventually put pressure on the older classical canon, when reading no longer meant a small number of books read by a small number of people. Before the canon began to shift under such pressure, it first became an object of attention, as living authors and readers attempted to estimate the importance of their own age in relation to the glorious works of the past. Congreve's reputation was already well established by the time Dryden wrote his laudatory epistle "To Mr. Congreve," and the poem only established even more strongly Congreve's place in the lineage of great poets. Numerous works began to be dedicated to him: for instance, Steele's *Poetical Miscellanies* (1714) and Pope's *Iliad* (1720), a sign that the poet-celebrity was beginning to replace the noble patron as muse-on-earth and that the gifted individual was finding at least as prominent, if not

more prominent, a place than hereditary authority could offer.[57]
Pope himself was to discover what it meant to be a poet-celebrity; the *Dunciad* and the "Epistle to Arbuthnot" suggest both the positive and the negative aspects of this status. The rise of the portrait and of the author frontispiece accompanies this rise in the status of the author.[58] Kneller's Kit-Cat portraits and the very popular engravings made from them are only one example of the ways in which portraiture helped promote convincing images for authors and thereby promote sales. Many early-seventeenth-century books carry author portraits, but as the century wears on, such portraits become increasingly part of an elaborate scenario. An unidentified hand may be offering bays to the author, who is dressed as Virgil or Ovid; the poet's pen may be shown as emitting a fluid landscape. It was important to look right for the part, and widely distributed portraits could help. Congreve was pleased with Kneller's portraits of him and with the engraving John Smith made of one of these. According to Congreve, this engraving was "generally liked," and he sent it out with copies of his books.[59] (He was less pleased with Hugh Howard's portrait of him, which he thought "too chuffy" and never had reproduced.)[60] Within a few decades of Kneller's Congreve, the reshaping becomes even more marked. The various portrait illustrations for Pope's works, for instance, highlight the strong bones of his face; they show him discreetly swathed and seated or leaning in such a way that his physique is concealed.[61]

It is nearly impossible to find a poem about poetry between about 1695 and 1710 that does not place Congreve (sometimes next to Dryden) at the top of the poetical hierarchy, and poetic folios and miscellanies are littered with such verse compliments as the following:

> All Wives distress'd invoke your Name,
> And distant Husbands dread your Fame:
> Or if you Worship more delight in
> Our vows that do affect your Writing.

John Smith's 1710 engraving of Sir Godfrey Kneller's portrait of Congreve, painted in 1709. (By permission of the Trustees of the British Museum.)

May *Critic's* ne'r disect your Plays,
Provoked by what they want, your Praise,
Nor Poet envy you the Bays.[62]

If fame meant that admirers could confuse his poetic with his
seductive powers, it also meant that they granted him an immortal life through the continuity of poetic tradition. As the
author of "The Mourning Poets" wrote in his or her "Account
of the Poem's on the Death of the Queen":

In *Congreve Dryden's* ours, to Him we owe
The tuneful Notes which from *Alexis* flow. . . .
Not so lamented *Græcian Bion* fell,
Nor *Venus* mourn'd the lovely Boy so well;
Poets unborn shall make his Lays their Theme,
And future *Rapins* take their Rules from him.[63]

This poetic immortality is fused with dramatic immortality
in the last few decades of the seventeenth century, when writers
on the drama use with greater insistence than ever the word *poet*
to denote a dramatist.[64] In the "Essay of Dramatic Poesy," for
instance, Dryden writes of Shakespeare as the author who "of
all Modern, and perhaps Ancient Poets, had the largest and
most comprehensive soul."[65] The usage appeared in the four-
teenth century and continued through most of the eighteenth
century. But the use of *poet* to denote *dramatist* is at its height
at the end of the seventeenth century. The insistence of the
usage is due, in part, simply to the impact of Greek and Latin.
But it suggests a further desire on the part of the dramatists to
stress their position in the canon of the classic poets. Dryden
and Congreve usually referred to themselves (and to each other)
as poets when they were speaking of their role as dramatists.
The word was not merely reserved for tragedians (although a
comedy was rarely referred to as a poem). Even before Congreve
had written *The Mourning Bride*, he considered himself a dramatic poet. *The Double-Dealer* is dedicated to Halifax because
he is "a Lover of Poetry" (p. 119), and the prologue to the
play claims that "the Poet's sure he shall some comfort find"

(p. 125). William Winstanley, like most late-seventeenth-century critics, dealt with the distinction between drama and nondramatic poetry in his *Lives of the Most Famous English Poets* (1687) by referring to "Dramatick Poetry" and "other kinds of Poetry."[66] But as literary genres became a point of debate, and thus separable, drama itself was more frequently seen as entirely distinct from poetry of other sorts, not simply a special kind of poetry.[67] In the *Dictionary* (1755), Johnson still defines drama as "a poem accommodated to action"; the poet is still "an inventor; an author of fiction; a writer of poems," suggesting the broader usage. But he adds immediately that the poet is "one who writes in measure," a definition that would exclude most comedy and much tragedy. By the end of the eighteenth century, plays are nearly never *poems*, and playwrights are never *poets* unless they also write nondramatic poems.

The emphasis on the word *poet* to identify a dramatist suggests an awareness of the loss of the poetic (that is, the oral) in a drama fixed in print and a desire to maintain that oral quality. It suggests a subtle resistance to what was to come in the eighteenth century: prose tragedy and its abandonment of many of the older aural patterns of the theater. To label the dramatist, with persistence, a "poet," especially when the first prose tragedies are beginning to appear, is to attempt to claim for drama a high place among the genres and to insist on its distinction from the increasing quantities of prose fiction that were appearing. If the drama is to be a genre that is not just an oral art but also an art that expresses itself through print, it must then claim the best of that print world. By acknowledging (in his preface to *Incognita* and in his shelf arrangement) that "drama" is a separable category, and at the same time insisting that the dramatist is a poet, Congreve attempts to keep for the drama a privileged place among the shifting categories of knowledge and arts that touch his library.

The catalog upholds the privileged place not only of the drama but also of the dramatic poet. The emphasis on authorship as a central ordering principle in the catalog further canonizes the elevated poet-dramatist and separates this dramatist from the communal realm of the theater. A play can be performed only with the collective authority of the company, under the patronage of royal authority. But a play can be written in solitude by an author who, through the manipulation of the printed page, usurps the older forms of collective and hereditary authority. It can be written in solitude by the individual genius as the adornment of a library for those individuals who read in solitude. The systems of eighteenth-century standardization and categorization seem to be public in that they are "for the benefit of the public." But they are actually devised for a world in which privacy and individualism have eroded older systems of shared knowledge, systems that were communicated orally—for instance, through the educational system. Cross-referencing and alphabetization, for example, help organize logically a world in which idiosyncratic listings or the categories of the medieval university have proved to be dependent on an oral communication that is now insufficient.

Congreve's cross-listings and alphabetization, while identifying the print realm in which he chooses to situate his drama, replace the fading public mode with a system designed to facilitate private attainment of knowledge. But he has not fully turned his back on the older shared assumptions or on the live stage. His catalog and shelves move between the systems of the medieval university and the standardized public categorization of the eighteenth century. The catalog and shelves mix the two, exploring their connection to the past and their usefulness for the modern era, their connection to the age of sacred books, and their place in the age of mass production, in which books are so plentiful that their only aura consists in the layers of dust that fall from the older ones in the private library. Both systems inform the soon-to-be articulated notion of the drama that Congreve's shelf only begins to suggest, a notion that will dominate eighteenth-century drama and that increasingly binds the oral drama in a printed form. Congreve's move from work for the active stage in the seventeenth century to work on editions and on his own library in the eighteenth century parallels this shift in the idea of the drama. While the urge toward the solitary pleasures of the library is for Congreve partly a traditional Horatian resistance to the frivolity of town life, it is also a more modern gesture. It contains the attraction to private consciousness that will take hold of the serious drama and that in the late eighteenth century will produce, in "closet drama," a drama most eminently suited to the library, a drama made for the library text conceived in the mind of the solitary celebrity, who is connected to the public only through a publisher like Tonson.

CHAPTER THREE

The Technologized Muse: Oral Ancients, Print, and Rhetorical Style

We hav[e] no *Chorus* to sing our Odes.
—Congreve, "On the Pindarique Ode"

Congreve's placement of himself in a dramatic lineage depended on a relation to the ancients and to knowledge in general that was fundamentally changed by the accumulation of commentary produced by print.[1] Throughout his life, from the Greek lectures at Trinity College, Dublin (which he never failed to attend), to the compilation of the library catalog, Congreve paid close attention to current critical and scholarly discussion of the classical past.[2] His poems and translations (of Horace, Homer, Juvenal, and Ovid) are themselves replete with scholarly commentary, explication of the problems inherent in the text, justification of his own choices. Congreve's principal model was still the general learning of the sixteenth and seventeenth centuries, but with the apparent increase in knowledge, this model no longer seemed possible for the merely human drudge. The choice between unreasoning and mechanical assimilation of vast quantities of material and deliberate ignorance was not appealing, but it seemed an unattainable task to know the past with any thoroughness. The alternatives (both of which many in the late eighteenth and nineteenth centuries finally accepted) were equally unattractive: to become a historical specialist led the way of pedantry; to reject historical knowledge altogether in favor of imagination led the way of chaos and dangerous individualism.

In poems, plays, and criticism, Congreve negotiates his way among three attitudes: the print-culture scholarship (largely Renaissance) that is delighted with the newfound possibilities of accumulation and comparison; the later print-culture stress on distinctions and the rejection of false evidence; and the continuing oral tradition identified with the ancients. The school system provided young scholars like Congreve with an environment in which classical poetry was communicated orally. But scholars such as Richard Bentley, William Wotton, and Sir William Temple and periodicals such as the *Journal des Sçavans* were circulating serious inquiry about the classical world by means of print, which had replaced not only oral disputation but also the scholarly manuscript.[3]

By the time Congreve was working closely with Tonson, collecting the best editions of Greek and Latin texts for his library and doing translations and imitations of Greek and Latin poetry, he must have known the classical world primarily as a phenomenon of print. And yet oral habits and values persisted both in his readings and in his imitations of the ancients. If he, like many of his contemporaries, was interested in imitation, this interest was not surprising for a poet in an era poised between a culture primarily defined by the oral and one primarily defined by print. The exploration of the past through imitation was itself inherently both an oral gesture and a literate one. Formal structures and formulae were mnemonic devices, helpful to rapid oratorical composition. At the same time, to insist on the poetic forms of the ancients was to insist on poetic standardization, on unity for a history that could now be checked through the pages of print.

The ancients and moderns debate, in which most writers, willingly or otherwise, partook at the end of the seventeenth

century, emerged partly from a desire to formulate a new relation to the physical volumes that lined library shelves.[4] The
older battles of oral disputation had been transposed into a battle not of voices, but of books (in which the stakes themselves
were, in a sense, the old oral voices). As many have noted, the
two sides were not at first so much rigid antinomies as descriptive categories.[5] For scientists such as Bacon and Newton,
knowledge of the ancients and modern discovery were inextri-
cably linked. One was essential to the other. The modern accuracy that they had helped develop was just as necessary to classical scholarship as it was to the scientific discoveries that had
discredited Aristotle as a scientific authority.

Although the terms *ancients* and *moderns* had been important
distinctions in scribal culture,[6] in the seventeenth century they
became increasingly forms of classification. Toward the end of
the century, when the sheer bulk and materiality of printed
matter seemed to call for some control, they became more fierce
terms of alignment. But the real "battle of the books" was that
between living speech and the books themselves. By the time
Swift wrote the "Battel of the Books" (written in 1697, although not published until 1704), he imagined the war between the ancients and moderns to be fought over a piece of
material property, the hill of Parnassus. "Whole Rivulets of
Ink" are exhausted in the cause, and libraries become cem-
eteries.[7] When Virgil is mentioned, "we are not to understand
the Person of a famous Poet, call'd by that Name, but only certain Sheets of Paper, bound up in Leather, containing in Print,
the Works of the said Poet."[8] The ancients had become a collection of books rather than a series of stories, a scholarly object
rather than a cultural memory, and their relation to their oral
past had to be redefined.

Using the scholarly tools that print provided seemed to Congreve to be one way of properly appreciating his place in relation
to that past. In the "Amendments of Mr. Collier's False and Imperfect Citations," for instance, he responds to Collier's pedantic use of Aristotle and the classical stage with his own more

precise distinctions, between *Comicus* and *Comædus*, *Tragicus* and *Tragædus*? He uses his scholarship even more extensively as corrective in his attempt to reestablish the true Pindaric ode:

There is nothing more frequent among us, than a sort of Poems intituled Pindarique Odes; pretending to be written in Imitation of the Manner and Stile of *Pindar*, and yet I do not know that there is to this Day extant in our Language, one Ode contriv'd after his Model. What *Idea* can an *English* Reader have of *Pindar*, (to whose Mouth, when a Child, the Bees brought their Honey, in Omen of the future Sweetness and Melody of his Songs) when he shall see such rumbling and grating Papers of Verses, pretending to be Copies of his Works?[10]

Congreve's scholarly restoration of the true Pindaric, which uses oral myth to support its claims, serves as an antidote to the "rumbling and grating Papers of Verses," the false copies of the true original. In the invocation, "Memory," the best servant of oral recitation, is still the Mother of the Muses. (She would become Fancy or Imagination in the nineteenth century.) But Congreve's phrasing—his desire to restore the "Honey" of Pindar's mouth, the "Melody of his Songs"—suggests that this orality must be saved from the mechanical noise of the press.

Scholarship, itself a production of the press, is the means of countering the printed with a new orality, but that very orality can be contained only within the printed and must be revised by it. Congreve's careful historical delineation of Pindar's intentions stresses the way the structure of the ode serves the motions of the chorus. But there is no chorus to sing the odes any longer. "We having no *Chorus* to sing our Odes, the Titles, as well as Use of *Strophe*, *Antistrophe*, and *Epode*, are Obsolete and Impertinent."[11] Print scholarship permits the restoration of the true Pindaric structure, with its elaborate choral articulations, only to show that such structure is "Obsolete and Impertinent" in a world in which writing has eroded the oral.

Similarly, scholarly knowledge of classical criticism helps Congreve support his claims for a living theater against pamphlet attackers like Collier, but those claims can be made available only in the context of late-seventeenth-century printed scholarship and scholarly traditions. The things Congreve learned from "the learned Holyday" or the young scholar, Lady Grace Gethin, for whom Congreve wrote a glowing commendatory epistle, help illuminate Congreve's knowledge of the comic tradition, the progression from Aristotle through Theophrastus, Plautus, Menander, and Terence. "As *Terence* excell'd in his Performance," Congreve wrote in his dedication to *The Way of the World*,

So had he great Advantages to encourage his Undertakings; for he built most on the Foundations of *Menander*: his Plots were generally modell'd, and his Characters ready drawn to his Hand. He copied *Menander*; and *Menander* had no less Light in the Formation of his Characters, from the Observations of *Theophrastus*, of whom he was a Disciple; and *Theophrastus* it is known was not only the Disciple, but the immediate successor of *Aristotle*, the first and greatest Judge of Poetry. (p. 391)

These commentators and practitioners are allied through another progression to the more general thinkers, Diogenes, Epictetus, and Pliny, who frequently appear to support Congreve's claims or to excuse him, as companions in both his theatrical and scholarly endeavors. "I will only make this general Answer in behalf of my Play," he writes in the dedication to *The Old Batchelour*, "(an Answer, which *Epictetus* advises every Man to make for himself, to his Censurers) viz. *That if they who find some faults in it, were as intimate with it as I am, they would find a great many more*" (p. 30). If the models—Menander, Plautus, Terence—teach him to find faults in his work, Epictetus teaches him the discretion of acknowledging them. He is not alone in the community of playwrights through history. Like his book, his dedication (which also serves as apparatus more authoritative than that possible in a performed play) is not alone but is surrounded by the crossing voices of scholarly comment. The annotation and the drama are fully linked. But they are linked only when the drama's voice is not heard.

Like the passage describing a historical progress from Aristotle through Terence, Congreve's serious works on purely classical or purely conventional models, his preservation of formal propriety in poems like his later Pindaric odes, and his reliance on a classical idiom in his serious epistles and odes suggest his eagerness to connect with a classical past that at once preserves its integrity and leads in a continuous line to his own poetic productions. "The Birth of the Muse" (1697), his poem on the way that poetic production arises to give immortality to political greatness (that of William III in concluding the Treaty of Ryswick), shows his own muse to be the culmination of past muses, who would have sung the end of the War of Spanish Succession (had they been available to do so). And yet Congreve recognizes the problem of self-glorification. This recognition emerges most clearly when he is detailing his relation to Charles Montagu, Lord Halifax, leading Whig politician, the man to whom Congreve dedicated both *The Double-Dealer* and "The Birth of the Muse," and his patron. In the "Epistle to Halifax," the dedicatory poem that heads the 1710 edition of his poems, he is more modest about his muse's relation to the ancients:

> In high *Parnassus* she no Birthright claims,
> Nor drinks deep Draughts of *Heliconian* Streams
> Yet near the sacred Mount she loves to rove,
> Visits the Springs, and hovers round the Grove.
> She knows what Dangers wait too bold a Flight,
> And fears to fall from an *Icarian* Height:
> Yet, she admires the Wing that safely soars,
> At Distance follows, and its Track adores. (S: p. 138)

His muse wanders near the realms of the highest achievements of the Greeks. (Though the context suggests, in conventional encomium, that Halifax himself has "the Wing that safely soars," Congreve clearly means this wing to be his precursors'.) Congreve takes nourishment from them, but he recognizes that to attempt to imitate too closely, to attempt to appropriate a classical loftiness of tone, is to be in danger of leaping into bombast or plunging into bathos. The extension of traditional characters, places, and events may circumscribe

what it is possible, or at least natural, for him to imagine in
such a poem. The poem may be connected with familiar figures
in familiar places doing familiar things, recurring characters
from the great distended epic that classical literature had become, but however familiar these characters may be, they remain part of a distant golden age, in which more perfect representations of action and emotion were possible, in which the
literal application of nontechnological forms could never appear
excessive, in which neither bombast nor bathos threatened, and
in which the originals fought and loved in a natural and mem-
oryless realm.

Congreve's favorite version of classical form is the pastoral,
which he uses in his two major elegies ("The Mourning Muse
of Alexis" [1695] and "The Tears of Amaryllis for Amyntas"
[1703]), many of his songs, his opera *Semele*, a number of occasional poems, and of course *The Judgement of Paris*, his only
masque, which opens with Paris "seated under a Tree, and playing on his Pipe; his Crook and Scrip, &c. lying by him."[12] In
Congreve and elsewhere, the pastoral has an odd combination
of effects. Traditionally, it has been a means of simultaneously
isolating and criticizing perennial human problems (often urban and aristocratic) and of describing a realm in which "modern" problems need not exist. On one level it claims a sophistication about classical convention and literary tradition, while
on a more explicit level it claims an absolute innocence and a
voice not contrived by the sophisticated arts of convention.[13] In
"The Mourning Muse of Alexis," when Alexis mourns, "Ah
Woe too great! Ah Theme, which far exceeds, / The lowly Lays
of humble Shepherds Reeds!" (S: p. 39), Congreve invokes the
rhetorically sophisticated inexpressibility topos to claim distance from the loftiness of rhetorical art. Pastoral uses a historical nostalgia that relies on books containing such "history" (literary texts from the past) in order to invoke an imagined ahistorical past. It uses history to reach the ahistorical. If that
nostalgia relies on history, it also encourages further historical
investigation; for the more the poems proffer as the ideal an im-

age of the rural land of Virgil's *Eclogues* (themselves, of course, only Roman rural nostalgia), the more they encourage a scholarly investigation of the primitive and a poetic proliferation of such images. Ironically enough, the more that nostalgia urges a technical and scholarly gathering of information about the past, the more that nostalgia longs for a past free of both that technology and that scholarship.[14]

In this lies Congreve's essential distance from the objects of his nostalgia. It is not merely that he can never achieve the lofty voice of Pindar, nor is it that his Pastora and Alexis are far distant in time; it is that Congreve is perpetually confronted with the technological distance between that imaginary Greece and Rome and his own London.[15] Human nature may remain perpetually the same ("Believe it, Men have ever been the same," he writes);[16] the ancient Greeks and the modern English may share an infinite number of desires, humors, foibles; but the Greeks, those mythical-historical creatures, do not have the long hall of reflecting mirrors that the accumulation of books and the reduplication of reduplications have created. The pastoral land of the golden age is oral, and the Greeks and Romans have a literacy closer to the oral in their innocence of print.

The idealized images of orality that pervade Congreve's work and his scholarly interest in pretechnological culture are closely related. Congreve was aware, at least to a certain extent, of Homer's oral method of composition. There are a number of classical arguments for the orality of Homer (that of Josephus, for instance).[17] In the 1670's, the Abbé d'Aubignac had argued that the *Iliad* and the *Odyssey* were merely bits of folksong that had later been compiled. Likewise, Richard Bentley claimed that although Homer had in fact existed, his "songs" were not put together until several hundred years later.[18] Congreve himself writes, in a note to his translation of the Homeric "Hymn to Venus" (which he believed to be Homer's), "After the Decease of *Homer*, there were such Persons who made a Profession of repeating his Verses; from the Repetitions of whom, and of their Descendents or Successors (for they became a Sect) the entire Poems of *Homer* in After-times were collected and put in Order"

(S: p. 165).¹ These Homeric repeaters, like the shepherds, have a small community devoted to singing. Their pure form of oral culture, a culture of song and performance, resonates in Congreve's scenes of classical golden age life.

In "The Mourning Muse of Alexis," Alexis mourns at first only in the wordless music of sighs and tears, which are echoed by "Each whistling Wind, and murm'ring Stream," until Menalcus urges him to vent his grief "not in Sighs, but Words" (S: p. 40). In "A Pindarique Ode Humbly Offer'd to the King On His Taking Namur" (1695), the figure of "Fame," who pervades classical and Renaissance literature, is still the recipient and carrier of the oral, with her "thousand Ears" and "Tongues" (S: p. 45). In "The Tears of Amaryllis for Amyntas," all nature remains silent in respect for Amaryllis's mourning cries:

> Ev'n Eccho fear'd to catch the flying Sound,
> Lest Repetitions should her Accents drown. (S: p. 68)

(Perhaps one might read here an anxiety about the drowning of the poetic voice by reduplication, whether the now-excessive reduplications of oral copia or those of mechanical reproduction, but again transmuted into a classical figure representing the oral/aural.)¹⁹ In "The Mourning Muse," one of the greatest tragedies of Queen Mary's death is that:

> No more, the Nymphs shall with soft Tales delight
> Her Ears, no more with Dances please her Sight;
> Nor ever more shall Swain make Song of Mirth,
> To bless the Joyous Day, that gave her Birth. (S: p. 41)

However much this mourning can be transposed into a regret for the loss of a queen who delighted in the numerous birthday odes written for her and the numerous theatrical performances in her honor, it remains a lament also for the lost oral narrative of the pastoral golden age. At the dinner of utopian simplicity that Congreve reimagines in his translation of Juvenal, oral recitation is colored by literacy:

> Yet with your Taste your Hearing shall be fed,
> And *Homer*'s sacred Lines, and *Virgil*'s read;

> Either of whom does all Mankind excel,
> Tho' which exceeds the other, none can tell.
> It matters not with what ill Tone they're sung,
> Verse so sublimely good, no Voice can wrong. (S: p. 17)

Homer and Virgil are read, but read aloud (*heard*, in the first lines). A few lines later, we are told that they are "sung," but that the quality of the performance matters little. If "Verse so sublimely good, no Voice can wrong," then no voice can wrong, either, verse read silently in a long-literate culture. The Homeric and Virgilian texts stand on their own, independent of oratory.

The passage negotiates between the literate and the oral in much the same way that Congreve's poems and prose pieces reveal a shifting balance between orality and literacy in his stylistic, rhetorical, and formal values. Naturally, Renaissance style and rhetoric had been deeply affected by the invention of print, just as eighteenth- and nineteenth-century styles were to retain many oral instincts and values. But many stylistic effects of Renaissance poetry and prose that can be identified as oral residue are replaced during the decades following the Restoration by effects that can be identified with print (although they are not solely attributable to print and although orality retains its hold).[20] Renaissance copia, for example, was more than an aesthetic principle. It was more than an ideal of rhetorical abundance in which a writer was to express an idea with as much elaboration and in as many ways as possible. (Erasmus's *De Copia*—which offers, for instance, 200 ways of saying in Latin, "I shall remember you as long as I live"—exemplifies the device most fully.) Copia was also a method of composition based on the values and recipes of oral improvisational composition, although in the Renaissance it was transposed onto the printed page. It embodied the kind of speedy proliferation that is difficult in extempore poetry and oratory and thus highly valued in cultures where oratory is the principal mode of communication—oral cultures. Copia's effective use relied on the notion that human memory is essential to cultural preservation, and thus repetition and abundance are to be valued. The common-places were at once bits of cultural memory and composition aids, always of service when, in the face of hungry listeners, a speaker's inspiration might be lacking. The rejection of copia by some seventeenth-century claimants for the "plain style" can be associated with a rejection of residual orality.[21]

Many of the older clichés about shifts in seventeenth-century styles and attitudes, from "humanist" and "baroque," for instance, to "Augustan" and "neoclassical," might also be seen as shifts from residual orality to newly interiorized postprint values. For instance, the humanist interest in collecting all available documents of human achievement can be identified with oral culture's interest in preservation, despite the fact that the humanist collections were made possible partly by means of print. Augustan skepticism about the possibility of attaining sure knowledge and thereby improving the human condition can be seen partly as a reaction to an abundance of printed matter. Baroque literature might be linked with the ornate rhetoric and abundance valued by orality, which uses rhetoric as a memory aid and which prizes the verbosity of the unhesitating speaker.[22] The neoclassical value for simplicity, clarity, and restraint might be seen partly as a reaction to the combination of this abundance and the already multiplying forms of print, a reaction that perceives the necessity of control.

With the interiorization of print values, copia was no longer felt as abundance. It seemed largely to be excessive and unnecessary repetition in a world in which mechanical memory could render extensive human memory obsolete. Any hack (or plagiarist) could throw together a book out of commonplaces gathered easily from other books. Erasmus, in his four thousand *Adages* and eight books of *Apophthegms*, had used print to bring copia to its furthest limits. Congreve and others like him had to invoke different values to combat the excesses that print made possible. The standardization of form that print allows encourages attempts at the kind of regularity that can be checked on a page, though later writers will rebel against what they perceive to be an excess of such regularity. (Perhaps the interest in the free-form "Pindaric ode" during the period can be seen as an early reaction to rigid formalism.) The union of fancy and restraint is an earlier version of such a reaction to print. Fancy and restraint are the ideal partners in a postprint world in that they avoid reduplicating the function that discursive books provide much more effectively. Fancy and originality replace cultural memory, for books already serve as better memory devices. Restraint replaces copia, for books already provide abundance, if not excess.

Congreve had always been interested in the virtue of restraint that adherence to formal principles could offer. The emphatic discussion of "design" and "decorums" in his prefaces and the use of these principles in the plays show one manifestation of the desire for containment and control of excess, particularly in prose. This control extends both to notions of plot and to notions of diction.[23] Over the years, he grew increasingly interested in regularity: he regularized the "numbers" for the 1710 edition of *The Mourning Bride*; he smoothed out pentameters in the poems. For Congreve, control does not enslave language, but actually frees it from the barbarity and confusion of copia. The freedom and "ease" of a simpler style are particularly important for poetry, which must learn to resist excess without destroying "fancy." The elimination of copia by no means eliminates variety, freedom, and metamorphosis, as Congreve was eager to point out in his "Epistle to Halifax." His muse moves freely:

> By no one Measure bound, her Numbers range,
> And unresolv'd in Choice, delight in Change;
> Her Songs to no distinguish'd Fame aspire,
> For, now, she tries the Reed, anon, attempts the Lyre.
> (S: p. 138)

The perfect regularity of the first three lines of the quatrain and the irregularity of the last demonstrate the union of freedom and formal restraint that Congreve sought to achieve. The identical placement of the caesuras in the first couplet and the last line further suggests the way in which Congreve is careful with his measures; however varied the collection may be, each poem retains its own decorum. His claims for freedom and change are nearly always themselves qualified by further claims for the "Skill" by which fancy must be "both temper'd and re-fin'd."[24] In his syntax and diction, Congreve avoids the repetitions, additive structures, accumulations of vocabulary, and epithets characteristic of oral style. He opts, rather, for simple sentences. He pairs opposites, rather than accumulating synonyms, here in "To Sir Godfrey Kneller":

> Judgment and Genius so concur in thee,
> And both unite in perfect Harmony. (S: p. 146)

He prefers description of a dramatic scenario to elaborately drawn conceits, as in "Song":

> Pious *Selinda* goes to Pray'rs,
>   If I but ask the Favour;
> And yet the tender Fool's in Tears,
>   When she believes I'll leave her. (S: p. 78)

It is only at his most impassioned, his most self-consciously "poetic," his loftiest version of the lofty strain, that plain style is subsumed in the repetitions, the epithets, the additive style, the sense of immediate action that is characteristic of oral composition. In "The Mourning Muse of Alexis," the fawns, nymphs, and satyrs can hardly be said to mourn Queen Mary with restraint:

> In prickly Brakes their tender Limbs they tear,
> And leave on Thorns, their Locks of Golden Hair.
>   With their sharp Nails, themselves the *Satyrs* wound,
> And tug their shaggy Beards, and bite with grief the ground.
> (S: p. 42)

Perhaps the comic undertone of this scene reflects a discomfort on Congreve's part with such nonverbal expressions. At any rate, in its strongly oral effects, this passage can serve to contrast with Congreve's more habitual periodic structures. Additive style helps speakers appear to have mastered the fluidity and unbroken abundance valued by orality. A sustained periodic style, however, is nearly impossible for speakers, who cannot look down at a page to remember the directions that their sentences were originally taking. Periodicity comes naturally to the writer, who can peruse the page and return, after a long absence, to a sentence's grammatical origin, but who can also stop to think.

Congreve's "Pindarique Ode Humbly Offered to the Queen" (1706), written when he had largely retired from the stage and had already spent time working with Tonson and building his library, offers an example of literacy's subordinate style in a poem that celebrates the aurality of music:

> High in the Starry Orb is hung,
> And next *Alcides'* Guardian Arm,
> That Harp to which thy *Orpheus* sung,
> Who Woods, and Rocks, and Winds, cou'd charm;
> That Harp which on *Cyllene's* shady Hill
> When first the Vocal Shell was found,
> With more than mortal Skill
> Inventor *Hermes* taught to sound. (S: p. 87)

Both the syntax of the individual sentence and the careful counting of lines and measures, whose precise numbers would be difficult to count aurally, are expressions of an absorption of formal qualities that can be identified as literate. Absolute strictness of form, although it characterizes some nonliterate religious ceremonies and some manuscript poetry, can be principally identified with print culture, which provides with ease the pleasure to be found in "correcting" the "abuses" of any deviation from that form.[25] Congreve's interest in correcting the abuses (his own past offenses included) of the Pindaric ode is part of that pleasure. In the "Discourse on the Pindarique Ode," he claims that most such English odes are "a Bundle of rambling incoherent Thoughts, express'd in a like Parcel of irregular Stanza's, which also consist of such another Complication of disproportion'd, uncertain and perplex'd Verses and Rhimes."[26] His concern over the exact form of the "true" Pindaric ode and his interest in a perfect mechanical structure for his plots suggest some of the ways in which print was challenging the oral values he had inherited from the preceding generation and from his classical models.

It would be wrong to suggest that preprint or early-print writers had no interest in strict form, even leaving aside the fact that oral recitation relies on precisely definable metrical sequences. To know otherwise, one only has to look at Dante or Petrarch: or to think of the role that numerology played for many in the precise relationships between meter, stanzas, and larger subdivisions; or to remember the intricate patterning of long verse cycles in the early Renaissance. Italian playwrights as early as the quattrocento struggled hard to conform their impulses to the five-act structure. Sidney worried about the unities; Jonson worried more.[27] But self-conscious defenses of precise form, whether metrical or structural, and attacks on those who fail to conform with the exigencies of such form are hard to find before the late sixteenth century and are abundant in the late seventeenth. Something happened in the interval. Writers discovered the possibility of checking formal properties against numerous printed examples of the same form, they easily were able to promulgate critical discussion of such properties, and they were aided in seeing the use of form in language by the spatial clarity of print. But they also felt the need to control the expansion of printed matter by distinguishing a technically knowledgeable elite from the slovenly mass of scribblers. That technical elite, which print makes both possible *and* necessary, defines its prowess by recuperating with self-conscious precision the metrical and structural forms of preprint expression.

The irony in print culture's interest in the exact preservation of oral form is not far from the irony in print's preservation of the nostalgia for the innocent song of the "untutor'd tongue." Classical and late-Renaissance models provided Congreve with oral values and structures and with the means of replacing them with the values and structures of literacy. The classical and Renaissance poets sung of an oral world in additive, formulaic strains, full of commonplaces and often full of the copious phrases of orality. Congreve received their works through the forms of literacy and passed them on in concise and unrepeating phrases, built on measured grammars of subordination. Only a knowledge of the exact forms, meters, and grammars of Greek and Latin poetry brought Congreve the very different rhythms of his own phrases. Only the distance between the culture of the nymphs' soft tales or the recitation of Homer and Virgil and that of the printing press and the stamped page, only that brought Congreve the possibility of imagining an innocent oral culture.

CHAPTER FOUR

"Asterisms":
Pedantry, Knowledge, and the
Struggle with the Past

You may put that into the marginal Notes, tho' to
prevent Criticisms—only mark it with a small asterism.
—Congreve, *The Double-Dealer*

𝕴f to Congreve, as to many of
his contemporaries, writing about and by the ancients was an
act of reverence, and if "imitation" meant control over temporal
loss, then the physical forms of scholarship also threatened the
older relation to a more distant past. Scholarly precision allowed
historians to mark time in new ways and thus to see history as
a long expanse separating the present from the past and distinguishing the two, but it also allowed a proximity through the
microscope of scholarly detail. Proximity meant a necessary redefinition of time and of the modern's placement in time.[1] Such
proximity did not always mean that the ancients seemed more
immediate to Congreve and his contemporaries. As Swift suggests in "The Battel of the Books," the older relation offered a
warmth and immediacy that seemed to be disappearing under
the distance and weight of scholarship. Swift's satire mockingly
attempts to reclaim that immediacy by imagining the books as
the warriors of classical epic, in whom presence is still tied to
an oral mode. When Congreve separated ancients and moderns

on his library shelves, he was doing the opposite of Swift, but for the same reasons. Congreve's separation, like Swift's battle, was an attempt to acknowledge the redefinition called for by print.

Furthermore, both were ways of acknowledging combat with a past as full of frailties as the present. Improvements in printing and the greater number and greater dissemination of classical texts permitted Congreve his intimate familiarity with those texts. Increasing speed in the dissemination of texts and in the exchange of scholarly information offered him more abundant physical detail with a greater sense of historical accuracy, even if the increasing quantities of historically suspect material produced something of a countereffect.[2] If technical sophistication, however, urged a nostalgia for a past that had lacked such sophistication, and if dissemination of classical texts urged a longing for the golden age portrayed in those texts, the physical details revealed by scholarship also made that classical world appear more human, more idiosyncratic, more replete with the mundane details and grotesque exigencies of the ordinary. Thus, at the height of the admiration for the classical, the classical was brought into alignment with the detail of the ordinary. The combination of scholarly minutiae and the exploration of previously little-read classical satires (for instance, those of Persius, available in Dryden's translation in 1693) gave a familiarity to the classical that made it seem, in many ways, less sacred.

Congreve's translations of Juvenal and Ovid underline the physical decadence of their social environments. In the eleventh satire of Juvenal, the gluttonous excesses of the Romans grow more and more greasily explicit:

> For scarce a Slave, but has to Dinner now,
> The well-dress'd Paps of a Fat Pregnant Sow. (S: p. 13)

(Congreve's footnote tells the reader, with just a touch of irony, that this is "A Dish in great Esteem among the *Romans*.") If the finest platters are not used, "Something's amiss, he knows not

what to think, / Either your *Ven'son*'s rank, or *Oyntments* stink"
(S: p. 15). A wanton woman completes the scene:

> Apace she warms, with an immod'rate Heat,
> Strongly her Bosom heaves, and Pulses beat;
> With glowing Cheeks, and trembling Lips she lies,
> With Arms expanded, and with Naked Thighs,
> Sucking in Passion both at Ears and Eyes. (S: p. 17)

In Ovid, the decay of womanly beauty is equally explicit and
equally invades the regions of ideal praise:

> Let not the Nymph with Laughter much abound,
> Whose Teeth are black, uneven, or unsound. (S: p. 100)

> Let her who has no Hair, or has but some,
> Plant Centinels before her Dressing-Room. (S: p. 99)

> I need not warn you of too pow'rful Smells,
> Which, sometimes Health, or kindly Heat expels,
> Nor, from your tender Legs to pluck with Care
> The casual Growth of all unseemly Hair.
> Tho' not to Nymphs of *Caucasus* I sing,
> Nor such who taste remote the *Mysian* Spring. (S: pp. 97–98)

The body exudes, the flesh sprouts, women must torture their
"tender Legs" (the connotations are culinary) and deny themselves "Health" and "kindly Heat" to attract the ephemeral
male lovers who lurk in the shadows of *The Art of Love.* This
dressing-room advice (in Congreve's version, almost a parody of
classical antifeminism), its physical explicitness full of torture
and repulsion, is not intended for those who receive the highest
poetic diction of the passage, the "Nymphs of *Caucasus*" or
those of Mysia, whose remoteness suggests a sylvan innocence.
But Congreve's note tells us that the "Wild Inhabitants of *Caucasus* and *Mysia*" are from regions noted for the "Worthlessness
of [their] Inhabitants." In a poem that, even in Ovid's version,
encases the grotesque in an ironic sublime diction, Congreve's
version of Ovid's sublime diction is transformed, through the
footnote, into a further extension of ironic pastoral.

The connection between classicism, a culture of excess footnotes, and suspicion of attempts at the sublime (fear of bathos) emerges even more forcefully a few decades later in *The Dunciad* (1728) and "Peri Bathous" (1727–28). In the mock-pastoral and mock-heroic of the early eighteenth century, the ironic juxtaposition of sublime diction and intimate physicality would be taken to its logical extreme in such works as Swift's dressing-room poems, where juxtaposition becomes a more essential fusion (Swift's toilet accoutrements do, in fact, rise to heroic proportions). Much has been written on this problem, in Swift and in others, and there have been many attempts at a definition of the mock-heroic.[3] In some ways, mock-heroic may be seen as a rebellion against the past in general and against the Renaissance in particular.[4] The Renaissance, insofar as it involves classical revival, may be seen partly as a version of naive classicism against which burlesque and mock-heroic struggle. Mock-heroic, burlesque, and parody of the classical, then, were less (as a traditional definition might put it) ways of registering disappointment with the modern world in relation to the classical ideal than they were reactions of surprise at the things a partial and idealized classical world had concealed.

Though this kind of mock-heroic response was not unique to the seventeenth century, it was particularly prevalent during that century, when certain kinds of scholarship still seemed relatively novel. The combination of actually reading certain more obscure classical texts (rather than relying on the descriptions of an admiring tradition) and discovering, through increasing scholarship, the physical realities of ancient Greece and Rome made the classical world seem closer to modern England. When one imagined the heroic descriptions of the classical texts applied to a world much like England, in which human beings and manners had remained essentially the same, the result was that such texts, great as they seemed in poetic terms, seemed absurd as descriptions of the real world. The *Aeneid* could finally either be burlesqued with destructive glee or be understood itself to be a version of mock-heroic, a commentary on the decay of Augustan Rome.[5]

In Congreve, mock-heroic remains mostly gently implicit, as if classical and heroic utterance were not altogether absurd, but merely slightly misplaced in a world whose essence cannot absorb it. But it is there, nonetheless, and Congreve's poems in this respect can be considered typical of the late seventeenth century. If Ovid could apply such diction (in Congreve's interpretation of it) to a Rome of odoriferous and plucked ladies, underlining the ironic gap between the ideal and the real, Congreve could apply the same diction (that learned from translation of classical texts) to his homegrown version of such a lady, in "Doris":

> DORIS, a Nymph of riper Age,
>   Has every Grace and Art;
> A wise Observer to engage,
>   Or wound a heedless Heart.
> Of Native Blush, and Rosy Dye,
>   Time has her Cheek bereft;
> Which makes the prudent Nymph supply,
>   With Paint, th'injurious Theft.
> Her sparkling Eyes she still retains,
>   And Teeth in good Repair;
> And her well-furnish'd Front disdains
>   To grace with borrow'd Hair. (S: p. 142)

This simultaneous mockery of high poetic diction and nymphs of riper age is not the only sign of Congreve's recognition, through scholarship and his intimate confrontation with classical satire, of the frailty of the classical ideal. The gods themselves, and the myths in which they play the roles of jealous lovers and nagging wives, are vulnerable to unflattering parallels with some of the lower and more comic elements of English life. In *The Old Batchelour*, to call Setter Mercury is to remind us that Mercury was a procurer for Jupiter. Congreve is not afraid to be explicit:

SHARPER   Here again, my *Mercury*!

SETTER   Sublimate, if you please, Sir: I think my Atchievments do
deserve the Epithet.—*Mercury* was a Pimp too; but, tho' I blush
to own it at this time, I must confess I am somewhat fall'n from
the Dignity of my Function; and do condescend to be scandal-
ously employ'd in the Promotion of Vulgar Matrimony. (V.i,
p. 105)

Congreve, like many of his contemporaries, seems both troubled and pleased by this reminder of the true nature of the god.
Dryden, for instance, in his *Amphitryon* (1690), shows his discomfort with and his amusement at what he sees as the skewed
morality of the myth. Congreve's satire against the Setters of
the world and the scheming Sylvias for whom they procure has
its own element of discomfort. But there is, at the same time,
a certain joyous abandon in playing with the doubly sacred gods
(sacred because they are gods, albeit pagan, and sacred because
they are made venerable through classical tradition). Congreve's
explicit claims for the superiority of the ancients are tempered
by his pleasure in dethroning them. Wide dissemination and
easy availability made the gap between the ancients and moderns—who could exist side by side in the same binding—seem
much narrower, and made rivalry seem more possible.[6] This rivalry only encouraged an idea of the history of poetry as a sort
of Olympic game in which one always tried to throw a discus
of one's fancy a little farther, tried to soar a little higher. (The
contest was one in which success lay in sublimity as much as in
decorum or wit, particularly after Boileau's French translation
of Longinus's *On the Sublime* in 1674.)[7] This was no "anxiety of
influence." But Congreve and many of his contemporaries, in
choosing those models, set themselves the task of striving to
outdo antiquity. It was important to them to make a fair estimate of their success or failure; and when they attempted to
surpass the Greeks and Romans in such poetic gestures as burlesque, parody, and "wit," they were often able to turn these
tools playfully against their models.

However modest Congreve may be about his muse, which follows at a distance the "Wing that safely soars" (in the dedicatory epistle to his collected poems), elsewhere he is less reticent about the possibility of competition with the ancients. For instance, in his conventionalized lament for his failure to live up to the poetry of the past (in "The Mourning Muse of Alexis"), he maintains a personal modesty but at the same time suggests an unbroken line of greatness that, like the comic line in the dedication to *The Way of the World*, might resolve itself in him. The rhetoric he uses is one of "If . . . then," with the implication that the "If" is not quite so implausible as one might think:

> O could I sing in Verse of equal Strain,
> With the *Sicilian* Bard, or *Mantuan* Swain;
> Or melting Words, and moving Numbers chuse,
> Sweet as the British *Colin*'s mourning Muse;
> Could I like him, in tuneful Grief excel,
> And mourn like *Stella* for her *Astrofel*;
> Then might I raise my Voice, (secure of Skill,)
> And with melodious Woe, the Valleys fill. (S: pp. 39–40)

Homer and Virgil are separated from Spenser and Sidney by a mere descriptive distinction, and the elaborateness of the latter end of the distinction (in contrast with that of the former) suggests that Congreve is more interested in the poetic qualities of the English poets. Homer and Virgil get no encomiastic epithets, where Spenser and Sidney are "melting," "moving," and "tuneful." Congreve's fate as a poet is bound up with that of the English moderns; the gradually accumulating adjectives of poetic praise, which gather momentum as the passage progresses, ensure the skill of his "melodious Woe." In the "Epistle to Halifax," England is no longer the nearer end of a long line of greatness, but the explicit rival of Greece, if not an altogether successful one:

> O had Your Genius been to Leisure born,
> And not more bound to aid us, than adorn!

Albion in Verse with ancient *Greece* had vy'd,
And gain'd alone a Fame, which, there, seven States divide.

(S: p. 139)

Halifax's choice of politics over poetry has disadvantaged England only temporarily in its poetic competition with Greece; the nation awaits the birth of a muse capable of singing the glories of an empire unified by political brilliance—that, for instance, of such Whig heroes as Halifax, as Marlborough, as William III himself.[8]

In "The Birth of the Muse" (dedicated to Halifax and devoted to William's praise), Congreve slyly, if only implicitly, suggests his own claim to patronage of that English muse, in suggesting that the muse was created principally to sing the glories of William III. Congreve's experiment in political-poetic mythmaking proposes a God who, before the creation, glances through the Book of Life, and notices that even the acts of the good and the great are destroyed by time:

> Bright in his View the *Trojan* Heroes shine,
> And *Ilian* Structures rais'd by Hands Divine;
> But *Ilium* soon in Native Dust is laid,
> And all her boasted Pile a Ruine made:
> Nor Great *Aeneas* can her Fall withstand,
> But flies, to save his Gods, to foreign Land.
> The *Roman* Race succeed the *Dardan* State,
> And first, and second *Caesar*, God-like Great. (S: p. 55)

Congreve collapses the essentials (in the poet's eyes) of classical history into this short passage. That history is contained in the two great epics: the fall of Troy, Aeneas's flight, the founding of Rome, and the reigns of Caesar and Augustus (these leading out of Dardanian heroism with as little difficulty or time lapse as for Virgil). All this greatness is destroyed by Time, the villain of the poem, who wipes out the ages of the past: the glorious and inglorious, the divine architecture of Ilium whose "boasted Pile" (the hint of mockery is not accidental) is "a Ruine made," the great empire of Elizabeth that crumbles into a *"Series* of

Inglorious Reigns" (S: p. 56). (Congreve, not as interested in
the medieval as Dryden and Pope are, skips everything between
Augustus and Elizabeth.) But Time, like Milton's Satan, is a
villain fated to be the unwitting machine behind a Fortunate
Fall, for the destruction of the past has made way for a new
reign, which breaks into the course of history:[9]

> *Britannia*, rise; awake, O Fairest Isle,
> From Iron Sleep; again thy Fortunes smile.
> Once more look up, the Mighty Man behold,
> Whose Reign renews another Age of Gold. (S: p. 56)

William has come to the throne, conquered, and awakened
England from the sleep caused by the erasures of Time, the sev-
ering of memory. Must Time destroy this greatness too? asks
Congreve. No, he answers, for Congreve's (and William's) God
is the benevolent God of late-seventeenth-century latitudinar-
ianism. He does not affect the course of human history but simply creates a being to record it; he does not interfere much in
affairs human, but when he does, he is principally concerned
with rewarding virtue and justice. (Through poetic mythmaking, Congreve is able to imply that William has heavenly connections and that his reign is backed by the divinity, without
needing to invoke the rhetoric of divine right, with all its suggestions of Jacobitism.)[10] God favors merit only, and he will
reward William for his "soaring Genius" and "deathless Fame"
by making his reign immortal:

> The Great Creator soon the Grant resolves,
> And in his mighty Mind the Means resolves.
> He thought; Nor doubted once, again to chuse,
> But spake the Word, and made th'immortal *Muse*. (S: p. 59)

Congreve has here used both the Creation (the speaking of "the
Word") and the making of Christ the Redeemer (the immortal
being who defeats the villain) in his creation of the muse, who,
nonetheless, has many secular-historical tasks. She must resus-
citate the fame of all the ages of greatness, all the forgotten con-

querors: the "Dardan Prince," the "Caesars," "Eliza." But her
most important task, that task for which she was created, is to
sing the praises of William:

> *And yet, O* Muse, *remains the noblest Theme;*
> *The first of Men, Mature for Endless Fame,*
> *Thy future Songs shall grace, and all thy Lays,*
> *Thenceforth, alone shall wait on* WILLIAM'*s Praise.* (S: p. 59)

The English muse who sings William's praises, and thus she
who sings his praises in "The Birth of the Muse" (as it turns
out, Congreve's muse), has priority over the muse who sang the
praises of Ilium and the Roman race, for she could not preserve
the fame of these great specimens of humanity, whose deeds
must now be restored by the new power born to celebrate William. Whether or not Congreve recognized the irony inherent
in writing a panegyric for his own muse, which writes pane-
gyrics on a king who shares his Christian name, it is impossible
to know. (The typography—full capitals for WILLIAM—
makes the name hard to ignore.) Certainly Congreve's explicit
intent in the poem is to demonstrate the connection between a
powerful and just monarch and powerful and just poetry, a poetry revolutionized in 1688 by political revolution. (The four
preceding Stuart monarchs, in their disgrace, are relegated in
the poem to the words *"Series* of inglorious Reigns.") But beneath this explicit intent there is an important implicit parallel:
the celebration of the overthrow of the old and tyrannical mon-
archy parallels the celebration of the overthrow of the ancients'
muse.

In "To Mr. Dryden on his Translation of Persius" (1693),
Congreve makes a stronger claim for the priority of the English
poetic voice. The poem is a triple tribute: a tribute to Dryden
as poet and man; a confirmation of Dryden's own high critical
estimation of English moderns; and in its deliberate Dryden
echoes, a flattering imitation of Dryden's verse as poetic model.
Congreve praises Dryden for redeeming Persius, who was held
in "small Esteem," by suggesting that the English master is ca-

To thee, the Dardan *Prince shall owe his Fame*;
To thee, the Cæsars *their immortal Name.*
Eliza *sung by thee, with Fate shall strive,*
And long as Time, *in Sacred Verse survive.*
And yet O Muse, *remains the Noblest Theme*;
The first of Men, Mature for Endless Fame
Thy future Songs shall grace, and all thy Lays,
Thenceforth, alone shall wait on WILLIAM's *Praise.*
On his Heroick Deeds, thy Verse shall rise;
Thou shalt diffuse the Fires that he supplies.
Thro' him thy Songs shall more sublime aspire;
And he thro' them, shall deathless Fame acquire :
Nor Time, *nor* Fate *his Glory shall oppose,*
Or blast the Monuments the Muse *bestows.*

    This said ; no more remain'd. Th' *Ætherial* Host,
Again impatient Crowd the Cryftal Coaft.
The Father, now, within his fpacious Hands,
Encompafs'd all the mingled Mafs of Seas and Lands ;
And having heav'd aloft the pond'rous Sphere,
He Launch'd the World to float in ambient Air.

F I N I S.

Congreve's 1697 panegyric on William III, *The Birth of the Muse*, published by Jacob Tonson. (By permission of the British Library.)

pable of a voice that uncovers the worth (a questionable one) of
the Roman poet:

> *Persius*, before, in small Esteem was had,
> Unless, what to Antiquity is paid;
> But like Apocrypha, with Scruple read,
> (So far, our Ignorance our Faith misled). (S: p. 23)

That Persius wrote in antiquity has given him whatever prestige
he might have had, for the modern age pays empty homage to
those things falsely dignified by antiquity, without knowing
whether they are worthy. The label "antiquity" is here figured
as the label "apocrypha," which the superstitiously religious
read out of blind "faith" and by which they are misled. But the
figure switches direction in the next lines, in which the Christian
is absorbed into the pagan, the religious into the poetic,
and apocrypha is miraculously transformed into genuinely sacred
matter:

> 'Till you, *Apollo*'s darling Priest, thought fit
> To place it, in the Poet's Sacred Writ.

As a priest of Apollo, Dryden has the magical power of writing;
translation becomes, more than anything, a process of switching
sacred orders by reinscribing. This process is emphatically
one of writing, rather than speech, but in the next lines, writing
becomes a form of imprinted image:

> As Coin, which bears some awful Monarch's Face,
> So your bright Image, which we here behold,
> Adds Worth to Worth, and dignifies the Gold.

The period's recurrent trope for print is the stamped coin, an
important image during the recoinage crisis of the 1690's. In
the metamorphoses of early-seventeenth-century alchemical
poems, base metal becomes gold; in late-seventeenth-century
alchemical poems, gold is given the more precise form of coins
or medals. Authors are usually described as "stamping" their
images in the metal and leaving numerous "copies" of themselves
behind; Grub Street productions are often envisioned as

"counterfeits." The context is nearly always one that suggests a mechanical reproduction analogous to that of the printing press. Both result in the diffusion of numerous identical images. Perhaps the choice of the image itself (stamping in gold) registers some longing for reproductions on indestructible matter, rather than on cheap and ephemeral paper. Coins were, of course, the first form of printing, and the late seventeenth century took a lively interest in this antecedent of a process that seemed so familiar. The relatively new science of numismatics was being perfected during the last decades of the century and was used extensively by historians like Wotton, who understood that archaeological sources could often be superior to traditional or literary sources. The early Church iconoclasts may have seen money as the prototype of the graven image, at once explication and embodiment of the commandment against the vanity of images;[11] but for an era inundated with the ephemeral, coins could represent the dignity of lasting matter. (It was printed paper money that would, a few decades after the Persius poem, receive scathing attacks analogous to literary attacks on printing like *The Dunciad*.)[12]

In imagining Dryden as a monarch on a medal, Congreve may intend subtly to rewrite (translate) the figure in Dryden's *The Medal* (1681–82), making it a positive image in a post-revolutionary England (a strange tribute from a Whig to a Jacobite and Tory). In any case, to secularize the sacred by suggesting that the pagan god of poetry (Apollo) is the true god is to pave the way for the suggestion that the true, divinely justified monarch, the monarch who has connections with the heavenly (inspiration), is the monarch of poetry (a perfectly reasonable claim for a Whig poet devoted to the sublime). Dryden has a right to that honor. The simile equates a great monarch's face imprinted in gold with Dryden's image imprinted in Persius's text (both raise the value of the thing in which they imprint themselves). The metonymy ("image" for translation) suggests an analogy between this process of imprinting and translation. A larger metaphor contains the others and suggests that modern printing, analogous to the coining of metal and to the process of translation, has dignified the base matter of ancient writing.

Tonson's beautiful edition (the Juvenal and Persius in which one of Congreve's first publications appears) has made Persius sacred for the sake of a new enlightened religion (the poetry of the moderns); the printing press becomes a tool of enlightenment:

> Else, whence proceeds this great Surprise of Light!
> How dawns this day, forth from the Womb of Night! (S: p. 23)

Print improves and remakes the past, just as it improves nature through its poetic re-creations and through its mechanical (superior) enactment of memory. If Time, in "The Birth of the Muse," is the destroyer, then the muse (Congreve's poetry) is the redeemer, at once Christ likeness, created to save humankind, and printing press, created to save history from oblivion (though perhaps the analogy should not be pushed too far). The press is a further form of translation: as Dryden translates Persius into modern English terms, improving him in the process, so the press translates Dryden's hand into the finished form of the art work, Tonson's folio. And the modern work is, finally, greater than the ancient:

> And as before, for *Persius* our Esteem
> To his Antiquity was paid, not him:
> So now, whatever Praise from us is due,
> Belongs not to Old *Persius*, but the New.
> For still Obscure, to us no Light he gives;
> Dead in himself, in you alone he lives. (S: pp. 23–24)

Here, the point about false tributes to antiquity is repeated as a way of substantiating Congreve's claim for the superiority of his best-beloved modern, the source of poetic illumination. He implies discreetly that all admiration for the ancients may be superstitious, but admiration for the moderns is clear-sighted and enlightened.

For Congreve, not all translation dignifies base material or illuminates an obscure poetry to which readers once paid only superstitious tribute. When the work to be translated deliberately uses base material as one of its poetic strategies, the competitive contract of translation is slightly altered. The less-dignified elements of classical culture (those of Congreve's Ovid translation, for instance) find a congenial home in the comically colloquialized diction of upper-class English domesticity. Such diction forces superstitious admirers of antiquity to confront the reality of the world they are admiring, without rejecting the Roman poet himself. Thus, Ovid's Roman woman adorning herself is "a Lady at her Toilet" snatching "in haste the Tour she wore" (S: p. 99); his glamorous Dido becomes an "Eliza" (an Anglicized version of Elissa, S: p. 93); his gambling women become "Gamesters" who know how "To raffle prettily, or slur a Dye" (S: p. 102). Congreve modernizes less radically than do some of his contemporaries and near-contemporaries. This is not Dryden's or Butler's transposition of the Greeks and Romans into the most vulgar of Londoners, for Congreve was too uncomfortable with vulgarity of expression for that.[13] But he, like many of his contemporaries, refuses antiquity the dignity of distance, here by rendering Ovid in familiar diction and by choosing the most common of parallels in that rendering. The Roman fashion for imitating the luxury of the Greeks, Congreve writes in a footnote, is identical to the English fashion for imitating the French (S: p. 21, n. 22). In this footnote, Romans quietly become English for Congreve's English readers.

Here and elsewhere, Congreve does not challenge the notion of translation that Dryden proposed when he wrote, in his dedication to *The Aeneis* (1697), that he has "endeavoured to make Virgil speak such English as he would himself have spoken, if he had been born in England, and in this present age."[14] Cowley, too, accepted that translation was a matter of rewriting a work for a modern and rational world when he wrote, in the preface to his *Pindarique Odes* (1656), "If a man should undertake to translate *Pindar* word for word, it would be thought that one *Mad man* had translated *another*."[15] For Congreve, as for Cowley and Dryden, no strangeness is to be left in the strange; it is rather to be absorbed into the modernity and Englishness of the printed text. That which cannot be absorbed—that which is too entangled in obscure custom, unfamiliar landscape, vocabulary without equivalent—either is eliminated or remains in mock-heroic juxtaposition, undermined by the contrast of its soaring claims and the lowly forms with which it is allied. Or the alien may be duly annotated, another way that the English historians, curious and acquisitive, collect it, encasing it in the neat pages at the back of the volume.

Despite this brand of assimilating historicism, which attempts to estimate each element of antiquity in terms of its modern equivalent, such annotations retain a strange mixture: they are both tonally credulous about myth and the gods and historically enlightened, longing to unmask classical superstition. A note in Congreve's Juvenal translation tells his readers that Romulus and Remus were "Twins, and Founders of the *Roman* Empire; who the Poets feign were nurst by a Wolf: The Woman's Name being *Lupa*" (S: p. 21, n. 23). Here, by explaining away the myth about the wolf-mother with a name origin, Congreve proudly uses history to debunk classical dogma (in a gesture similar to the biblical historicism that would, during the Enlightenment, so joyously "debunk" the "myth" of Christianity by finding mechanical explanations for miracles). The next note claims that "Formerly the Statues of the Gods were made of Clay: But now of Gold. Which Extravagance was displeasing even to the Gods themselves." This note contains no implication that the same feigning poets who created the myth of the suckling Romulus and Remus might have created those disapproving gods; in fact, the word *now* even suggests that Congreve locates himself in this world in which golden images are offered to the gods, and the gods register their displeasure. Congreve's debunking of myth, his rather imperious suggestion that he holds the key to enlightenment, mingles with a tonal reaffirmation of myth, a return to the age of belief in mysteries; competition mingles with reverence.

Congreve's portrayal of scholarship and satire of pedantry in the plays are similarly ambivalent. He was aware of the dangers of pedantry, as he acknowledges in the critical apparatus to the printed versions of his plays, writing in the dedication to *Love for Love*, "I hope I may be excus'd the Pedantry of a Quotation, when it is so justly apply'd" (p. 210).[16] The apology for his own "pedantry" is a small reflection of the anxiety he expresses in his much larger-scale satire against those who have usurped the classical inheritance, those who become false progenitors through the fecund presses: the pedants.

Of course the satire of pedantry is nothing new in the late seventeenth century; it is not restricted to a culture with a fully developed press. The learned doctor who gets cuckolded while he is reciting Latin (or pseudo-Latin) tags is a staple of the Italian Renaissance comedy; Aretino's pedant in *The Stablemaster* mixes up astrology and scholastic philosophy with his Latins and Greeks; Holofernes in *Love's Labour's Lost* spews Latin set speeches. But pedantry on the Renaissance stage is of an entirely different character than that on the late-seventeenth-century stage. It is almost always oral: the doctors and scholars know Latin commonplaces, with a few citations of Virgil and Horace; they know the *sententiae* that make up moral education and serve oration; they are not primarily readers, and certainly not writers. In most cases, pedantry on stage before the late seventeenth century is not so much satire of an affectation as it is a virtuoso display of Latin, a way of consolidating a community of listeners by excluding those who do not understand (women, for instance), an occasion for a good joke among the boys who got thrashed for the same misconstructions of Ovid. In *The Merry Wives of Windsor* (IV.i), when Sir Hugh Evans grills little Will on the cases, little Will of Stratford with his schoolroom-Latin puns is just in the background. By the late seventeenth century, the satire has changed. The joke has become more central, more insistent, shriller, less merely a foil for the lively and industrious scheming of a lover; it has taken on the apparatus of literacy, the books and papers and the itch of the pedant to write. Pedantry has left the learned doctors and the schoolmasters and seeped into the margins, into the speech of those who do not seem to have a right to such knowledge—women and social climbers, for instance.[17]

In *The Double-Dealer*, the concern about the democratization of pedantry serves as a mirror for the larger problem of the play: there is a powerful parallel between Lady Froth's (or woman's) scholarly usurpation and Maskwell's (or the lower-class male's) attempted dynastic usurpation.[18] Brisk has agreed to assist Lady Froth with her academic-heroic epic (already in print, in her mind), which she has named, in honor of her husband (Lord Froth), *The Sillibub*. When Brisk suggests that her use of the words *bilk* and *fare* (to describe her, now pastoralized, coachman Jehu's work in the poetic dairy) belongs too much to a hackney coachman, he is satisfied with her defense that Jehu was once a hackney coachman:

BRISK   Was that he then, I'm answered, if *Jehu* was a Hackney Coachman—you may put that into the marginal Notes, tho' to prevent Criticisms—only mark it with a small asterism, and say,—*Jehu* was formerly a Hackney Coachman.

LADY FROTH   I will; you'd oblige me extremely to write Notes to the whole Poem.

BRISK   With all my Heart and Soul, and proud of the vast honour, let me perish. (III.i, p. 165)

Brisk and Lady Froth not only desire the lofty "asterism," with its authority and prestige, but feel that, in the dangerous and combative print world that they wish to enter, they cannot defend themselves without it. At the heart of the play, at the heart of their jubilant exchange, lies this mark, the glittering symbol of starry knowledge, or the winking symbol of vast astral foolery. Marginal notes, marked by stars, express the heights of pedantry. They have lost even their connection to the medieval scholiast's manuscript, under the weight of print's accumulated conventions. In the theater, their contrast with the aurality of true poetry, the unnecessary materiality and visualness of their forms in a world that is already made of vocal poetry, becomes all the starker.

Brisk's and Lady Froth's footnotes are matched by their wild accumulation of sources, which serve as the foundation for their plans. Brisk asks her, "I presume your Ladyship has read *Bossu?*" (perhaps hoping for a negative answer so that he can enlighten her). "O yes," she replies. "And *Rapine*, and *Dacier* upon *Aristotle* and *Horace*" (II.i, p. 142).[19] The altered spelling (and probably pronunciation) of Rapin's name suggests the nature of Lady Froth's actual work with these scholars: they have provided her with the opportunity for theft and plunder of both sources and scholarly suggestion. Print has provided her, like Bayes in *The Rehearsal*, with the opportunity to plagiarize. The reaction to print has taught Congreve, like Buckingham, to struggle against cultural reduplication, using the increasingly strong notion of plagiarism itself as a weapon. Thus, Congreve reacts with postprint assumptions to a woman who is not ashamed of her facile rattling of names, her glee in the cumulative effect of the randomly constructed list, her misuse of printed scholarship in an oral formulation. In fact, Lady Froth's literacy is so misplaced because she has not, after all, found her muse in the library, nor, even, at the bookseller's. Though she uses in vain, to buttress her pretensions, the names of Rapin, Aristotle, Dacier, and Horace, her fancy is made of nothing but air, the rancid air of the lady's closet. When she was in love with Lord Froth, she confides to Cynthia:

LADY FROTH   Between you and I, I had whimsies and vapours, but I gave them vent.

CYNTHIA   How pray, Madam?

LADY FROTH   O I Writ, Writ abundantly, . . . Songs, Elegies, Satyrs, Encomiums, Panegyricks, Lampoons, Plays, or Heroick Poems. (II.i, p. 138)

Again, the list appears, a list whose style reflects the abundant accumulations of orality, but whose items are now the products of print (divided into genres made more precise by print's impulse toward categorization and labeling). The texture of the list is the vented vapor, ephemeral flatus, which yields up, as in Swift and Pope, the solid matter of the press.

Lady Froth's explanatory etymology, a few moments later, suggests as strongly her part in print-world fecundity. Using the words *Phosphorous* and *Hemisphere*, she asks Cynthia condescendingly, "Do you understand those Two hard Words? If you don't, I'll explain 'em to you" (II.i, p. 139). Cynthia is not learned, but she is naturally wise, wise enough to know how to escape one part of the folly around her: "Yes, yes, Madam, I'm not so Ignorant.—(*aside*). At least I won't own it, to be troubled with your Instructions." She cannot, however, escape altogether, for pedantry is self-generating; it has no capacity for dialogue. Thus, Lady Froth perseveres: "Nay, I beg your Pardon; but being derived from the *Greek*, I thought you might have escap'd the Etymology."[20] Lady Froth is surprised that Cynthia is not as self-generating, as infinitely reproductive, as she: "But I'm the more amazed, to find you a Woman of Letters, and not Write! Bless me! how can *Mellefont* believe you Love him?" Cynthia does not attempt to superimpose a culture of "asterisms" on natural everyday oral discourse: "Why Faith, Madam, he that won't take my Word shall never have it under my Hand." The oral word, once again, must be the foundation for the written, but the written may control the oral. Cynthia asserts the power of direct relations between the simple spoken word and the written over the meaningless production of written language, the overpowering cumulation of words written about words, which are no more than imaginary physical excretions, whimsies and vapors. As the mistress of natural wisdom, Cynthia knows her own ignorance: this humility seeks a connection between orality and literacy and is able to leave a space for dialogue (the basis of dramatic form).

The Double-Dealer shows the contortions of artificial pedantry; *The Old Batchelour* begins by denying affected knowledge altogether so that wit and pleasure can run their course more smoothly. The play begins with the rejection of "Business" and then proceeds quickly to the rejection of learning, which often hides under the inaccurate title of "Wisdom." As Bellmour tells Vainlove:

> Ay, ay, pox Wisdom's nothing but a pretending to know and believe more than really we do. You read of but one wise Man, and all that he knew was, that he knew nothing. Come, come, leave Business to Idlers, and Wisdom to Fools; they have need of 'em: Wit be my Faculty; and Pleasure my Occupation; and let Father Time shake his Glass. (I.i, p. 37)

Wisdom, here, is affected wit, and true wit is a natural "Faculty," like seeing and hearing, which suggests Bellmour's oral preference. Socrates is not named (nor are the Epicurean skeptics who silently inform this passage), for only the writers of "wise" dissertations (writers who have need of artful wisdom) would name him. The naturally wise need not cite those registered as authorities, for they accept the fact that knowledge is already registered in their speech, and they recognize the magnitude of the collection of human knowledge. And yet the refusal to name authorities is a reaction to the pedantry fostered by print. In the culture of infinite printed discourse, which portrays scholarly knowledge as too vast to be attainable, the wise recognize the impossibility of a true knowledge that could go beyond the natural faculty of wit. Only the pretenders, the artificial pedants, assert their claim on such a knowledge. By the late seventeenth century, the Socrates figure has ceased to be one of humility in the face of human self-deception and has become one of exhaustion in the face of scholarly accumulation, exhaustion that turns back for relief toward an oral state (the pure wit of those who refuse the world of scholarly accumulation).

Valentine, then, is chastised by orally oriented wit for his attempted retreat from public (and thus oral) wit into the world of books. In the first scene of *Love for Love*, Jeremy's mocking commentary serves to juxtapose, similarly, natural appetite and the artificiality of the philosophic inheritance embodied in Valentine's "musty Books." Valentine wants to "digest" the books, and Jeremy, hungry (interested in another form of the oral), questions whether Epictetus is a "real Cook" or simply a writer of recipes. Valentine responds:

> Read, read, Sirrah, and refine your Appetite; learn to live upon Instruction; feast your Mind, and mortifie your Flesh; Read, and take your Nourishment in at your Eyes; shut up your Mouth, and chew the Cud of Understanding. So *Epictetus* advises. (I.i, p. 216)

But Jeremy, master of the knowledge of natural necessities, asks:

> Does your *Epictetus*, or your *Seneca* here, or any of these poor rich Rogues, teach you how to pay your Debts without Money? Will they shut up the Mouths of your Creditors? Will *Plato* be Bail for you? Or *Diogenes*, because he understands Confinement, and liv'd in a Tub, go to Prison for you? 'Slife, Sir, what do you mean, to mew your self up here with Three or Four musty Books, in commendation of Starving and Poverty?

Here, if the philosophers are authorities, voices that add weight to the opening of the play and a philosophical import to Valentine's choice of confinement, they are also victims of Jeremy's antischolarly witty scholarship. A knowledge of the stoics can be picked up by any servant who, like Jeremy, has attended a master at Cambridge. It can do little in the face of starvation and debt. And when such knowledge becomes mere citations, the fragments of a gentleman's education, it can do nothing for natural needs. Citations are isolated and disoriented in modern oral discourse, at home only in what Jeremy calls "Three or Four musty Books, in commendation of Starving and Poverty." In the world of Valentine and Jeremy (Jeremy seems to imply), on the gestural witty stage, such citations have decayed and grown hollow. Long ago constructed on the oral discourse of the classical philosophers, the cumulations of oral-rhetorical culture have been appropriated ironically enough by the culture of footnotes, of the printed frozen text. Scholarship cannot live in the remaining regions of the live voice—conversation or the theater—for there it is against nature and belongs only to the artificial wit of pedantry. And yet, even there, the forms of print (pedantic accumulations, the "asterism") have come to circumscribe the oral and theatrical.

In his earlier "theatrical" novel, *Incognita*, Congreve is similarly aware of the state of the theatrical circumscribed by the world of print, of the novel's status as a literate genre and the insufficiency of the purely theatrical. *Incognita* may be modeled on the theater in its plot, contexts, and characterizations ("I resolved . . . to imitate *Dramatick* Writing," writes Congreve to the reader).[21] But only plot and character follow theatrical form. Congreve signs the dedication "Cleophil"; and whether we take "Cleo" to mean "Clio," the narrator of the novel is very much a "lover of history," a writer as interested in historical technique as in dramatic narrative. *Incognita* relies heavily on techniques inappropriate to or impossible on the stage: a great deal of detailed historical description; a pseudohistorical narratorial voice; and claims to the truth of that voice, claims suggesting that a redemption of the theatrical is possible only through the scholarly voice of a narrator exposed to historical books. *Incognita* is filled with historical and geographical detail about Italy, most of which Congreve probably found in John Raymond's *Itinerary Contayning a Voyage, Made through Italy* (1648).[22] Siena, Florence, the Church "di Sancta Croce," "Porta Romana," and "Poggio Imperiale" are all in their proper places. Like London, Florence is a city with lodgings, and in this as in other details, Congreve is skeptical about using the romance as the principal model for the medieval archaism of *Incognita*, choosing instead the travel narrative.

In his preface, he insists on the verisimilitude of his novel, which he distinguishes carefully from romance:

Romances elevate and surprize the Reader into a giddy Delight, which leaves him flat upon the Ground whenever he gives of, and vexes him to think how he has suffer'd himself to be pleased and transported . . . when he is forced to be very well convinced that 'tis all a lye. Novels are of a more familiar nature, . . . delight us with Accidents and odd Events, but not such as are wholly unusual or unpresidented, such which not being so distant from our Belief bring also the pleasure nearer us.[23]

Congreve articulates here for the English a distinction already implicit in such antiromances as *Don Quixote* (1605), Charles Sorel's *Berger extravagant* (1627–28), or Paul Scarron's novels, and in prose fiction like Behn's *Oroonoko* (1688)—a distinction that would be crucial for the eighteenth-century novel.[24] The "Novel" (and Congreve is unusual here in abandoning the claim to history that is a premise throughout the narrative) resists the imaginative excesses of romance without being willing to abandon "Accidents and odd Events." It has a higher claim to truth than the actual "true History" that it imitates in that it chooses verisimilitude (events that are not "so distant from our Belief") over what it conceives to be a strict account. But this classical verisimilitude, borrowed from Aristotle and the French stage, was no longer sufficient in the world of print. For the more that improvements in scholarship seemed to show, with increasing detail, ways of distinguishing truth from fiction, the more writers of prose fiction felt that the old higher forms of truth simply would not do. But neither, for many, was the naive empiricism of the "true History" acceptable. For the problem, as Congreve and others found, was that it was not so easy as one might think to find a true account, because even once one had gotten beyond literary convention, the conventionality of language kept getting in the way. The only way, then, to have a truth truer than the old verisimilitude or the "true History" was by negation: inspired partly by the antiromances of Cervantes, Sorel, and Scarron (which gave Congreve demonstrations of the antiromantic "true History" topos), writers like Congreve found a way of negotiating between the "lies" of romance and the naïveté of radical empiricism. Much of *Incognita*'s Florence may function according to codes of chivalry; the games may be those of Arthurian legend: "While the running at the Ring lasted, our Cavaliers alternately bore away great share of the Honour.

That Sport ended, Marshals were appointed for the Field, and every thing in great form settled for the Combat."[25] Nevertheless, such fictional chivalric modes are understood by the characters themselves to be fictional. Aurelian and Hippolito, for instance, on seeing a large shield with a lady painted on it in the tilting arena, "thought themselves obliged, especially in the presence of their Mistresses, to vindicate their beauty," but discover later that "the thing was only designed for show and form" (*I*: p. 42).

The narrator repeatedly makes claims for his own scholarly care and historical accuracy. This pretension to historical accuracy, this blazoning of scholarly knowledge, is partly an attempt to overcome the nonverisimilar quality of the printed word's imitations (by contrast with the physical verisimilitude of theatrical imitations), an attempt to gain the presence of the theater, which the written or printed word lacks. But the playfulness and irony of such claims suggest a further discomfort with the pedantry of claims to historical accuracy.[26] For Congreve, the scholarly claims of his narrator would be, in a genuine "historical" work, at once pretentious and naive. But the fictional basis opens a space for them. The narrator's historical pomposity is made possible by the patent fictitiousness of the work, by the words *a Novel* flashed on its title page (an unnecessary warning in later works, as the genre becomes more common, and the claims to truth are protected by an implicit contract between the writer and the "knowing" reader), and by the authorial intrusions themselves. The recognition of the lack of inherent verisimilitude of the form permits (even requires) more strenuous claims to reach nature, or truth.

As the mock-historian, Congreve not only can use the knowledge he has gathered from his wide reading, but also can joyously partake (without danger of pedantry) in the pleasures of the historian's voice, its care, its revisions, its connection with the sources of knowledge, its tone of emanation from the cellars of the deepest and most carefully compiled wisdom. The historian is scientific in analysis of circumstance: "By Computation now . . . *Hippolito* entred this Garden near upon the same Instant, when *Aurelian* wandred into the Old Monastery" (*I*: p. 59). The historian is honest when ignorant: "The Fellow . . . snatch'd up the Lanthorn from the Ground; either to have given Light only to himself, or to have put out the Candle . . . but which of the Two he designed, no Body could tell but himself" (*I*: p. 52). The historian only cautiously attributes cause on the basis of motivation: Aurelian "groped for the Knots, and either untied them or cut them asunder; but 'tis more probable the latter because more expeditious" (*I*: pp. 52–53). The historian is thwarted by lack of evidence: "And if the Reader have a Curiosity to know, he must blame *Aurelian*; who . . . ran him immediately through the Heart, so that he drop'd down Dead at his Feet, without speaking a Word" (*I*: p. 52).

In a novel that underlines its fictitiousness with highly artificial romance names, a preface explaining its artistry, and an overriding mock-preciosity in the characters' speech, subtle (and specious) claims to truth can serve three purposes simultaneously: they invoke the verisimilar presence of the theater; they mock the pedantry of the actual historian; and they emphasize the author's understanding of historical methodology. But they also serve a further and more pedagogical purpose: they teach the reader to beware of the falsely historical, of lies masquerading in the dignity of scholarly formulation and the pomp of print. They teach the reader not to remain in passive awe of the printed word, but to question its power and to lift the mask of the page to discover the truth of the living voice.[27] Toward the end of the novel, Incognita, the principal heroine, offers a brief relation of her adventures, which the reader can recognize to be untrue. Congreve's warning affixed to her lie serves as the explicit pedagogy of his mock-historical narration:

I would Caution the Reader by the bye, not to believe every word which she told him . . . to be accurately true. It was indeed truth so cunningly intermingled with Fiction, that it required no less Wit . . . as the Reader shall understand ere long: For we have another Discovery to make to him, if he have not found it out of himself already. (I: p. 57)

The cautious reader is fully capable of making discoveries independently, but truth is often cunningly mingled with fiction; one must learn to be suspicious.

Even such superstitious characters as *Love for Love*'s Foresight, in Congreve's view, can learn to reject what were once fully credited "historical" texts. "Thou Modern *Mandevil*!" Foresight cries in accusation against Sir Sampson, "*Ferdinand Mendez Pinto* was but a Type of thee, thou lyar of the first Magnitude" (II.i, p. 241).[28] Mandeville's and Pinto's texts are no longer merely versions of geographical or astrological observation, but lies, valuable only for their curiosity or as subjects for satire. Abundant sources may make it impossible to be master of all knowledge. They may make it possible for pedantry to thrive. They may threaten the presence of the living voice. But when they are combined with scholarly exactitude and the proper suspicion, they also make it possible, with much study, to know truth, or, at least, to come closer to it.

Here, the patient historian/reader can distinguish truth from apocrypha (as in the poem to Dryden on his translation of Persius) with the help of print. And thus, here the distinction between fiction and what would eventually be called "nonfiction" begins to find a more rigid formulation. If Congreve mingled, on the same shelf in his library, Mandeville's travels, Addison's serious remarks on his travels in Italy (1703), *Gulliver's Travels* (1726), and a copy of his own works, it was not without a sense of irony. The deliberate amalgam of fictional and historical method in the prose of the seventeenth and eighteenth centuries was largely an acknowledgment of new distinctions between the fictional and the historical. It was an attempt to confront with claims of truth the arts of scholarly accumulation and the resulting precision (yet distance) of the printed word. Such claims had the power to achieve both the presence of verisimilitude and the reliability and modernity claimed by such serious scholarship as Congreve's (without falling into the traps and falsehoods of rigid signification). *Incognita* offers an attempt at a voice that can confront print scholarship with its own tools. In the eighteenth century, both scholarship and the ironic use of it (from the satire of pedantry to the novel's mock-historical methodology) would increasingly isolate the historical, leaving the fictional a clearer territory for mobility, a space to dance among the forms of theater, scholarship, art, and nature. Like *Incognita*, other fictions would struggle to find an approach to nature (whether through claims to truth, assumption of historicist technique, or naturalism) that could overcome the artifice of the book. As in *Incognita*, print would use the techniques of print to preserve the living qualities of orality, but that orality would never free itself from its containment in print.

The relationship of novelistic and antipedantic orality to print is analogous to that between nostalgia for golden-age orality (encouraged by print's classical revival) and the scholarship that undermines such nostalgia. Repeatedly reinforced by reduplicating footnotes, scholarly knowledge continually challenges reverence and nostalgia and allows Congreve to win certain battles against the ancients, even when he wishes most to lose. If proximity to antiquity through wider dissemination of classical texts has brought him nostalgia for a golden world of innocent belief (of pastoralism and oral song), that proximity has also brought clear-sighted skepticism. When he asserts, in the "Letter to Viscount Cobham," that human nature is unchanging, he is not offering a mere critique of modern folly:

> Believe it, Men have ever been the same,
> And all the Golden Age, is but a Dream. (S: p. 178)

That perfect golden age, which he portrayed in his pastorals as celebrating the purity of the untutored oral tongue, does not exist. Here, the oral is subsumed in the literate, and in Congreve's scholarly works, the ancients themselves no longer belong either to an oral or to a manuscript culture, but now fully to the late-seventeenth-century printed texts that embody them; they belong to the "asterisms" that both defend and assault them.

Conversely, the essential modernism of Congreve and his contemporaries (who do recognize that they are moderns) lies in their connection to the past, a past that must nevertheless be rewritten, but a rewriting that repeatedly finds itself jostling with the stubborn follies of modernity.[29] It is not without irony that Congreve chooses Horace's "Interdum tamen, vocem Comœdia tollit" ("Nevertheless, sometimes even Comedy elevates her voice") as his epigraph to *The Double-Dealer*, a play partly about the follies of attempting a heroic poem in a comic world. Whatever Congreve's affinity with Homer, Pindar, Juvenal, Ovid, whatever his connection to the stage of Menander, Terence, Plautus (and whatever his belief in a timeless taxonomy of human nature), he knows that his models cannot live unbroken in him; nor can his translations or imitations cover them with a complete opacity. The ancient and the modern must, in the skin of the same work, remain forever in a playful battle for supremacy. This battle takes place not only on the stage, not only in the words of a bodiless text; it is the fundamental stance of a blossoming print culture, which resuscitates the past to watch it struggle, at one and the same time, to preserve itself and to assimilate itself to a form inherently alien.

CHAPTER FIVE

Scandal's Portraits:
Engravings
and Visual Imitation

If Satyrs, Descriptions, Characters, and Lampoons are
Pictures.   —Congreve, *Love for Love*

O, impotence of Sight!
Mechanick Sense, which to exteriour Objects,
Owest thy Faculty—
                              —Congreve, *The Mourning Bride*

The distance of the Stage requires the Figure represented, to be something larger than the Life; and sure a
Picture may have Features larger in Proportion, and
yet be very like the Original.
                              —Congreve, "Concerning Humour in Comedy"

The late seventeenth century,
on the brink of the great expansion of engraving in the eighteenth century, had not yet entirely come to accept the printed
image as a dignified medium for representing the world.
Printed images were scorned as imitations of imitations of imitations, useful for visual relief in books or the decoration of
taverns, necessary in meat markets and privies.[1] The biblical
prohibition "Thou shalt not make to thy self any graven image"
seemed to identify engraving as a particular violation of the in-

terdiction of idols and gave the general Puritan suspicion of the image special point in the case of printed images. But several of the numerous printsellers and engravers living in London between 1660 and 1700 made energetic attempts to establish the prestige of fine engraving, which was so useful, for instance, to the growing body of virtuosos, natural scientists, collectors, and others among the curious. Evelyn's history of and guide to engraving, *Sculptura* (1662), makes a defensive distinction between use and abuse. He is certain "that in *Moses* we have the Tables of stone, engraven by the Finger of God himself; where the commandement is expresse, even against the abuse of this very Art, as well as an instance of the Antiquity of Idolatry attesting that of Sculpture: THOU SHALT NOT MAKE TO THY SELF ANY GRAVEN IMAGE."² If the finger of God himself engraved, surely human instruments might also be permitted the art, so long as they are nonidolatrous.

Printed "sculptures" (and the less elegant "cuts") altered the London they both adorned and described. The relation of late-seventeenth-century playwrights to their visual medium, the theater, was complicated by the increasing body of printed pictorial images during the period, images that challenged the theater's role as the principal popular visual medium (both the theater and the popular woodcut being means of education and entertainment for the nonliterate). Although there had always been some illustration of the printed drama, from the 1493 Lyons edition of Terence on, most printed drama would be unillustrated until the eighteenth century. And so the two visual forms remained rivals, but rivals in opposition to the strictly verbal printed text. The theater is distinguished from the printed text not only by its oral presentation but also by its visual effects, both pictorial and spatial. But print too (as opposed to the oral) is visual: we use eyes, not ears, to read; print teaches ways of precisely demarcating space—for instance, with title pages, charts, and maps.³ Poised between, on the one hand, the predominantly gestural medieval theater and predominantly spatial Renaissance theater, and on the other, the pictorial theater of the eighteenth and nineteenth centuries, the late-seventeenth-century theater had to determine its relation not only to print culture in general but also to the printed pictures sold beside Tonson's fine octavos.

None of Congreve's plays was illustrated during his lifetime, and it is significant that there are no visual renderings of any performance of his plays until the eighteenth century. What, then, is the meaning of the environment of images in which his characters live? Mellefont's ancestors watch from the gallery walls as he plots to preserve the ancestral line. Lady Wishfort's portrait mocks the peeled wall of her face. Tattle's collection, whose purpose is to lure ladies into his closet (the ancestor of "let me show you my etchings"), loses out to Scandal's scandalous collection:

> SCANDAL   Yes Faith, I can shew you your own Picture, and most of your Acquaintance to the Life, and as like as at *Knellers*. . . . Pride, Folly, Affectation, Wantonness, Inconstancy, Covetousness, Dissimulation, Malice, and Ignorance all in one Piece. Then I can shew you Lying, Foppery, Vanity, Cowardise, Bragging, Lechery, Impotence and Ugliness in another Piece; and yet one of these is a celebrated Beauty, and t'other a profest Beau. (*DD*, I.i, p. 233)

If Scandal's "portraits" have little affinity with Kneller's—with the serious portraits of the beautiful and the celebrated, so popular during the decades following the Restoration[4]—his "Beauty" and "Beau" do suggest "portraits" like the individually sold satiric print probably intended to represent a Covent Garden coffeehouse keeper named Rothmel.[5] Scandal's other portraits—his "Hieroglyphicks" and social-occupational images—may have a partial genesis in emblems like those of Francis Quarles, the author of the most popular book of seventeenth-century emblems.[6] (Congreve would not have listed in his library such ephemera as the ballads and broadsides that carried the woodcuts; but like Heartwell in *The Old Batchelour*, who fears he "shall be hang'd in Effigie, pasted up for the exemplary Ornament of necessary Houses and Coblers stalls" [III.i, p. 63],

"Rothmel, Who Kept a Coffeehouse in Covent Garden." (By permission of the Trustees of the British Museum.)

he must have lived with them as everyday presences.)[7] Scandal's pictures of "a Beau in a Bagnio, Cupping for a Complexion, and Sweating for a Shape" and "a Lady burning of Brandy in a Cellar with a Hackney-Coachman" (I.i, p. 233) share with many of the woodcuts the moralist's penchant for satire. Such woodcuts share the lower-class milieu with images like Jeremy's "Spirit of Famine" in *Love for Love*, who appears

> sometimes like a decayed Porter, worn out with pimping, and carrying *Billet-doux* and Songs; not like other Porters for Hire, but for the Jests sake. Now like a thin Chairman, melted down to half his Proportion, with carrying a Poet upon Tick. . . . And lastly, In the Form of a worn-out Punk, with Verses in her Hand, which her Vanity had preferr'd to Settlements . . . as if she were carrying her Linnen to the Paper-Mill, to be converted into Folio Books, of Warning to all Young Maids, not to prefer Poetry to good Sense. (I.i, pp. 218–19)

Jeremy's "bilked Bookseller, with a meagre terrify'd Countenance, that looks as if he had written for himself, or were resolv'd to turn Author, and bring the rest of his Brethren into the same Condition" (I.i, p. 219) suggests a woodcut entitled "The Compleat Auctioner" (BMS 1415, ca. 1695)—with its open-air bookstall, behind which stands the poorly dressed and desolate bookseller. The 1692 "Emblem of Ye Athenian Society" (BMS 1283) shows the collective descent into chaos that characterizes Scandal's collective satires—for instance, that "representing a School; where there are huge Proportion'd Critics, with long Wigs, Lac'd Coats, *Steinkirk* cravats, and terrible Faces; with Catcalls in their Hands and Horn-books about their Necks" (I.i, pp. 233–34). Scandal's "Hieroglyphicks" (I.i, p. 233) imitate the symbolic disfigurement that one could see in the popular visual hieroglyphics:

SCANDAL   I have a Lawyer with a hundred Hands, two Heads, and but one Face; a Divine with two Faces, and one Head; and I have a Soldier with his Brains in his Belly, and his Heart where his Head shou'd be.

Come Sirs, and view this famous Library,
'Tis pity Learning should discourag'd be :
—'res Bookes (that is, if they were but well Sold)
—'t maintain't are worth their weight in Gold

THE
COMPLEAT
AUCTIONER

Then bid apace, and break me out of hand :
Ne'er cry you don't the Subject understand :
For this I'll say -howe'er the Case may hit,
Whoever buys of me. -I teach em Wit.

A Choice Collection of Books
being the Library of the late
famous Unborn Doctor, are
to be put to Sale this Day, and
to continue untill all be Sold
at Mr L—ys Auction in the
North West Corner of Middle
Moorfields. Catalogues may
be had at most of the eminent
Booksellers in the four Quarters
of Moorfeilds Gratis: the Books
may be Seen before or at the
time of Sale.

Sutton Nicholls excudit

"The Compleat Auctioner" (ca. 1695). (By permission of the Trustees
of the British Museum.)

"The Lawyer's Arms" (ca. 1692). (By permission of the Trustees of the British Museum.)

Close to Scandal's emblems are the traditional professional prints (of lawyers, clergymen, and doctors), such as "The Lawyer's Arms" (BMS 1284, ca. 1692), with its wolf-headed lawyer whose body issues, like extra limbs, hundreds of writs inscribed with scraps of legal phrases.

The woodcuts of the period partly parallel Congreve's subject matter; the elegant engravings of the period partly parallel his style. Congreve and the makers of pictures were drawing on some of the same cultural images, working on many of the same impulses, and the correspondence that does exist between Congreve's references to the pictorial and the larger pictorial culture is revealing. But the misalignment of the two is even more revealing. Congreve's "portraits" have little to do with the lower-middle-class audience and subject matter of most of the woodcuts; nor do they have either the political specificity or the grand allegory of the engravings. Jeremy's "Spirit of Famine," rather than haunting the vast porticoed plains crowded with struggling armies of flesh, appears in coffeehouses, at the paper mill, on door stoops. Scandal's portraits appear in the bagnio, a school, the cellar. Valentine's prophetic pictures of "the Horn'd Herd" buzzing in the Exchange, "Coffee-Houses . . . full of Smoak and Stratagem" and the "cropt Prentice" dirtying "his Sheets" (IV.i, p. 289) are located in the shops, the exchange, the bedchamber of the apprentice's master. The images are intimate, the human forms neither specific to great figures nor grandly allegorical, but instead familiar to any wanderer in London streets. By the end of the first decade of the eighteenth century, engravings would grow closer to the style and subject matter of the portraits Congreve conjures. Engravers and illustrators would begin to fuse the social and moral satire of the woodcuts with the exact lines and sophisticated compositions of the high-quality engravings. There would be an increase in fine book illustration, in which pictures would begin to narrate the texts themselves, rather than relying on the verbal text to interpret the relevance of the print's abstracted classicism. Illustration of scenes from the theater, scarce in the seventeenth century, would become popular. But none of this had yet happened during the decade in which Congreve was writing for the stage.

Congreve's "portraits," however, cannot simply be classified as part of a transition between the world of linked representations of the Renaissance collector and the pictorial-narrative world of the eighteenth- and nineteenth-century gatherer of prints. They belong to a moment apart, a moment in which both writers and makers of pictures were trying to find a relation to the relatively new ease with which one could reproduce the image. Easy reproduction put pressure, for Congreve and others, on the sense of the larger power of pictures to represent.

MRS FRAIL   I hear you have a great many pictures.

TATTLE   I have a pretty good Collection at your Service, some Originals.

SCANDAL   Hang him, he has nothing but the *Seasons* and the *Twelve Caesars*, paultry Copies; and the *Five Senses*, as ill represented as they are in himself: And he himself is the only Original you will see there. . . . No, no;—come to me if you wou'd see Pictures. (I.i, p. 232)

Once pictures are readily reproducible, they can no longer have value as "originals," and so one is forced to ask more questions about their significative power. Tattle's collection, the "Originals" or "paultry Copies," is the site of the conflict between the painted and the printed image, a conflict that does not yield a victory for either side. Rather, it pushes to the forefront the question of the representative power of the image. Like many, but unlike those who were already beginning the advancement of the pictorial that would occur in the next century, Congreve's way of dealing with the question is to prefer the image most easily translatable into social language. Tattle's collection, according to Scandal, is composed of the Seasons, Caesars, and Senses—all conventional series prints, belonging, for Congreve, to a meaningless and immobile tradition of pictorial allegory. Scandal can challenge Tattle's images with his more genuine pictures, not because Scandal's are painted originals (which he never claims) but because the most significant pictures, for Congreve, are those whose meaning rests primarily in their translation into language. Like Quarles's emblems, like the printed satires, like the scientific diagrams of the epoch, Congreve's portraits, although they draw on the culture of printed images that surround him, choose translation into language as their primary means of expression.

The implicit debate about the value of "paultry Copies," then, is a debate as much about the value of copied language (printed words) in comparison with original language (the live voice of the stage) as it is about the physical portraits on Tattle's wall. The physical portraits are mostly mirages, imaginary constructions created by Tattle's tattling words. Behind Tattle's external collection—his Seasons, Caesars, and Senses, his "paultry Copies"—lies a collection of painted female portraits (his "Closet of Beauties"):

SCANDAL   All that have done him Favours, if you will believe him.

TATTLE   . . . Those are Sacred to Love and Contemplation. No man but the Painter and my self was ever blest with the Sight. . . .

VALENTINE   As Tattle has Pictures of all that have granted him favours, [Scandal] has the Pictures of all that have refus'd him: If Satyrs, Descriptions, Characters, and Lampoons are Pictures.

SCANDAL   Yes, mine are most in black and white.—And yet there are some set out in their true Colours. (I.i, pp. 232–33)

Congreve maintains, as far as possible, the ambiguity between verbal and visual here as a way of dislocating the visual, stressing the figurative meanings of "black and white" and "true Colours," reminding us that even colored images are comprehensible primarily insofar as they reflect verbally identified states, in this case ones identified by "Satyrs, Descriptions, Characters, and Lampoons."

In Congreve's multileveled denials of the visual and of vision itself, he stresses verbal precedence again and again. He openly declared his disdain for the spectacular nature of the entertainment (opera and other forms of spectacle) that he, and many others, complained was taking over the stage.[8] The irritation with spectacle was a commonplace (for writers in particular) long before print. Horace had complained, in the *Epistle to Augustus*, of the unsteady nature of the eye, which is drawn toward "vain delights."[9] But playwrights like Congreve invoked with alacrity the older commonplace, as they tried to define the nature of their theater. For the practitioners of verbal arts, the visual is always to be secondary. But for Congreve and many other playwrights, the indictment of the visual sense was particularly important.[10] Vision is the faultiest of faculties, and any sight on which it chances, the most trivial of perceptions. In *The Mourning Bride*, Osmyn, echoing Horace, speaks for Congreve when he says,

> O, impotence of Sight!
> Mechanick Sense, which to exteriour Objects,
> Owest thy Faculty—
> Not seeing of Election, but Necessity.
> Thus do our Eyes, like common Mirrours
> Successively reflect succeeding Images;
> Not what they would, but must; a Star, or Toad.
>   (II.ii, p. 345)

The eye takes "paultry Copies" (like Tattle's cheap reproductions) of the lowest objects. It debases even the divine by mixing it with the common, for it cannot discriminate. And for Congreve, however much visual art may try to correct the faults of the eye, the eye can never approach the mind or the word. Painting and music are merely lesser subdivisions of poetry, as Congreve suggests in his "Discourse on the Pindarique Ode" (S: p. 85).

The notion that painting is less important than poetry is not unusual for the late seventeenth century. The many advice-to-a-painter satires of the seventeenth century—Waller's "Instructions to a Painter" (1666) or Marvell's "Last Instructions to a Painter" (1667), for instance—make it clear that the lesser sister art serves primarily as a trope and that the painting figure is simply a way of emphasizing the mimetic element of the poems.[11] Even the greatest promoters of painting, those ostensibly trying to gain for it the prestige of epic poetry, repeatedly undermine their own arguments. Dryden, in his "Parallel Betwixt Painting and Poetry" (1695), attempts to give homage to

his sister art, but he is able to write only an essay on poetry with
a few half-hearted references to painting, and even these have
odd satiric edges to them, similar to those in his ostensible panegyric to Kneller.[12]
   Congreve also offered Kneller a panegyric, his single sustained effort at praising visual art. His "To Sir Godfrey Kneller"
is equally unconvincing as a defense of painting. Congreve does
indeed make a genuine effort at the beginning. He claims that
Kneller's descriptive power is superior to his own, for it has
caused him to fall in love with the painted image. Why? Because he can recognize the subject:

> Others some faint Resemblance may express,
> Which, as 'tis drawn by Chance, we find by Guess.
> Thy Pictures raise no Doubts, when brought to View,
> At once they're known, and seem to know us too. (S: p. 146)

To offer, as the highest tribute to the greatest painter of the era,
praise for achieving a recognizable likeness does not show much
sophistication about the painter's art. And indeed, Congreve
can hardly wait to return to familiar ground, which he neatly
does by praising Kneller for having been praised by Dryden:

> Ev'n He who best cou'd judge and best cou'd praise,
> Has high extoll'd thee, in his deathless Lays;
> Ev'n *Dryden* has immortaliz'd thy Name;
> Let that alone suffice thee, think That, Fame.
> Unfit I follow, where he led the Way,
> And court Applause, by what I seem to pay.

Congreve almost chastises Kneller here for daring to find Dryden's Kneller poem insufficient fame. The praise for Dryden, in
fact, so dwarfs the praise for Kneller that the poem becomes a
panegyric upon Dryden. Dryden could judge and praise best.
Dryden leads the way. Perhaps Congreve even "court[s] Ap-
plause" by applauding, not Kneller, but Dryden. He writes
such a poem, the lines suggest, not primarily because he admires Kneller or because he admires the art of painting, but

because Dryden wrote one. Ostensible praise of the visual is here turned to praise of the verbal. The visual is subordinated to the superior powers of language.

Those—namely, the poets—who have a stake in preserving the prestige of the elder sister art from encroachment by the younger are not alone in this attitude. Congreve is not alone in his verbalization of his pictures, his suggestion that the visual holds no interest except as metaphor for the verbal. The most popular pictures themselves—the printed woodcuts, engravings, and illustrations—defer to the verbal: the emblematists mistrust the visual when it lacks verbal defense; the scientists drown their engraved diagrams in narrative. Many of these images have no meaning without words to interpret them. Hogarth's later use of images that require verbal puns to explain them is a continuation of this tradition of deference to the verbal. The emblems, from Quarles and the post-Restoration interpreters to the political and occupational hieroglyphics, require their explanatory headings and poems. The woodcuts, with their interchangeable subjects, require the ballad or narrative that explains who is being satirized or what quality being decried (or promoted). The satiric prints require their texts and the labeled streamers that identify the objects of the satire. Most scientific illustrations—like Robert Hooke's, in *Micrographia*, with its elaborate explanations—rely on a dominant text. And the serious portraits, when (as often) badly rendered and badly printed, require the name beneath as identification.

Congreve had an acute awareness of the problem of likeness and identification, as he shows not only in his Kneller poem but elsewhere: for example, Scandal warns Tattle, "Take notice, if you are so ill a Painter, that I cannot know the Person by your Picture of her, you must be condemned, like other bad Painters, to write the Name at the bottom" (I.i, p. 230). Angelica is troubling because "she is a Medal without a Reverse or Inscription" (IV.i, p. 297), because the text that explains her image is not legible. Even if the prints were not accompanied by texts, they would have to be "read" in a verbal way. Before one can

understand "The Prodigal Sifted," for example, one must recognize the sifter with its correct name ("strainer" will not do),
recall the two uses of the word, and read the pun. The emblematic images function in the same way. Viewers can understand
them only if they hear the actual words represented in the pictures.

One can only speculate on the reasons for this preponderance
of words and images requiring the reader/viewer to verbalize the
visual. The altered proportion of printed words perhaps suggested an imbalance between the two realms in the literary and
visual imagination. The flood of verbal printed matter after the
Restoration may have made it difficult to conceive anything (including pictures) without a verbal commentary, explanation of
the commentary, and further commentary on the explanation.
Pictures, perhaps, appeared minor adjuncts to the mighty current of language washing through London bookstalls. Furthermore, those with an interest in the verbal may have felt threatened by the growing prestige of the visual, which would find a
fuller form in the eighteenth century.[13] Defense of painting
would blossom into sophisticated discussions of the visual by
Jonathan Richardson, Hogarth, Reynolds, and others. Thus, in
the late seventeenth century, the older verbal interests may have
tried with increasing energy to preserve themselves in literature
and images as they felt their territory shrinking to make room
for visual theory.

This increase in the number of printed images in the eighteenth century and accompanying improvements in reproduction technology may also have partially caused changes that
took place in literature. If great numbers of exact, cheap
printed images can be easily produced, exact reproductions become increasingly essential to those actually producing images.
Viewers become accustomed to technical proficiency—that, for
instance, of the mezzotint (with its subtler grading of tones),
which was introduced by Evelyn's *Sculptura* and had grown extremely popular by the turn of the century. Viewers become accustomed to the imitations of the world accompanying that

proficiency and can no longer regard an imitation of the general idea of things as truly mimetic. Visual imitations must follow the exact outlines and detail all the shadings of color in the thing they portray, rather than offering a general or idealized version of vision. In rejecting general or idealized imitations, audiences come to conceive of mimesis in more narrow terms than they had before.[14]

Many who linked themselves with the technical in the late seventeenth century chose to celebrate this narrow mimesis that owed nothing to tradition, language, or the abstraction of nature. Cowley, in his "Ode to the Royal Society," allied himself with the scientists when he wrote:

> Who to the life an exact Piece would make,
> Must not from others Work a Copy take;
>   No, not from *Rubens* or *Vandike*
> Much less content himself to make it like
> Th'Idaeas and the Images which lie
> In his own Fancy, or his Memory.
>   No, he before his sight must place
>   The Natural and Living Face;
>   The real object must command
> Each Judgement of his Eye, and Motion of his Hand.[15]

Cowley, Hooke, and the emblematists all conceive of their imitations as literal representations of God's nature, untransformed. Cowley's "Eye" and "Hand" are echoed by Hooke's requirement that the true observer have a *"sincere Hand*, and a *faithful Eye*,"[16] as Hooke himself strove to do when he drew the creatures of his microscopic world. One can easily imagine the emblematists calling for the same, although the meanings of *sincere* and *faithful* would differ. Such faith and sincerity require humility. This is not merely a humility before man and God, but a humility before things. One must revere even the most common object. Ordinary things contain an infinitude of mysteries. Visual representation of them must be just to their power and complexity.

Both the emblematists and the scientists call for direct correlation between representation and represented, although their methods differ. One cannot debate that an emblematic cupid with horns represents the devil and only the devil, just as one cannot debate that the engravings of the scientist's faithful hand and eye represent nature and only nature. Such direct representation depends on the faithful hand and eye, which are ideally to be machines free of the arrogant intervention of human emotion or thought. The human faculties are instruments, simply faultier versions of the technical machines that could improve them. Memory is a lesser version of print. The nose is a lesser version of a machine Hooke projected for shooting vast quantities of odoriferous air at high speed up the nostrils.[17] The eye is a lesser form of the microscope.

Such ideas had a tremendous impact on nonscientific writing, as well as on scientific discourse itself. If the senses are merely technical instruments, then all observation is a scientific process to be recorded with the utmost objectivity. The result is literary notions of naturalism, with their narrow interpretations of imitation. In poetry, one finds descriptive lists; in prose fiction, the minute record of the common observed life.[18] But if science encouraged notions of a secular and narrowly conceived mimesis, the microscope and telescope also contributed to a continuing tradition of abstracted mimesis and a literature of the fantastic. The improvements in these instruments reopened realms that had once belonged only to pseudoscientists and dreamers. Such speculations as Hooke's, that by further improvements "we may perhaps be able to discover *living Creatures* in the Moon, or other Planets,"[19] fed the visual imaginations of both panegyrists (like Dryden in *Annus Mirabilis*) and satirists (like Butler, Shadwell, and Swift), and there are many traces of the micro- and macroscopic vision in *The Dunciad*. In Hooke, it is no surprise to feel the microscope's openings and shuttings when he writes, for example, that he hopes his slight labors will not be compared to the greater works of others, any more than "my *little Objects* are to be compar'd to the greater and more beautiful *Works of Nature*, a Flea, a Mite, a Gnat, to an Horse, an Elephant, or a Lyon."[20] Perhaps one can see something of Hooke's microscope, too, in Milton's insistent use of the Virgilian tag comparing great things with small and small with great in *Paradise Lost*, published two years after *Micrographia*.

The scientists, then, contributed to arts founded in both abstracted and narrower imitation. The latter became increasingly popular, since it satisfied an expectation for exact reproduction instilled by the technology of mechanical reproduction (whether words or engravings). The older abstracted imitation needed a champion. It found it in the invention of "high art," a concept developed in the eighteenth century, when such art had to define itself against the increasing numbers of cheap visual images. The theoretical voices of "high art" claimed the privilege of recognizing a truer kind of imitation (closely representational imitation being too easy to recognize) and stressed the lack of "fancy" in such imitation, in the typical rhetoric of antiprint romanticism.[21]

Congreve's defense of abstract imitation might be seen as an early form of resistance to the naive literalism and plodding banality of mechanical imitation. Like many of his contemporaries, he relied most comfortably on visual images that reminded him of a continuing tradition of abstracted imitation: the emblematic secular "Hieroglyphicks," with their concealed intentions; classical portraits that could change their subjects with a few new strokes; satirical portraits representative of a political idea or class of human beings. In his essay "Concerning Humour in Comedy" (1695), Congreve stressed the importance of such abstract imitation for the theater:

If this Exactness of Quantity, were to be observed in Wit, as some would have it in Humour; what would become of those Characters that are design'd for Men of Wit? I believe if a Poet should steal a Dialogue of any length, from the *Extempore* Discourse of the two Wittiest Men upon Earth, he would find the Scene but coldly receiv'd by the Town.[22]

Theater is the only artistic form that, in its imitations, uses the same materials as those things it imitates—human bodies. Music does not use actual birds to create its tones, figurative painting does not use actual trees or streets in its canvases, printed poems do not need live voices to exist. But the theater does need actual humans, and in this sense it is most literally a reproduction of the things it imitates. It can, however, evade some of that literalness by favoring the imitation of actions and speeches that are not altogether verisimilar, that are abstracted from life. In urging this kind of abstract imitation, Congreve may be registering his discomfort with the theater's inherent proximity to life. Such proximity of the imitation to the imitated is matched by the dangerous physical proximity of the audience to the actors, who need only cross the boundary of the stage (and the imaginary threshold of the theatrical) to eradicate the difference between art and life. Theater has always needed to emphasize its distance, its difference from the dangers of overly close imitation. Its tradition of abstract imitation and its interest in disguise and the mask allow it freedom from a naturalism that would be grotesque in its proximity to reality.[23] So it is dangerous to copy exactly an oral dialogue ("*Extempore* Discourse"),[24] for the oral world on the stage is just beyond the proscenium: "the Town" is separated from the actors only by the narrow boundary of abstracted imitation. Orality relies on abstract mimesis for safety.

As in his evocations of the golden-age orality of antiquity, Congreve expressly defends the oral and theatrical and the notion of imitation tied to those values, but the way he frames his argument suggests a less-conscious ambivalence: "The distance of the Stage requires the Figure represented, to be something larger than the Life; and sure a Picture may have Features larger in Proportion, and yet be very like the Original."[25] The choice of the word *Figure* and its apposition with "larger than the Life" already suggest a being that could not be human, but only a representation of the human. The immediate comparison to "a Picture," without the usual framework of simile (*as* or *like*), suggests that in fact this Figure is not an actor, but a "Figure," or visual design.[26] It is hard to reconcile such rhetoric with a live theater, but it is much easier to identify it with the inanimate visual images that surrounded Congreve, the kind of satiric images on which he drew, for instance, for Scandal's portraits. The invocation of the visual is again, here, principally a rhetorical technique for clearing an arena for language (just as the spatial visuality that the printed page encouraged was a visuality that served the purposes of language). As with Scandal's portraits, in which the visual is temporary scaffolding for the verbal satire, here "Picture" is immediately subsumed in the discussion of "Wit," "Dialogue," and "Discourse." "Ut pictura poesis" is still about the "poesis" side of things.

Congreve learned a great deal from the visual format that print provided: the visual figures (subordinate as they are) in which he is interested are strongly identified with the inanimate (printed) picture and the spatial form of the printed page (which serves as an arena for language, as the stage serves as an arena for the oral language of theater). He learned, most of all, the ways that fixed images and text could be brought together. He was living between two eras. Heroic painting and the designs that emerged from it could no longer rely on convention to explain them, for the textualism of print culture seemed to subsume all explanation, to question all formula. The eighteenth century would seek new nonconventional modes of pictorial illustration through scientific verisimilitude, attempting to free itself from textual explanation. But the late seventeenth century needed the text to bridge the two modes. The visual could not be trusted. In the plays, where the visual and the verbal are allied (the theatrical and the literate), the visual belongs to the world of print. And just as the printed dramatic text, in translating the stage into words, attempts to replace the visual stage with its own visual format, Congreve's visual references are immediately appropriated by verbal translation of them. His identification of the visual in his plays with the inanimate visual forms of the printed picture and his transformation of those visual forms into language suggest his transformation of the theatrical into dramatic textualism. If Congreve's theater is a place in which "Wit" can, for a moment, be animated, a place in which the physical form on the boards gives motion to the abstraction of language, a place in which *"Minerva* walks upon the Stage before us,"[27] it is nonetheless a theater of words in a culture of verbal effusion, mistrustful of effects, disdainful of spectacle, interested in the rigid images of the pictorial world but committed to their textual translation.

The Dictionary and the Monkey: Words and Gestures, Words and Things

For words are wise men's counters, they do but reckon by them; but they are the money of fools, that value them by the authority of . . . [any] doctor whatsoever, if but a man. —Hobbes, *Leviathan*

Another means whereby the *Eye* misleads our Judgement is the *Action*. . . . This thing of *Action* finds the blindside of humane-kind an hundred ways. We laugh and weep with those that laugh or weep; we gape, stretch, and are very *dotterels* by example.
—Rymer, *A Short View of Tragedy*

When, in the preface to *Incognita*, Congreve tells us that the Minerva who walks upon the stage is there to assure us of the presence of "Wit,"[1] he does not say more about the nature of that "Wit," why we need to be assured of its real presence, and its relation to the physical embodiment of wisdom that Minerva represents. What is the relation of language to the concrete physicality of the stage? What is the relation between the presence that constitutes orality and the inscription that constitutes literacy in the theater of the period? There are no simple equations, for Minerva's *viva* *voce* is both embodied (in her body) and disembodied (separate from the tangible page). The theater's orality offers a physical embodiment of the word and thus provides a link between language and materiality, the kind of link the era was seeking. And yet orality does not make the word into an object (as print does) and so leaves it floating in the realm of the immaterial.² Just as the stage (as spectacle) and print each require a strongly developed visual sense, so does each offer a different format for the incarnated word. Theater preserves the link between the human body and language; print makes the word itself (a separable and fully formed entity on the page) seem to be a thing, not simply a sound. This sense of the word as thing, rather than resolving the old debate over the relation between words and things, exacerbated the sense of anxiety over the referentiality of language: words, since they had become things in themselves, seemed to refuse to refer outside of themselves. By the seventeenth century, it was difficult to avoid in some way confronting language theory, whose productions only added to the sense of the instability of language.³ Playwrights were forced to come to terms with this problem by the very nature of their genre, a genre whose form constantly confronts words with gestures and things.

The verbal universe of the late seventeenth century, the universe in which Scandal's and Tattle's visual portraits have far more to do with verbal satire than with the pictorial image, is filled with scraps of written matter, writings that become confused with one another, writings under which other writings hide. These are, of course, mostly manuscripts, but print is responsible for the sense of the necessity of textual explanation, for the sense of textual overabundance that the manuscript makers try to match. The world was beginning to seem made of texts, as it would be more fully for the novel during the eighteenth century—in *Robinson Crusoe*, *Clarissa*, and *Tristram Shandy*, for instance, in which the heroes "write themselves."⁴ Although the playwrights' image of this manuscript profusion would become, in the eighteenth century, explicitly an image of print profusion, the sense of textual excess is already powerful.

That Congreve's plays are "literate," that the characters continually engage in the act of reading and writing, is obvious to even the most cursory reader or viewer. Vainlove shows Silvia's letter to Bellmour, and Laetitia's appears soon after (*OB*, I.i, pp. 38–39). Bluffe tries to prove himself by showing letters "from Persons of great Quality" (*OB*, V.i, p. 103), just as Petulant tries to prove himself by sending himself a letter from a person of quality (*WW*, I.i, p. 405). Lady Plyant tries to read her letter from Careless under the cover of Lord Plyant's (*DD*, IV.i, p. 173), and Millamant is "persecuted with Letters" (*WW*, II.i, p. 419). Zara sends an impassioned note to Osmyn, which we hear in a fragmentary form when the King reads it (*MB*, V.i, p. 374), and Osmyn finds the fragment of his father's scribbled prayer (*MB*, III.i, p. 350). Lady Plyant sees herself as "a fair Sheet of Paper, for [Mellefont] to make a Blot upon" (*DD*, II.i, p. 145), and Valentine corroborates this view when he tells Angelica that women are "Paper, when you first are Born; but you are to be scrawl'd and blotted by every Goose's Quill" (*LL*, IV.i, p. 292).[5] Letters or written sheets have become so common that they may be used for anything, and we find them not only in prison cells, on trees, in the air, but tucked in the curls of Millamant's hair. She "hate[s]" letters, "And yet one has 'em, one does not know why—They serve one to pin up one's Hair" (*WW*, II.i, p. 419).

The images of printed matter are not as insistent in Congreve as they will be in Fielding, for instance. In drawing on an earlier dramatic tradition, Congreve invokes letters, rather than printed books, as pivots for his plot, recalling the manuscript culture from which the theater partly emerges. But in Congreve, letters seem to have lost their identities as manuscripts. There are so many of them, and they are so impersonal (those Millamant receives, for instance) that they seem no longer to be part of the correspondence of intimates, but to have joined the ranks of the mechanically reproduced. These letters, which appear continually and from nowhere, serve as a dramatized figuration for the continually increasing flood of printed matter that must have seemed to be filling London streets, shops, houses, alleyways. And books themselves consume oral discourse (even illiterate oral discourse) when Witwoud begins converting the "illiterate" Petulant's few words into printed books ("Thou hast uttered *Volumes, Folio's*, in less than *Decimo Sexto*, my Dear *Lacedemonian*, Sirrah *Petulant*" [*WW*, IV.i, p. 453]). Orality disappears into the book. (The technical descriptions of size, despite the contradictions, only emphasize the fact that Witwoud is fully a man of print.) When the written dominates (in the form of print), words become reified, as Petulant's are, and as Jeremy's are in the face of Valentine's creditors:

VALENTINE   And how the Devil do you mean to keep your word?

JEREMY   Keep it? Not at all; it has been so very much stretch'd, that I reckon it will break of course by to morrow, and no body be surpriz'd at the Matter. (*LL*, I.i, pp. 220–21)

The words of Jeremy's "plain downright English" stretch, break, perform a variety of physical tasks. But they do not represent, at least not things as they are.

The interest in the relationship between words and the material world that they were supposed to express—an interest that had been increasing throughout the seventeenth century and that found a firm formulation in the linguistic work of, among others, Hobbes, Lancelot and Arnauld, Sprat, and later Locke (and, in England, of the Royal Society as a body)—partly resulted from the way that verbal effusion (and attendant "nonsense") called into question semiological (and so epistemological) stability.[6] By the end of the 1660's, the attitudes that were to make up the Royal Society's view of language had been worked out by Bacon, Hobbes, Arnauld, and by members of the society itself, such as John Wilkins.[7] Their concern, like Hooke's in his attack on earlier scientific method and his assertion of visualist principles, was not only that (as the old argument would have it) the rhetoric of the poets was a form of lie.[8] It was not only that the spoutings of "fanatick" preachers (the "enthusiasm" that Swift would later mock) distorted religious truth. It was that all words, proliferating words, themselves took up so much space that there was no more room for the things they were supposed to represent.

If the rhetoric of the dissenting preachers made many people wish for a pure language of words attached to things, the dissenters themselves had a powerful awareness of the truth status of the word, which originated in their desire for the purer textuality of the Bible but was carried on in their continual interpretation of the world-as-text, in their distinctions between verisimilar (true Christian) and nonverisimilar (un-Christian) texts. Even the broadest parody of the dissenters picked up on this—for example, in Congreve's rendering of Fondlewife, who must interpret Bellmour's story about his "attempted" seduction of Laetitia: "Ha! This is Apocryphal," cries Fondlewife. "I may chuse whether I will believe it or no." In typical late-seventeenth-century fashion, Bellmour obfuscates matters: "That you may, Faith, and I hope you won't believe a word on't.—But I can't help telling the truth, for my life" (*OB*, IV.iv, p. 95). Congreve's interest in the apocryphal (here and in the poem on Dryden's translation of Persius) suggests his concern for the truth status of texts. Like Maskwell, and like many other characters of the period, Bellmour tests the margins between truth and lying. As for many, those margins consist in named ways of telling stories, of representing things (or states or events) with words.

Congreve's contemporaries very consciously considered themselves part of a "dissembling age," a "flattering age," an age in which words must be read backwards, meanings read in inverse, if they are to be read at all. Bellmour knows that Belinda loves him because "she never speaks well of me" (*OB*, I.i, p. 41). For Careless, the most that one can ask from language is that it be melodious nonsense: "Your Fools grow noisy—and if a man must endure the noise of words without Sence, I think the

Women have the more Musical Voices, and become Nonsence better" (*DD*, I.i, p. 127)? If words are signs, then they are empty signs, signs full of the nonsense scratching of writing or the wind of sound. When the Renaissance spoke of signs, such signs contained all that they signified; mystics like Jakob Boehme, in *The Signature of All Things* (1622), could see, quite clearly, the Being of Beings in a pewter dish.[10] For the late seventeenth century, the word *sign* meant false, insubstantial representation or indication of a thing without substance, as in Sharper's identification of Bluffe as "that sign of a Man there— That Pot-gun charg'd with Wind" (*OB*, III.i, p. 69), or the more usual use of "sign of a man" to indicate cuckold, a man without the essential quality of manliness (an active phallus).[11]

The seventeenth-century argument for "plain style" is essentially an argument for a stylistics of a more precise and literal method of signification, and the debate that opposed plain style to rhetorical ornament ("copia," for instance, and what were viewed as its most outlandish absurdities) can be seen largely as response to the anxiety over semiological dissolution resulting, in part, from print.[12] The problem, of course, reaches back to Greece: the most vociferous claimants for plain style—Bacon, Jonson, Hobbes, Sprat, Cowley, and Dryden—nearly all invoke Quintilian against what they perceive to be Ciceronian rhetoric. But this division of plain style and rhetorical ornament into classical camps nearly always involves the nostalgic primitivism that is itself a reaction to print's perceived oversophistication.[13] For instance, Sprat writes that the Royal Society is in the process of undertaking a reformation of language: "The only *Remedy*, that can be found for this *extravagance* [is] a constant Resolution, to reject all the amplifications, digressions, and swellings of style: to return back to primitive purity, and shortness, when men deliver'd so many *things*, almost in an equal number of *words*."[14] Like Congreve's primitivism, in which the golden age is reached through footnotes and finally subsumed by them, the argument for plain style attempts to attack the problems of print culture with more print.

This attempt is only one of a number that respond to the sense of dissolution by encouraging even more forms of printed matter: dictionaries and encyclopedias, such as Pierre Bayle's *Dictionnaire historique et critique* (1697), which try to stabilize definitions;[15] scientific writings (Hooke's and other Royal Society treatises, for instance), in which the firm foundations of empirical methodology are celebrated; scholarship (that of Bentley, Wotton, and even Congreve), in which the methodical investigation of the past, it was hoped, would eliminate "fantastical" myth and replace it with a neat historicism grounded in truth; and philosophic-linguistic investigations, such as Hobbes's or Locke's, which strive for definitions, consistent usage, and a grammar to stay linguistic flux. For Hobbes, proper definitions can prevent the multiplication of errors that arises from the multiplication of books. As books increase, so do errors: "From whence it happens, that they which trust to books do as they that cast up many little sums into a greater, without considering whether those little sums were rightly cast up or not . . . but spend time in fluttering over their books."[16] In definitions, such as those Hobbes is about to give in his own book, lies the first use of speech, "which is the acquisition of science: and in wrong, or no definitions, lies the first abuse . . . which make those men that take their instruction from the authority of books, and not from their own meditation, to be . . . below the condition of ignorant men." Nonetheless, even proper definitions cannot alter the fact that words are merely a form of currency, with no intrinsic value: "For words are wise men's counters, they do but reckon by them; but they are the money of fools, that value them by the authority of . . . [any] doctor whatsoever, if but a man."[17] The "if but a man" seems appended, a way of countering accusations that nominalism equals atheism. The recognition of the emptiness of words, however, and the distress that this recognition must have caused were quite close to the sense of the emptiness of religious form that the religious skeptic must have felt. For Hobbes, one feels, there is little true hope for a redemptive language.

For Locke, there is more hope. Just as many tried to fortify themselves against late-seventeenth-century atheism, Locke tries to fortify himself against skepticism about the referential power of language. For Locke, it is clear ideas and consistency of usage that may result in a comprehensible language: "They who would advance in knowledge, and not deceive and swell themselves with a little articulated air, should lay down this as a fundamental rule, not to take words for things, nor suppose that names in books signify real entities in nature, till they can frame clear and distinct ideas of those entities."[18] Dictionary makers, like Locke, hoped that "clear and distinct ideas" could make names "signify real entities." With proliferating pages, the books of the plain-style advocates and the results of those books—dictionaries, grammars, and increasingly rigid notions of the proper use of the language—were also proliferating, infusing the English with a great sense of the seriousness of words and of the ways that words must be attached to the physical world or not permitted at all.

These attempts at a language that would perfectly and absolutely adhere to things, whether a scientific, philosophical, or literary language, called forth numerous satiric responses, most notably satires on the Royal Society and its endeavors.[19] They also called forth more subtle and only half-conscious responses in the form of reactive, energetic bursts of wit against the repressions of linguistic fixity. The "wit" of the comedies might be seen as the stage's struggle to subvert such linguistic fixity (although wit has its own forms of entrapment). The capacity to detach a word from its ordinary dictionary definition is more than a form of power used against the power of the dictionary and the linguistic establishment: in the "wit comedies" of the 1670's, it is a necessary defense in a world in which scandal becomes social law, in which the shifting winds of such detachable language can alter social and material status. To take one of the more insistent cases, the ability to play with the word *honor*—used as a weapon, in self-defense, as a social and class determinant, or merely as "noise"—liberates the characters from the atmosphere of disease and death that pervades Wycherley's *Country Wife*. Adultery is "not an injury to a husband till it be an injury to our honors," Lady Fidget assures Mrs. Dainty Fidget and Mrs. Squeamish.

LADY FIDGET   So that a woman of honor loses no honor with a private person. . . . But still my dear, dear honor. . . .

SIR JASPER FIDGET   Ay, my dear, dear of honor, thou hast still so much honor in thy mouth—

HORNER (*aside*)   That she has none elsewhere.[20]

Lady Fidget uses the word to liberate herself from the social constraints of marriage; Sir Jasper uses it in its legal sense; Horner, who combines plain dealing with wit to suit his purposes, twists Sir Jasper's use of the word back to the denotative meaning that suits the situation. Horner has, in fact, already put the case quite plainly early in the play, when we have had only a glimpse of the three "women of honor." "Your women of honor, as you call 'em," he tells the quack, "are only chary of their reputations, not their persons, and 'tis scandal they would avoid, not men."[21]

Horner's forthright asides remind us of the way in which he uses language in public places and point out the way a single term can split into mutations of itself, mutations that have taken flight from rigid definitions. Horner's commentary, too, teaches us to hear the language of others differently—Lady Fidget's, for instance:

> But, poor gentleman, could you be so generous, so truly a man of honor, as for the sakes of us women of honor, to cause yourself to be reported no man? No man! And to suffer yourself the greatest shame that could fall upon a man, that none might fall upon us women by your conversation? . . . But I have so strong a faith in your honor, dear, dear, noble sir, that I'd forfeit mine for yours at any time, dear sir.[22]

Here Wycherley gives five permutations of the word *honor*: (1) kindness ("so truly a man of honor"); (2) reputation for virtue ("us women of honor"); (3) capacity for secrecy and (4) sexual prowess ("faith in your honor," for both meanings); and, finally, (5) sexual fidelity ("forfeit [my honor] for yours"). Lady Fidget uses at least two other words in similarly fragmented ways: *conversation*, which in this case means both verbal interchange and sexual intercourse; and *shame*, which in this case means both feeling and the language of scandal that causes that feeling.

Medley, in Etherege's *Man of Mode*, has something of Horner's attitude toward language: he both notes its fragmentation from concrete definitions and uses its capacity for fragmentation to his own advantage, in this case not to seduce women (as Horner does), but to take the privileged position of town gossip. He can observe, for instance, that "marriage has lost its good name"[23]—that the name, the word for marriage, is no longer firmly attached to the physical forms for which it stood. But he also, according to Lady Townley, "improves things so much" that "one can take no measure of the truth from him. Mr. Dorimant swears a flea or a maggot is not made more monstrous by a magnifying glass than a story is by his telling it."[24] Etherege emphasizes Lady Townley's comment on Medley's manipulations of words by allowing her her own linguistic manipulation in the ironic juxtaposition between the verb *improves* and *made more monstrous*, the adjectival phrase held off as long as possible. *Improves* had come to mean, among other things, any kind of verbal change, particularly a change for the worse. Medley here is portrayed as the creator of fictions, a type for the playwright, who has chosen to free himself from pedestrian signification.

The playwright's ability to make alternate, or "false," realities has always disturbed those who wished to reform or abolish the theater. Such verbal construction of reality is a nightmare for dictionary makers and is untenable for their allies, those religious realists who, like Jeremy Collier, registered concern over the nature of language in the comedies: "As Good and Evil are different in themselves, so they ought to be differently marked," he wrote in his *Short View* (1698). "To confound them in Speech, is to confound them in Practice."[25] For Collier, language is already fixed to specific and unchanging moral forms. To have a flexible language is to be in danger of having a flexible morality.

If both the witty hero and heroine and the witty satiric target liberate language from an imprisonment in specific and rigid referents, there are characters who themselves represent the inflexible and brutish forms of the literalized language, if not with Collier's purity of intention. In *The Man of Mode*, Old Bellair asks the minister, "Please you, sire, to commission a young couple to go to bed together a God's name?"[26] In *The Country Wife*, Pinchwife, similarly, proclaims that "I must give Sparkish tomorrow five thousand pound to lie with my sister."[27] Horner's victory at the end of the play consists in having successfully seduced, without scratching his own reputation, the wife of Pinchwife, the only man in the play who tries to guide his life according to rigid and inflexible verbal rules that show no capacity for flexible response to changing situations. Pinchwife becomes the representative of linguistic imprisonment. The precept-loving Pinchwife, at his most Collier-like, reprimands Alithea early in the play for letting Margery know that Alithea is leaving the house. "Good precepts are lost when bad examples are still before us," he tells her. "The liberty you take abroad makes her hanker after it."[28] Pinchwife becomes the guardian of the inflexible word, while Alithea is, in his view, the mistress of action. We, of course, know that it is not Alithea, but rather Pinchwife himself, who, in his unwitting foolishness, is making Margery long to see the pretty player men and the handsome man who has fallen "in love" with her. Liberty is opposed to precepts, and the irony of the situation lies partly in the fact that Pinchwife is duped because of his belief that his inflexible verbal rules can protect him.

Even Dorimant comes dangerously close to becoming a man of precept, and the lesson he must learn is that the attainment of desire and of freedom can coexist, even within the bonds of matrimony, as long as one retains the liberating power of disjunctive wit. When, in witty debate with Harriet, Dorimant tries to move from sustained metaphor to a language of sincerity, Harriet simply walks away, saying, "Mr Bellair! let us walk, 'tis time to leave him, men grow dull when they begin to be particular." Similarly, when he tells her that he "will renounce all the joys I have in friendship and in wine, sacrifice to you all the interest I have in other women," she responds, "Hold! Though I wish you devout, I would not have you turn fanatic."[29] If Etherege is interested in testing the limits of the ethical and temperate life, he is even more interested in shaking the rigid tenacity to inflexible verbal structures, unbinding the fanaticism that leads men mechanically to attach their actions to verbal absolutes. Sir Fopling, similarly, is the perfect example of the verbal fanatic who, rather than subscribing to moral or religious law, subscribes to the laws and defined codes of fashion:

SIR FOPLING   In Paris the mode is to flatter the *prudé*, laugh at the *faux-prudé*, make serious love to the *demi-prudé*, and only rally with the *coquetté*.[30]

Sir Fopling has adopted the French desire to methodize, to create an external structure like those the academy was creating for the French language.

The "plain dealer," one of the favorite humours characters of the late-seventeenth-century stage, is another version of the dictionary maker, visibly an adherent of rigid signification. (The period is especially interested in plain dealers who are double-dealers or dupes.) The plain dealer's words, like Hooke's microscope, strive to show only the accurate portrait of the most traditionally ugly natural forms, claiming that the beauty of their accuracy supplants the conventional human estimation of beauty. The drama does not, on the whole, treat the plain dealer well: Molière's misanthrope, Alceste, the model for most, has little conception of the nature of social behavior and is justly chastised by Philinte, as Wycherley's Manly, hypocritical and ill-natured in addition, is justly chastised by Freeman (the figure of the freeman who fights the constraints of plain style).[31] Congreve's plain dealers are equally rude or hypocritical or both.

Heartwell, who claims, "My Talent is chiefly that of speaking truth, which I don't expect should ever recommend me to People of Quality" (*OB*, I.i, p. 45), lies to all of his friends about Silvia. Scandal's name denotes the true nature of his "plain dealing," and Valentine's admonition serves as a larger warning for the play: "Learn to spare your Friends, and do not provoke your Enemies; this liberty of your Tongue, will one day bring a Confinement on your Body, my Friend" (*LL*, I.i, p. 221). (Here the ostensible liberty of plain dealing is actually connected to enslavement, and, again, plain speech is associated with confinement.) Mirabell views Petulant's plain dealing as simply a failure of wit: "What, he speaks unseasonable Truths sometimes, because he has not Wit enough to invent an Evasion" (*WW*, I.i, p. 404). Witty words do not correspond to things in the world. Petulant's inability to speak witty evasions cripples him; Heartwell's inability to "lie" (in both senses) with Silvia binds him slavishly to his love.

HEARTWELL   Lying, Child, is indeed the Art of Love; and Men are generally Masters in it: But I'm so newly entred, you cannot distrust me of any skill in the treacherous Mystery. . . . I tell thee I do love thee, and tell it for a Truth, a naked Truth, which I'm ashamed to discover. (*OB*, III.ii, p. 72)

The failure to lie is reflected inversely in the failure to recognize lies, which so interested the period. The numerous renderings of the Don Quixote figure brought forth in the late seventeenth century—for instance, in Butler's *Hudibras* (1663–78), D'Urfey's *Comical History of Don Quixote* (1694–96), and, later, Fielding's *Joseph Andrews* (1742) and Charlotte Lennox's *Female Quixote* (1752)—show that naïveté about the ways of the world can be a failure to recognize lies. That naïveté is partly the effect of a dominant print culture. The Quixotes have read too many romances; in *Tom Jones*, Partridge's experience with only the flat representations of the page has made him incapable of understanding that the embodied forms of the theater are merely representations. Like the dictionary makers, such figures fail to recognize that language is flexible. Not only does language have no fixed and limited referents, but it has innumerable variations of tropes, innumerable ways of swerving from the literalism that efforts at definition suggest. The creators of these characters here take revenge on the literalism of print standardization, trying to wean it from its self-important certainty. For the far end of naive literalism (that of the learned) is pedantry. Pedants, Quixote characters, and plain dealers all share an essential quality: they receive the abstractions of language as an ideal, which they bravely follow in defiance of custom. They fail to recognize that the abstractions of language are inherently lies.

The Double-Dealer is one example of a play largely about the failure to recognize lies, although Maskwell's lies are literal truths not believed. (In this, Congreve suggests that the fixity of the dictionary cannot help in a world accustomed to the "lies" of figurative language.) Similarly, witty literalism (less perniciously) speaks literally in a world accustomed to figuration, interpreting figurative language as if it were describing corporeal reality. Witty literalism is the obverse side of the naive failure to recognize lies. When Lucy warns Bellmour, "But if you do deceive me, the Curse of all kind, tender-hearted Women light upon you," Bellmour replies, "That's as much as to say, *The Pox take me*" (*OB*, V.i, p. 98). Bellmour redefines Lucy's words by connecting them with the material world, reinterpreting *curse* to mean physical disease and reinterpreting moral qualities ("kind, tender-hearted") as physical actions (sexual promiscuity). Bellmour himself has his figurative language wittily literalized by Belinda, who responds to his poetic wooing by saying to Araminta: "Lard, he has so pester'd me with Flames and Stuff—I think I shan't endure the sight of a Fire this Twelvemonth" (II.ii, p. 59). Yet Bellmour persists, stuck in his poetically contrived repetitions, encased in his tragic iambic pentameter: "Yet all can't melt that cruel frozen Heart." Belinda fights Bellmour's inflexibility with a mock-refusal of flexibility, which is actually flexibility in disguise. If the traditional wit hero disjoins words from things, showing that only fools understand words purely literally, such later wit heroines as Belinda fight the literally defined universe by showing that the direct linkage of words and things can never accurately represent the world. A witty use of words that falsely adhere to materiality is another version of the witty figuration that represents freedom from signification.

Rebellion against the constraints of rigid signification, rebellion expressed through disjunctive wit or through witty literalism, is nearly an automatic gesture in the drama by the time Congreve is writing, prescribing a flexibility for the ills of language chained to things. But in Congreve (and many others), the prescription of flexibility is only one response to problems of language in the late seventeenth century. Perhaps it is more a conventional one than an essential one, perhaps more a homage to such witty models as Wycherley, Etherege, and Dryden than pure defiance of dictionary culture. In Congreve's four comedies, such wit is as much mimetic and satiric as it is prescriptive. Horner and Lady Fidget may both be satiric targets, but they liberate the viewer from the weight of fixed referents. Petulant and Witwoud, on the other hand, going at each other "like two Battle-dores," convey only the ever presence of nonsense and remind the viewer (as the plain-style advocates did) that words must find some way of grounding themselves in the world (although such a grounding, for Congreve, cannot be found in a philosophical or scientific language, nor can it be found in a police state of linguistic regulation). Congreve complains, in the dedication to *The Way of the World*, that his audience could not "distinguish betwixt the Character of a *Witwoud* and a *Truewit*" (p. 390);[32] but the audience had claimed that the fools were too witty and that Congreve himself did not distinguish sufficiently. The audience of *The Double-Dealer* a few years earlier had objected to Mellefont on the grounds that he was "a Gull and a Fool," as much because he displays "wit" only in brief flickers as because he "is made a Fool and cheated" by Maskwell (as Congreve relates in his dedication, p. 120). It is not, as many critics have claimed, that there is in Congreve's plays simply a finer distinction between false wit and true.[33] Congreve's wits *are* less witty than their predecessors. His fools *are* too witty (or just witty enough to show the problems with wit), as his early critics justly noticed.[34]

The Old Batchelour is the only one of Congreve's plays that opens with an expectably witty Restoration exchange (I.i, p. 37), the exchange in which Bellmour and Vainlove discuss the purpose of wit (which is held in opposition to the seriousness of business and worldly concerns). The opening of *The Double-Dealer* reveals Careless and Mellefont in a serious exchange about a matter of great importance. Only with Brisk's entrance do the two begin to play a wit game, and Mellefont joins the game halfheartedly, since he cannot speak of the serious things on his mind in the terms that wit affords. Careless, here, takes on the role of the cruel wit:

BRISK   You're always spoiling Company by leaving it.

CARELESS   And thou art always spoiling Company by coming into 't. (I.i, p. 128)

Mellefont makes kindly but serious interjections and, after Brisk has gone, tells Careless: "Faith, 'tis a good natur'd Cox-Comb, and has very Entertaining follies—you must be more humane to him" (I.i, p. 129). Valentine, wittier than most of Congreve's "heroes," nonetheless allows Jeremy the monopoly on wit ("You are witty, you Rogue, I shall want your Help" [I.i, p. 218]); for the veracities of madness are more Valentine's mode.

Mirabell begins *The Way of the World* by showing that he is tired of games, fatigued with play that is only an abstract representation of "the play of the world." He responds to Fainall's witticisms with halfhearted quips. Like many of the central characters, whose wisdom is more important than their wit, Mirabell is less interested in displaying his wit than in watching the wit of others and exploring the meaning of wit. Similes, for instance, are now interesting as objects of attention, but dangerous in that they threaten the stability of the referential language associated with print. In this sense, the similes of the wits, "similitudes," are disjunctive rather than conjunctive. Although they bring together two ideas, they do so by wrenching one from the context in which it seemed to have meaning. Mirabell's nonfigurative observation and Millamant's similes are trespassed upon at her first entrance by Witwoud's "similitudes," which disjoin and redirect Millamant's. Mirabell tells her that she used to have "the *Beau-mond*" hovering around her:

WITWOUD   Like Moths about a Candle—I had like to have lost my Comparison for want of Breath.

MILLAMANT   O I have deny'd my self Airs to Day. I have walk'd as fast through the Croud—

WITWOUD   As a Favourite just disgrac'd; and with as few Followers.

MILLAMANT   Dear Mr. *Witwoud*, Truce with your Similitudes: For I am as Sick of 'em—

WITWOUD   As a Physician of a good Air—I cannot help it, Madam, tho' 'tis against my self. (II.i, pp. 418–19)

The rampant "similitudes," which are shown to be violent and regressive in Congreve's plays, can be seen in several ways as oppositions to print. On a fundamental level, their strong association with classical epic suggests that they are oral gestures. Like other aspects of orality, they are accumulative in that they add one term to another and do not eliminate the bridge between the two. They invoke the presence on which orality relies in their assumption that, for the world to be conceived as a series of analogical relations, both terms must be brought forth fully, not lost in the metaphysical absences of metaphor. Metaphors have the conciseness valued by a print culture in their contractions of the two terms into one. They assume that a web of implicit explanations of figuration already exists. They assume that there is a hermeneutics of analogy already inscribed in language. They are sophisticated in their recognition that figuration is a precondition of language. In the Restoration, the opposition of simile to print was further emphasized by the association of simile with the liberating disjunctive wit that opposed rigid signification. But in Congreve that wit is now approached differently. Rather than showing the unexpected ways that words indicating particular things can suddenly metamorphose themselves into new things, similes now plague the bearers of words. For sentences can never remain whole. They are always fractured by the infinite possibilities of figuration.

Mirabell's observation that Millamant is unattended suggests that, in the world outside the limits of the stage, there is a flock of fools, a stream of Witwouds, all redirecting each fragment of discourse, swerving it from its intended objects, with the violence of a fracturing language and against all entreaty:

MILLAMANT   *Mincing*, stand between me and his Wit.

WITWOUD   Do Mrs. *Mincing*, like a Skreen before a great Fire. I confess I do blaze to Day, I am too bright.

But Millamant herself has the same disease, and immediately after her warning to Witwoud, she answers Mrs. Fainall, who asks why she has taken so long:

MILLAMANT   Long! Lord, have I not made violent haste? I have ask'd every living Thing I met for you; I have enquir'd after you, as after a new Fashion.

WITWOUD   Madam, truce with your Similitudes—

And at last Mirabell is brought into the discourse of similitudes with a conventional joke on marriage:

WITWOUD   No, you met with her Husband and did not ask him for her.

MIRABELL   By your leave *Witwoud*, that were like enquiring after an old Fashion, to ask a Husband for his Wife. (II.i, p. 419)

His ponderous "by your leave" suggests the slow pace of the half-wit, and Witwoud's acclamation ("a hit, a hit, a palpable hit"), which makes the operation of Mirabell's wit seem self-conscious, only confirms the impression. Mirabell, like the others, can be infected, but he is wise enough not to wish to be. After this exchange, he remains silent for a long time, until addressed directly by Millamant. Then he simply asks her whether it pleases her to give pain, and when she replies in the affirmative, he offers two simple statements, two sententious statements: "You wou'd affect a Cruelty which is not in your Nature; your true Vanity is in the power of pleasing" (II.i, p. 420).

Unlike similitudes and other forms of wit, which disjoin words from things and apply them to other things, Mirabell's simple abstractions (*Cruelty, Nature, Vanity, pleasing*) cling to their conventional meanings, conventional in that their meanings have been quite carefully socially determined. In Mirabell's usages, he neither challenges social accord nor follows social forms unthinkingly, mechanically. In the earlier playwrights, witty verbal disjunction and similitudes are liberating because they show the possibility of flexible response to experience, of mutative power over language.[35] In many of Congreve's scenes, on the other hand, such wit (now, witless wit) is shown to be mechanical, rigid in its unthinking adherence to conventional language. The voices of parrots dominate. In Wycherley, when Lady Fidget juggles the word *honour* or when, in the china scene, she flaunts her semiological skill, she is exhilarated by her own playfulness. Here she breaks the bonds of language, just as, with Horner, she breaks the conventions that restrain the body. In Congreve, such semiological wildness is shown to be incapacity, rather than skill. When Careless complains that he cannot get an answer from Lady Plyant "that does not begin with her Honour, or her Vertue, her Religion, or some such Cant" (*DD*, III.i, p. 156), he is showing the incapacity of her language to free her from her imagined definition of marital fidelity, from her mechanical "cant" (with the negation implied by the pun).

The most fully formed of Congreve's mechanical "wits" are, of course, Witwoud and Petulant:

WITWOUD   Raillery, Raillery, Madam. . . . We hit off a little Wit now and then, but no Animosity—The falling out of Wits is

like the falling out of Lovers—We agree in the main, like Treble
and Base. Ha, *Petulant*!

PETULANT   Ay, in the main—But when I have a Humour to contradict—

WITWOUD   Ay, when he has a Humour to contradict, then I contradict too. What, I know my Cue. Then we contradict one another like two Battle-dores. . . .

PETULANT   If he says Black's Black—If I have a Humour to say 'tis
Blue—Let that pass—All's one for that. (*WW*, III.i, p. 435)

This mechanical language that Witwoud and Petulant have developed between themselves (echoing oral disputation without
its substance) is a mask of illogical logic with no connection to
action or feeling. It has a destructive, not a liberating, function.
Millamant complains that Petulant "has done nothing; he has
only talk'd—Nay, he has said nothing neither; but he has con-
tradicted every Thing that has been said" (III.i, p. 432). Although contradiction is Petulant's special gift, Congreve seems
to suggest that all so-called wit is contra-dictory, antispeech (if
we take the etymology to imply, in the limited sense, a language that means).

Wit is conventional social memory that denies language
through its mechanical nature, its action of meaning. Like the
similitude, it holds infinite possibility, but only finitude can
have the stability that allows meaning to occur. When Fainall
says that Witwoud "does not always want wit," Mirabell responds:

Not always; but as often as his Memory fails him, and his common place of Comparisons. He is a Fool with a good Memory,
and some few Scraps of other Folks Wit. He is one whose Conversation can never be approv'd, yet it is now and then to be
endur'd. (I.i, p. 401)

Witwoud, himself a piece of hackwork with his "few Scraps of
other Folks Wit," values memory in the way that preprint man
does, but such memory is now useless. His memory has been
filled with conventional versions of witty disjunction, the worst

combination of disjunctive wit and mechanical convention,
which, when combined with rudeness, becomes unendurable.
Mirabell complains that Witwoud and Petulant have been "putting the Ladies out of Countenance, with your senseless Ribaldry," and adds:

> Where Modesty's ill Manners, 'tis but fit
> That Impudence and Malice, pass for Wit. (I.i, p. 409)

Their ribaldry is senseless both in that it hurts the "Ladies'"
sensibilities and in its nonrepresentational nature.

Speakers must now strive to speak a language that is "sensible" in a number of ways. It must link words to sense (as opposed to nonsense) and to real things and qualities in the world
(with the empirical implications of "the senses"), but it must
not do so naively. It must link them to feeling, which need not
necessarily be identified only with the pieties of sentimental
generosity. Such feeling has ties, too, to the beneficial sensual-
ism that was part of late-seventeenth-century Epicurean libertinism and to empiricism, in that empiricism is a philosophy
of the senses. A "sensible" language may have to be sententious,
like Mirabell's, filled with the wise sentiments of the "sentimental" speaker.[36] For "sentimentalism" had at least as much to
do with righteous sentences as it did with emotions and is thus
as much about kinds of speech as it is about pious and generous
emotions. It posits a link between speech and feeling. Congreve
himself must find, whether here or elsewhere in the tangle of
inadequate words, a redemptive language. But that language
cannot be a language of plain terms, which have come to seem
naively unyielding and which the earlier playwrights taught
Congreve to resist. Not only figuration, but plain terms too
have been debased, shown to be inadequate and inappropriate
means of representing things, let alone emotions. To struggle
against the absurdities of flexible nonsense does not mean fully
to support the efforts to achieve a perfect scientific language.
Swift's Grand Academy of Lagado demonstrates the point later,
but ever since print had first attempted to fix language, even

those writers who felt the most need for a redemptive language had portrayed as naive the belief that words represent things just as they are.

Cynthia, who achieves more direct, precise, "sensible" evocations of feeling in her language than any other character, without falling into the traps of sententiousness, suggests, if only analogically, the way in which language produces meaning when she tells Mellefont:

> I swear it never do's well when the Parties are so agreed—for when People walk hand in hand, there's neither overtaking nor meeting: We hunt in Couples where we both pursue the same Game, but forget one another; and 'tis because we are so near that we don't think of coming together. (*DD*, IV.i, p. 168)

Two people who are too close together can never come together. It is distance, difference (not agreement), that produces both desire and union. Similarly, a language that agrees too well with itself, a language of rigid and literal signification, produces neither desire nor union: the words of such a language can never come together in meaning (although a language that contains too much difference is "Senseless"). If Cynthia and Mellefont cannot meet because they are too close, Tattle and Scandal "should never be asunder," according to Valentine: "You are light and shadow, and shew one another" (*LL*, I.i, p. 225). Their oddly affectionate differences, like those of light and shadow, like those of Witwoud and Petulant, begin to represent the outlines of things as they are.

Difference—whether between words and things or between things as they seem and things as they are—allows both desire and signification. Such difference is at the heart of Congreve's ironic disjunctions, which respond to a world in which not only language but ordinary social bonds have been debased by false sentiment or cruelty. The way that Congreve's irony enacts a separation between speech and feeling allows them to rejoin, and those reunifications produce the meaning that contains Congreve's "sentimental" sincerity. This is not the irony of disjunction, Witwoud's irony, which is afraid of sincerity ("a Wit shou'd no more be sincere," claims Witwoud, "than a Woman constant" [*WW*, I.i, p. 403]). This is, rather, the irony of things that differ in order to agree. For instance, after Sir Sampson has debased the idea of paternity, Valentine can only express paternal love for his illegitimate child with an ironic indifference that reveals true or "natural" affection. When the nurse and child appear on his doorstep, he says:

> Pox on her, cou'd she find no other time to fling my Sins in my Face: Here, give her this,
>
> *Gives Money.*
>
> and bid her trouble me no more; a thoughtless two handed Whore, she knows my Condition well enough, and might have overlaid the Child a Fortnight ago, if she had had any forecast about her. (I.i, p. 221)

Seemingly an affirmation of Valentine's heartlessness, the gesture of tossing money at the "two handed Whore" by "generous Valentine," who has hardly any, rather belies his cheerful recommendation of infanticide. An odd bit of intimately paternal affection, his reference to "my Boy" a moment later, stresses the impression that his tone conceals "natural" parental love, that love so noticeably missing in Sir Sampson.

The tender generosity that lies behind "generous Valentine['s]" angry nihilism is rewarded by the ironic gesture toward which the play moves: only when Valentine rejects all can he receive all. Only then can a union between the two very separate parties, Valentine's passion and Angelica's seeming indifference, be found. Valentine must kneel in order to rise.[37] Similarly, Millamant's startling and comically beautiful declaration, "Well, if *Mirabell* shou'd not make a good Husband, I am a lost thing;—for I find I love him violently" (*WW*, IV.i, p. 453), moves beyond debased referential language, beyond nonsensical figuration, and into a kind of irony of feeling, an emotive understatement, in which the "if . . . then" parts of the sentence are joined in the final phrase.[38]

That space between the differences of irony, like silent gesture, acknowledges the insufficiencies of words. The passage that preceded Millamant's declaration emphasizes the connections among irony, gesture, and silence:

MILLAMANT   Well then—I'll take my death I'm in a horrid fright—*Fainall*, I shall never say it—well—I think—I'll endure you.

MRS FAINALL   Fy, fy, have him, have him, and tell him so in plain terms: For I am sure you have a mind to him. (IV.i, p. 452)

"Plain terms" are not exactly what Millamant uses, and she will not allow Mirabell to respond in plain terms either:

MILLAMANT   Well, you ridiculous thing you, I'll have you,—I won't be kiss'd, nor I won't be thank'd—here kiss my hand tho'—so hold your tongue now, and don't say a word.

Silence is better than the "plain terms" advocated by Mrs. Fainall, the plain style advocated by seventeenth-century literalism, the rigid connections between words and things, but better, too, than the "Flames and Stuff" with which Bellmour pesters Belinda and which Millamant might fear from Mirabell.

Meaning occurs beyond the barrier of verbal signification, between the layers of "you ridiculous thing you" and "I'll have you," and that space between finds its semiological expression in a silent kissing of the hand. The element of irony that expresses its resistance to words as signs finds its completion in silence and gesture. This does not, however, mean that Congreve's theater successfully fights off the seductions of a verbal universe, asserting solely its primitive connection with gesture and physical action. If gesture, for Congreve, allows a means of signification beyond words, it is always *beyond* words, always aware of its role in responding to the failures of verbal signification, which is prior, and thus circumscribed by it.[39] The physical body may be an irrefutable thing on stage. Congreve's theater may show an understanding of the power that transcends language, of the stage's physical facticity: Lady Wishfort's reified state, against which her constant self-identifications, "as I'm a Person," try desperately to assert themselves; or the grotesque presence of the severed head and body on stage in *The Mourning Bride*. But Lady Wishfort is a thing partly because she asserts again and again, mechanically, that she is "a Person." And the severed head and body are the work of a mute who is not actually mute (Gonsalez disguised as a mute). Gesture may be inherently theatrical, an essential part of the physical materiality that is one of the particular tools of the theater. It may be deeply tied to the oral world of the stage. But it is not free, for Congreve, from verbal circumscription and its meaning as counterforce against the dissolution of language, just as the stage is not entirely free from the printed text that encases it.

In his criticism of spectacle and farce, Congreve resisted a theater of pure gesture. In the "Essay Concerning Humour in Comedy," Congreve complains: "Is any thing more common, than to have a pretended Comedy, stuff'd with such Grotesques, Figures, and Farce Fools? Things, that either are not in Nature, or if they are, are Monsters, and Births of Mischance; and consequently as such, should be stifled, and huddled out of the way."[40] For Congreve, these "Grotesques" were the representatives of a nonliterary theater, a theater wholly devoted to its physical forms. Several years later, in the dedication to *The Way of the World*, he expressed similar attitudes by identifying his own work with that of Terence rather than that of Plautus: "Some of the coursest Strokes of *Plautus*, so severely censured by *Horace*, were more likely to affect the Multitude; such, who come with expectation to Laugh out the last Act of a Play, and are better entertain'd with two or three unseasonable Jests than with the artful Solution of the *Fable*" (p. 391).[41] Congreve's complaint, again invoking Horace, is another version of the distaste for the visual, this time the visual in motion. The "Jests," almost certainly farcical physical gags, interfere with the text, "the artful Solution of the *Fable*." For Congreve, there is something inherently obscene in the connection of gesture and action to the body, in their inseparability from human flesh.[42] Sir Joseph's grotesquely explicit description of Araminta's imagined gestures are, in Waitwell's phrase, "the Antidote to desire" (*WW*, IV.i, p. 459):

SIR JOSEPH   Did not she pull up her little Bubbies? And—A-gad, I'm so over-joy'd—And stroke down her Belly; and then step aside to tie her Garter, when she was thinking of her Love. Heh, *Setter*. (*OB*, V.i, p. 103)[43]

Sir Joseph's "obscenity" here (his choice of matter more properly left "outside the scene," to take the word etymologically) lies not only in the particularly sexual nature of the gestures he describes but also in the mistaken assumption that the mere fact of managing the body itself is communication. To assume an inherent semiotics of the body is as absurd as to choose one, as Bellmour attempts to do. Recognizing the ineffectuality of words with Belinda, Bellmour tries a self-conscious version of stage gesture, the "Signs" of "dumb shew," in a dense synecdoche for the larger semiotics of gesture on the stage (and perhaps as an implied critique of the increasingly popular pantomime, which was threatening the success of the more traditional theater). In her response, Belinda describes perfectly the excesses of both the verbal and the gestural worlds:

BELINDA   O fogh, your dumb Rhetorick is more ridiculous, than your talking Impertinence; as an Ape is a much more troublesome Animal than a Parrot.

ARAMINTA   Ay, Cousin, and 'tis a sign the Creatures mimick Nature well, for there are few Men, but do more silly things, than they say. (*OB*, II.ii, p. 60)

Belinda, naturally, would except herself, but part of the joke is her own verbal gestural affectations. Speech consists in the mechanical repetition of parrots (based only in convention, and so meaningless). Gesture consists in the obscene mimicry of apes. But if both are meaningless, gesture is nonetheless circumscribed in speech and is only understood by Belinda in an analogy to speech ("dumb Rhetorick"), the primary term of the metaphor. Araminta devalues gesture even more in her claim that men "do more silly things, than they say," and she twists the argument to point out that human gesture is even further debased than animal gesture. In claiming that "the Creatures mimick Nature well," she suggests that animals have a certain polish of artifice in their imitations of men, who are implicitly identified with rude nature and who, in their gestures, are less artful, more grotesquely physical, more bestial than animals.[44]

The monkey, for Congreve as for many of his contemporaries, is the perfect representative of the absurdities of human gesture, as it had traditionally been the representative of art during the Renaissance.[45] But it is one that disturbs viewers with the knowledge of their proximity to the animal world (the world of the body without speech). In the "Essay Concerning Humour in Comedy," Congreve suggests in his complaint about farce that farcical grotesques not be shown so that

Mankind may not be shock'd with an appearing Possibility of the Degeneration of a God-like *Species*. For my part, I am as willing to Laugh, as any body, and as easily diverted with an Object truly ridiculous: but at the same time, I can never care for seeing things, that force me to entertain low thoughts of my Nature. I dont know how it is with others, but I confess freely to you, I could never look long upon a Monkey, without very Mortifying Reflections; thô I never heard any thing to the Contrary, why that Creature is not Originally of a Distinct *Species*.[46]

The monkey transgresses our sense of the boundaries between the animal species and the human species. Gesture without speech is disturbing in something of the same way, no longer simply ridiculous, but beyond the pale of laughter, "Mortifying," reminding us, as it does, of our mortal natures (the body, which, unlike the soul, dies).

If humans are inherently bestial, inherently obscene in the motions of their bodies, both Congreve's effort to banish farce and the refinements of the human social state have put gesture, even in the theater, in second place.[47] Language is now the first instinct, gesture only a secondary recourse, in a reversal of the ordinary notion of historical priority, in which language was invented as a system of signs that could represent gestures and things. Bellmour's "Apishness" is the servant of his words, a stand-in for the parrot, which then sets the parrot free from captivity, a temporary alternative to language that returns as the natural state:

BELLMOUR Well, I find my Apishness has paid the Ransome for my Speech, and set it at liberty—Tho' I confess, I could be well enough pleas'd to drive on a Love-bargain, in that silent manner—'Twould save a Man a World of Lying and Swearing at the Years end. Besides, I have had a little Experience, that brings to my mind—

When Wit and Reason, both, have fail'd to move;
Kind Looks and Actions (from Success) do prove,
Ev'n Silence may be Eloquent in Love. (II.ii, p. 60)

Again, the figuration suggests that gesture is like language, which is the primary term. Bellmour claims to prefer gesture because it keeps one from the usual abuses into which language draws the speaker and because gesture has an implicit connection with sexual action, which the diction of "drive on a Love-bargain" emphasizes. But only when speech is imprisoned does "silent manner" (which metonymically displaces gesture with the opposite of speech) emerge to set it free. Only when the speaker is exhausted with "Lying and Swearing," with the disjunctions between words and things, may gesture assist (as physical servants stand in for their verbal masters, Waitwell for Mirabell when his master's wooing of Lady Wishfort has proved ineffectual and exhausting). Gesture finds "eloquence" only as a replacement for failed "Wit and Reason."

Congreve's theater chooses its recourse to gesture only when words fail (chooses farce and buffoonery only when the audience fails to appreciate wit).[48] Similarly, action is fully absorbed in language. The view we get of Osmyn emphasizes the way that inscription, and writing in particular, circumscribes action. To a certain extent, most tragedy of the period understands action as essential to the heroic moment, and *The Mourning Bride* is, in many places, true to such a notion, a notion particularly appropriate to stage tragedy, which can represent action without language. Garcia has told the King of his "mute Valour" (muteness is a central theme of the play), and his description of Osmyn imprisoned shows Osmyn to be the perfect hero of action:

> If he speak
> 'Tis scarce above a word; as he were born
> Alone to do, and did disdain to talk;
> At least, to talk where he must not command. (I.i, p. 335)

But Osmyn, we realize when we meet him, actually talks all the time, to others, to himself. Like many Congreve characters, he finds himself enmeshed in words and must rely on his hermeneutic powers, applied to a text, to determine meaning. When he finds in his cell the torn fragment of writing, the last prayer of his dying father (whose living voice is gone, but who leaves a fragment of himself in writing), he struggles to interpret not only its explicit content but also its dissolving figural meaning. He reads the fragment aloud and then exclaims:

> 'Tis wanting what should follow—Heav'n, Heav'n shou'd
>   follow.
> But 'tis torn off—why should that Word alone
> Be torn from his Petition? 'Twas to Heav'n.
> But Heav'n was deaf, Heav'n heard him not; but thus,
> Thus as the Name of Heav'n from this is torn,
> So did it tear the Ears of Mercy, from
> His Voice. (III.i, p. 350)

The catachresis involved in mourning the fact that heaven did not "hear" with "Ears" the "Voice" of a written text suggests the way the theater has become confused with its written forms. The voice that prays cannot be heard by heaven because it is no longer a voice, but a text, which has subsumed the live voices of prayer, and even heaven itself (metonymy for God) has become a word scribbled on a scrap of paper. (The absent fragment and the traditional God transcend any concrete physical form manifest in the world, except insofar as they leave traces of the places they have been.)

Gesture, like this orality, which must work itself out through writing, finds a place in the plays only when it is inscribed in language or commented on as if it were a text. The scene between Young Bellair and Harriet in *The Man of Mode*, in which the two instruct each other verbally in the gestures of amorous awkwardness in order to trick their parents, who see only a "dumb shew" of passion, is the prototype for this gesture as verbal instruction.[49] Such verbal intercession with gesture, whether descriptive, prescriptive, or hermeneutic, becomes essential to physical motion in the plays, seeming to acknowledge that we arrive at any knowledge, even the most fundamental, through linguistic categories. Fainall tells Mrs. Marwood that he has "seen the warm Confession red'ning on your Cheeks, and sparkling from your Eyes" (*WW*, II.i, p. 413). The observation becomes not simply a way of letting the audience in the upper gallery see it too, but Fainall's way of tormenting Mrs. Marwood, showing his verbal power over her physical vulnerability.[50] Similarly, early in *The Way of the World*, Mirabell describes his visit with Lady Wishfort and Millamant the night before with much physical detail:

MIRABELL   Seeing me, they all put on their grave Faces, whisper'd one another; then complain'd aloud of the Vapours, and after fell into a profound Silence.

FAINALL   They had a mind to be rid of you.

MIRABELL   For which Reason I resolv'd not to stir. At last the good old Lady broke thro' her painful Taciturnity, with an Invective against long Visits. (I.i, p. 396)

Mirabell understands the gestures of the cabal but refuses to act until there is a verbal formulation of them in Lady Wishfort's invective; when Millamant confirms Lady Wishfort's invective, he leaves. The narrative of offstage action is told in gestures encircled by words: messages are contained in a description of grave faces or even further removed in a description of a description of the vapors.

In Shakespeare and others, such descriptions and the environmental scene painting are aids to the imagination. They are replacements for elaborate sets, better lighting, more verisimilar actors (real female faces, for instance). In Congreve (and Etherege), they are more ways of indicating that gesture is material for verbal manipulation. Thus, it is not redundant for Lady Wishfort to recount her gestures in her planned seduction of Sir Rowland even while she practices them and before she will actually enact them, even if it has the sense of reduplication that is part of the mechanicality of the comic:

> Shall I sit?—No I won't sit—I'll walk—aye I'll walk from the door upon his entrance; and then turn full upon him—No, that will be too sudden. I'll lie—aye, I'll lie down—I'll receive him in my little dressing Room, there's a Couch—Yes, yes, I'll give the first Impression on a Couch—I wont lie neither but loll and lean upon one Elbow; with one Foot a little dangling off, Jogging in a thoughtful way—Yes—and then as soon as he appears, start, ay, start and be surpriz'd, and rise to meet him in a pretty disorder—Yes—O, nothing is more alluring than a Levee from a Couch in some Confusion.—It shows the Foot to advantage, and furnishes with Blushes, and re-composing Airs beyond Comparison. (*WW*, IV.i, p. 445)

The foot "a little dangling off, Jogging in a thoughtful way," has humors of its own, in the gestural self-consciousness whose pathos personifies it. Lady Wishfort attributes thoughtfulness to it; we feel its poignancy. But the passage is not merely an encircling narrative, in which the various parts of her body become active characters (as do the objects of allegory, the natural forces inspired by pathetic fallacy in lyric, the biological functions in the understanding of the humors). It is marked even more by print's fine scientific distinctions in the analytical critique at the end of the passage, where Lady Wishfort distinguishes between gestures according to their effects, and where the contrast between the excitement of her erotic anticipation and her cool analysis contributes to the comic.

Lady Wishfort, in fact, has trouble keeping straight the differences between gesture and language. For her, both are acts that find an equal, if confused, place in her narration to "Sir Rowland" of Mirabell's offstage behavior:

> O Sir *Rowland*, the hours that he has dy'd away at my Feet, the Tears that he has shed, the Oaths that he has sworn, the Palpitations that he has felt, the Trances, and the Tremblings, the Ardors and the Ecstacies, the Kneelings and the Riseings, the Heart-heavings, and the hand-Gripings, the Pangs and the Pathetick Regards of his protesting Eyes! Oh no memory can Register. (IV.i, p. 458)

Mirabell's physical presence (hours), his bodily excretions (tears), his verbal acts (oaths), his descriptions of his physical responses (palpitations), his physical acts (kneelings, risings, hand-grippings), and the literary interpretation of all these (ardors and ecstasies) are an indistinguished jumble of effects. All these versions of body and gesture must be written, or inscribed, in Lady Wishfort's copious (in the rhetorical sense of "copia"), cumulative sentences. If her rhetoric reflects residual orality, it is because her description re-creates in her the violence of her physical longings at Mirabell's wooing (combining with that of her present eagerness) and threatens to overturn the language that controls and analyzes the event. She fears that the bodily effects will escape her ("no memory can Register") without an external inscription. Her language attempts to be that inscription in the hope that, through language, physical memory or the re-collection of bodies in the world will be imprinted.[51]

The external inscription is also what keeps the past alive in the theater (which is made of the present and the fleeting) through the narrative of action that takes place outside the enclosed realm of the stage—in Lady Wishfort's story about Mirabell's courtship or, for instance, in Mirabell's description of the cabal night. Such description is tied to print both in that it fights the theater's unstable temporality and in that it approximates the techniques of prose narrative. The novel, too, would learn to use much of theatrical technique, interweaving descriptions of "offstage" action increasingly over the course of the eighteenth century, with the descriptions becoming ever more complex, vivid, and entangled. (The epistolary novel offers a special case of this theatricality encircling theatricality, in its interlocking narratives of letters describing scenes describing scenes.)[52] In the novel, such a technique becomes a way of invoking the theater and increasingly a way of conjuring the presence that the printed page lacks—a presence fully achieved in the elimination of boundaries, which the *style indirect libre* of the nineteenth-century novel could bring about.[53] In the theater, such description is a novelistic gesture, one that tries to approximate the power of showing more than one scene at a time and the power of descriptive narrative, which are the prerogatives of the novel.

The late-eighteenth- and nineteenth-century closet drama carried on the marriage of theatrical and novelistic techniques in a drama that was to be read but not performed. The eighteenth-century popular stage did not learn more about this technique from the novel over the course of the century, nor did it return to the tradition of pure gesture essential to the formulaic plots on which the theater had relied for hundreds of years. Instead, it became increasingly interested in the spectacle of display, a display that integrated older forms such as pantomime in the kind of static visual presentations that had originated in the early seventeenth century with the masque. Over the course of the eighteenth century, greater efforts were put into costuming and scenery and into spectacles for which such displays were necessary.[54] In the early part of the century, Congreve was not alone in his complaints about the dominance of visual effects over the text. Steele, in the prologue to *The Funeral* (1701), wrote:

Gay Lights, and Dresses, long extended Scenes,
Daemons and Angels moving in Machines,
All that can now or please or fright the Fair
May be perform'd without a writer's Care,
And is the Skill of Carpenter, not Player.[55]

By midcentury, few of those involved in the theater were complaining any more. Garrick urged actors to wear period costumes, and playbills began to advertise as an attraction "Characters new dress'd in the Habits of the Times."[56] In the nonliterary theater, the motion and mutability of gesture were increasingly subordinated to the novelty and surprise of the image on the stage (conceived as a still frame analogous to the visual spatialism of the page), which would culminate in the nineteenth-century theatrical *tableau vivant*.[57] But Congreve was striving for a theater that had largely given gesture over to the word. The increasing pages of commentary suggested that no experience could escape linguistic formulations—however alien to language, however connected to the purely corporeal—even if the relations between the word and such experiences were unstable. In working out the way that language means and the relation of that meaning to physical form and motion, Congreve was able to formulate his attitudes toward the theatricality and the textualism of his medium. He found linguistic stability not in physical form, but in verbal difference; and he identified the silences of verbal difference and of irony with theatrical gesture, although a gesture that is, like such silences, circumscribed by the text.

CHAPTER SEVEN

Nature and Art:
The Theater, Print, and the
Solitary Mind

I warrant you, Madam; a little Art once made your
Picture like you; and now a little of the same Art, must
make you like your Picture. Your Picture must sit for
you, Madam.   —Congreve, *The Way of the World*

I know no effectual Difference between continued
Affectation and Reality.   —Congreve, *Love for Love*

𝕿he Renaissance topos of the
world as a book belonged partly to a culture that had discovered
the new possibilities of the press, but also to a world that still
believed in divine inscription, in a Nature written by God's
hand as a mysterious text to be understood by the faithful or the
graced.[1] By the late seventeenth century, however, the nature of
the book itself (and of the book of nature) had changed, through
both secularization and the abundance of print. The book was
no longer the mysterious object guarded by priests. It was no
longer an individual copy containing the precious secrets of
God and holy men who had the rare power of reading and
writing.[2] Although through much of the Renaissance, the
book's relative scarcity and association with the aristocracy had
allowed it to keep the aura of the sacred manuscript, by the late

seventeenth century it seemed less a mysterious object and more
the product of an often imperfect artifice, crafted by the hands
of workers for commercial use.[3] The many late-seventeenth-
century complaints about the hack (Jeremy's impoverished
poets, for instance) expressed the period's sense of loss, a sense
that Goethe was to express in a more precise form a century
later, when he wrote:

> Printing had been invented more than a century [before Shakespeare];
> nevertheless, a book was still regarded as something sacred, as we
> know from the bindings of the times, and hence to the noble poet it
> was a thing to love and to honor; whereas we put everything between
> covers and are hard put to it to respect either the binding or the
> contents.[4]

Congreve's 1710 edition of the *Works* may be seen as a concrete form of the same sentiment, an attempt to preserve the
sacredness of the book, making it "a thing to love and to honor"
by designing it to be a beautiful physical object. He hints at his
disappointment over the lost sacredness of the book (and perhaps, as a gentleman, over the lost upper-class connection with
the power of the sacred book) in Foible's comment as witness in
the last act of *The Way of the World*:

> *Madam Marwood* took a Book and swore us upon it: But it was
> but a Book of Verses and Poems,—So as long as it was not a
> Bible-Oath, we may break it with a safe Conscience. (V.i,
> p. 464)

Marwood has committed the sin of using a book of poems (perhaps a pornographic miscellany) in place of the Bible.[5] In that
substitution, as Foible and Mincing's retraction of their oath
suggests, ritual action surrounding a secular book is meaningless. Only the Bible keeps its aura of sacredness. If the world
and nature are a book, then they are artificial, human constructs, crafted and only to be understood through the artificial
terms of the book.

Thus, the world-as-book topos seemed, to many, debased.
The Puritans had overused the idea of biblical inscription (de-

spite their devaluation of writing and seeing, and their preference for hearing), with the result that the textuality of the
Puritan world appeared, at times, self-parody.[6] The abundance
of printed matter, furthermore, mocked the metaphor. The om-
nipresence of books made the world-as-book topos seem no
longer a suggestive analogy but a self-evident truism about the
literal physical world, and the topos began to grow more
scarce.[7] The seventeenth-century secular book was, unlike the
Renaissance Book of Nature, perceived as superimposed on the
world, no longer a part of that world, but instead a mask behind
which the world lay concealed. One could understand the nature of the human world by reading the book of the world,
which was no longer, on the whole, thought mysterious, but
could be interpreted by investigators like Hooke through careful empirical observation.[8] The abundance of printed matter at
the close of the century only emphasized the sense, already present in such emblems at Quarles's, that the world was made of
layers of concealment. The expanses of the world—geographical, intellectual, and imaginary—could be reached through
the printed world. And the more the printed word proliferated,
the more that pages seemed to be piled between readers and the
things they sought, the more readers felt they could know the
nature of things only by lifting page after page, by uncovering
the artifice of writing.[9]

   The idea of writing as art had existed as long as writing itself—for instance, in Plato's dismissive association of the two
in the *Phaedrus*. But through most of classical, medieval, and
Renaissance literature, metaphors identified writing and the
book much more strongly with the natural or divine world than
with the artificial world. In the middle of the seventeenth century, the Book of Nature metaphor began to shift. There can
no longer be one unique book, created by the master Author,
for mechanical reproduction has made the book seem inherently
an identically reproduced form. The Book has become books,
no longer the metaphor for totality, but rather the physical reminder of the artificiality of the world. In Congreve, folios and

playbooks and miscellanies abound, but they are almost never tropes for the divine world, and never for the natural.[10]

This change—from the book as metaphor for the natural to the book as manifestation of the artful—coincides with an intensified interest in one of the grand topoi of the seventeenth century: the nature and art dichotomy. The commonplace about the relation between nature and art, which was moving from orthodoxy into cliché, had been used to describe every manifestation of the divinely and the humanly created world, every wrinkle of human character, every aspect of learning, literacy, and the book.[11] Montaigne hopes that his readers will see him in his "natural" state without "artifice."[12] Jonson claims that, although Shakespeare's "matter, Nature be, / His Art doth give the fashion."[13] For Cowley, the muse rides a chariot with "the *Postillion Nature*" and "the *Coachman Art*."[14] Just as one could understand books by reading them, and the natural and divine worlds by reading them, one could understand the true nature of the human and social world by reading the text of art that concealed it. Nature and art were each presented in both positive and negative terms throughout the century. Art is good in that human effort can supply it and it endures. Throughout the century, the adage reminded readers: *ars longa, vita brevis*. Art is also bad in that it represents disguise, deceit, concealment, as opposed to the naked truth, *nuda veritas*. Nature is good in that it is generative, undisguised, has none of the "adulteries of art." It is bad in that it represents the chaotic, the savage, the insane. In *MacFlecknoe* (1684), Dryden suggests the good versions of both when he has Flecknoe ask, "What share have we in Nature or in Art?" thus dismissing him from serious poetic concern.[15]

Similarly, for Congreve, neither art (be it the calking on Lady Wishfort's face in *The Way of the World* or the perfectly turned verse) nor nature had either absolutely positive or absolutely negative connotations. Congreve knows that to prefer art, to fight the natural with it, is to choose to cover the excrescences of the body and mind, to dress them appropriately. At the same

time, other forms of artifice, the clothing of the natural nakedness of the human soul, can be disturbing or even dangerous.
Like most of his contemporaries, Congreve often finds disguise
and dissimulation troubling, either because they interfere with
nature (which must be left to destroy beauty undisturbed) or
because they deceive. *The Double-Dealer* is largely about the horrors of Maskwell's artifices, about the ways in which his mask
obscures his face. In *The Way of the World*, Mirabell's conditions
are largely attempts to prevent Millamant from exercising the
many available artifices of femininity, despite the fact that he is
an artist himself.

Sometimes even similar forms of art are both positive and
negative. For both women and men, heroes and heroines, art is
a form of power, sometimes positive, sometimes negative. In
The Old Batchelour, Bellmour's "counterfeit" of Mr. Spintext, in
which he disguises himself as a text and goes with a disguised
text in his hand (Scarron's *Innocent Adultery* counterfeiting a
prayer book), is portrayed as admirable bravado. Bellmour's
power comes from his disguise, just as the book's power comes
from the way it controls nature by disguising it. On the other
hand, Heartwell's attempt to conceal his true feelings for Silvia
shows his vulnerability. Maskwell's disguises are dangerous,
whereas Valentine's disguise of madness in *Love for Love* is com-
pelling. Mirabell's artifices, in his attempt to gain control over
Lady Wishfort, are meant to be viewed with sympathetic eyes.
Fainall's feignings are vicious. Nature and art are often shown
to be allies, which together indicate the span of the universe or
the full reaches of artistic imitation: "Nature and Art, in thee,
alike contend, / Not to oppose each other, but befriend," writes
Congreve to Kneller (S: p. 146). The figurative book of the Renaissance was the "Book of Nature," "Nature" was used to describe complex functions in the universe, and the poet imitated
"Nature."

All these forms were carried into the late seventeenth century,
where interest in orality and awareness of print focused even
more attention on nature and art. Print seemed to make learn-

ing an artificial process, and an attentiveness to the natural was needed to rebalance this state.[16] This attentiveness to the natural accompanied claims for orality, which was often identified with the nature side of the dichotomy during the period, whether in the pastoral celebration of the "untutored tongue" or in exclamations against insanity, ignorance, or mental deficiency ("natural" meaning congenital idiot).[17] In Congreve's "Mourning Muse of Alexis," Alexis wishes to sing of his grief, free from the tame and mechanized world of writing:

> *Alex.* Wild be my Thoughts, *Menalcas*, wild my Words,
> Artless as Nature's Notes, in untaught Birds;
> Boundless my Verse, and roving be my Strains,
> Various as Flow'rs on unfrequented Plains. (S: p. 40)

The birds whose oral song he wishes to imitate are artless and natural in that they are untaught. By imitating them, his words can be "boundless," free from the constraints of writing, free to move in "unfrequented" places where no formal limitations or models precede him.

Such praise found a place throughout the Renaissance and seventeenth century in pastoral. By the late seventeenth century, it also expressed itself in such noble-savage myths as Behn's *Oroonoko* (1688); and it would find its culmination in late-eighteenth-century primitivism. But the praise of illiteracy also had more urbane forms. When Fainall suggests that one of Petulant's possible failings is his illiteracy, Petulant becomes, through Witwoud's less pastoral version of praise for the natural voice, the ironic exemplar of the virtues of natural knowledge as contrasted with artful literacy. Petulant is illiterate in at least two ways: quite literally, he probably cannot read or write more than to sign his name, as we discover when Witwoud unfairly accuses him of signing with an X and when he himself says, "I read nothing" (V.i, pp. 476–77); and he is "unlettered," not scholarly. His illiteracy is, according to Witwoud, "his Happiness—His want of Learning, gives him the more opportunities to shew his *natural* Parts" (*WW*, I.i, p. 404, emphasis added). Petulant himself suggests later that his illiteracy not only permits him the freedom of natural conversation free from the book:

MILLAMANT   Ah! to marry an Ignorant! that can hardly Read or Write.

PETULANT   Why shou'd a Man be ever the further from being married tho' he can't Read, any more than he is from being Hang'd. The Ordinary's paid for setting the *Psalm*, and the Parish-Priest for reading the Ceremony. And for the rest which is to follow in both Cases, a Man may do it without Book—So all's one for that. (III.i, p. 436)

Here, other kinds of "natural Parts" provide him with all the tools necessary for the natural functions for which books are superfluous: sex and death. Education, or the attainment of the wisdom of books, is a form of clothing, and Petulant's illiteracy is a form of vulgar nakedness that, as he rightly observes, would hardly interfere with the natural act he intends to perform with Millamant.

If nature was associated with illiteracy, print made people more conscious of both nature and art. Just as nature was tied to illiteracy, "art"—which indicated a wide range of things, from the production of visual artifacts to behavioral modes— was often tied during the period to verbal artifice and thus, by analogy, to literacy or hyperliteracy. Despite their emphasis on hearing over seeing, for Milton in *Paradise Lost* and Cowley in "The Tree of Knowledge," the loss of the absolute natural and the discovery of "art" are intrinsically bound up with the discovery of books and learning. For Locke, the "learned Disputants, these all-knowing doctors" of the schools have an "*artificial* Ignorance" that prevails by the "*Artifice* of those" who amused the "Ignorant, with hard Words" (emphasis added).[18] For Congreve's Heartwell, "Lying . . . is indeed the Art of Love" (*OB*, III.ii, p. 72). Congreve argues for the introduction of true Pindaric form in the English ode on the grounds that "there is certainly a Pleasure in beholding any Thing that has

Art and Difficulty in the Contrivance."[19] (Here, "Art" is identified with intricate literary form and with "Difficulty," a stronger value in postprint culture, in which clarity is no longer an essential need.) Brisk similarly identifies art with the ornate poetic productions of Lady Froth, who has "the Art of Surprizing the most Naturally" (*DD*, II.i, p. 142), although Congreve wants us to recognize that Brisk is confused about the nature of Nature.

Congreve argues that the focus of his satire is words, rather than manners, physical appearance, or deformity of body: his characters are "ridiculous not so much thro' a natural Folly (which is incorrigible, and therefore not proper for the Stage) as thro' an affected Wit; a Wit, which at the same time that it is affected, is also false."[20] Self-conscious about the dangers of his own scholarship ("I hope I may be excus'd the Pedantry of a Quotation, when it is so justly apply'd"), Congreve was most interested in pedantry and artificial wit, particularly in the later plays.[21] For Congreve, literary artifice and pedantry are the central forms of the negative version of "art," the kind of art that eradicates (rather than imitates) nature. For him, these forms are almost always tied directly to the accumulation of books, whether Lady Froth's fashionable French critics, Valentine's dusty philosophic tomes, or Millamant's amorous miscellanies. Literary artifice has come to dominate the drama's notion of disguise, which, although always inherent in the very definition of theater, traditionally had less singular, more multiple ways of expressing itself.

It is needless here to stress the extent to which disguise is constitutive of the very idea of theater.[22] Disguise shows theater's resistance to its own physically identical imitations and to its dangerous proximity to its audience, for it offers protection. Like disguise, the mask, in both its material and its metaphorical forms, allows the theater distance from that enslaving physical identity.[23] Both the mask and disguise become analogous to the abstract representation of material, which the theater favors. The mask calls attention to the way in which art masks experience, the way in which life itself is a series of disguises. The mask's effects of physical concealment and distortion free the theater from excessive enslavement to the physical body.

The late seventeenth century had a sense of its identity as a theatrical construct and a construct of human texts, as a literate (as opposed to primitive) age. The period's sense of itself as an artful (as opposed to a natural) age (as a "dissembling" and "flattering" age), expresses itself in the vocabulary of the period: late-seventeenth-century works are replete with such words as *art, artifice, artful, design, plot, dissimulation, disguise,* and *contrivance.*[24] The lively discussion of verisimilitude and historical truth does not alter the fact that the plotted constructions of the drama and the highly self-conscious ordering principles of the book are both emphasized by the period's literary criticism. Such emphasis points out that literature is art that is different from nature, no matter how much critical attention the importance of proximity to nature received throughout the Renaissance and seventeenth century. If literature meant imitating poetic forms such as the true Pindaric ode or the rules of the stage, then it meant imitating nature through art.[25]

In an artificial age—in which life is theatrical and the book-bound world has begun to circumscribe the theatrical, in which the artificiality of the book dominates both the artificial and the natural worlds—not only does the book imitate life, but life too imitates the book. The period was fascinated by the workings of mimesis, the ways in which theatrical and literary imitations of the world could take place. It was similarly fascinated and disturbed by the inverse, the ways in which the world had begun to imitate the book. Don Quixote had set the pattern at the very beginning of the seventeenth century for the late-seventeenth- and eighteenth-century vogue for quixotic apparitions, which reflected the interest in the way humans imitate books.[26]

Congreve's quixotic figures call attention to his discomfort with the impact of the book on imitative human behavior. If Belinda in *The Old Batchelour* is an "affected Lady" (according

to the dramatis personae), a type of the "Platonick Lady" celebrated by the *précieuses*, she is courted by an equally book-formed
man. Bellmour is not only marked by the passionate speeches
of romance (which Belinda mocks), but instructed by the forms
of the salacious, and he uses Scarron's *The Hypocrites* and *The
Innocent Adultery* as guides in his intrigue with Laetitia. If Lady
Froth is constructed of the slippages of critical jargon, Lady
Plyant is a diluted form of the female Quixote, convinced by
her experience of the romance and the novel that all men desire
her.[27] Jeremy's wit was created by Cambridge lampoons. Foresight's certainties have been formed by the astrological almanac.
Lady Wishfort and Mrs. Marwood plan retirement according
to pastoral. Mirabell and Millamant understand each other
through the amorous wit of the seventeenth-century lyric. The
relationship between books and nature here is reciprocal, or,
more accurately, influence has become indeterminable.

The relationship between more general ideas of art and nature
functions in the same terms. Nature offers models for art. Art
regulates and reformulates nature. If the countryside serves as
a model for landscape, or if human speech serves as a model for
the language of tragedy, the imposition of aesthetics on the
landscape could invent *la belle nature*, or the imposition of stylistics on verse could create (through education) more perfect
patterns of everyday speech. The consciousness of the impact of
art on nature was certainly not new in the last years of the seventeenth century. The Renaissance artist had a distinct notion
of what it meant to be "self-fashioned." But the late seventeenth
century had to deal with the problem of the impact of art on
nature, an eternal human concern, in the context of particular
cultural conditions that had been slowly shifting since the Renaissance. The artificial forms that surrounded culture, and the
pedantry arising from a culture of machine-made pages, called
attention to the power of art over nature and over humans. They
called attention to the helplessness of human life in the face of
its own creations. For imitative artists came to recognize that
they did not wholly control art in the service of nature. It was

felt that art itself and the psychological institutions that were teaching the eye to see or the mind to understand were beginning to control the perceiver in their own service.

Addison would articulate this most clearly in his essays on "The Pleasures of the Imagination," when he described the way in which nature is transformed by the art of the mind.[28] But many had come to understand nature's imitation of art long before. Congreve repeatedly experiments with inversions of the traditional idea that art imitates nature. He exploits such inversions partly, of course, for their comic effects, but partly because they suggest so powerfully the ways in which the art of the book, in its complex reduplications, has confused the simple duality of nature and art. Foible expresses the problem most clearly in her reassurances to Lady Wishfort that the natural face can, in fact, imitate art:

LADY WISHFORT   Thou must repair me *Foible*, before Sir *Rowland* comes; or I shall never keep up to my Picture.

FOIBLE   I warrant you, Madam; a little Art once made your Picture like you; and now a little of the same Art, must make you like your Picture. Your Picture must sit for you, Madam. (*WW*, III.i, p. 429)

Foible captures here the sorrow implicit in the idealization of which art is capable. Art can always offer a more perfect, more enduring embodiment of that which nature attempts, and thus nature, in all its fragility, must learn to imitate art.

The traditional Renaissance and seventeenth-century coquette dissembles indifference and naturalness, "Affecting to seem unaffected,"[29] even when all know that lack of affectation is affected. Bellinda and Lady Brute, in Vanbrugh's *The Provoked Wife*, are obliged to affect a natural innocence during the smutty jokes at the theater because "if we quit our modesty [men] say we lose our charms, and yet they know that very modesty is affection."[30] Congreve offers many such coquettes, for instance, Silvia in *The Old Batchelour*, Lady Wishfort herself, or Amoret in "A Hue and Cry after Fair Amoret" (1704). The more sophisticated artist of disguise, more artful than the traditional coquette, dissembles at dissembling.[31] Maskwell's dangerous version of dissembled dissembling is simply to tell the "truth":[32]

> Now will I, in my old way, discover the whole and real truth of the matter to him, that he may not suspect one word on't.

> No Mask like open Truth to cover Lies,
>   As to go naked is the best disguise. (*DD*, V.i, p. 190)

When nakedness becomes the best disguise, convolutions of the topos of art and nature make it impossible to determine any original and genuine foundation from which art springs. In fact, Congreve suggests repeatedly that artifice is so multilayered that nature and art are indistinguishable in the end. According to Mirabell, Millamant's follies are "so natural, or so artful, that they become her" (*WW*, I.i, p. 399). According to Fainall, if Mrs. Marwood had "dissembl'd better, Things might have continu'd in the state of Nature" (*WW*, I.i, p. 397). Art both leads to a natural condition and is natural in itself. When Silvia complains that she fears she has no art with which to counterfeit love, Lucy wisely responds, "Hang Art, Madam, and trust to Nature for Dissembling" (*OB*, III.i, p. 62). Nature, or at least female nature (here), in itself dissembles. If art is artful, nature is even more so. Setter articulates the artificiality of the natural, the impossibility of distinguishing between the mask and the face, more concisely than any other character when he confronts Lucy by demanding that she "Lay by that Worldly Face and produce your natural Vizor" (*OB*, III.i, p. 65).

Mellefont offers a closer reading of Setter's expression, in answer to Careless's claim that "a Vizor disguises" the inclinations of women "as much as their Faces" do:

> 'Tis a mistake, for women may most properly be said to be unmask'd when they wear Vizors; for that secures them from blushing, and being out of Countenance, and next to being in the dark, or alone, they are most truly themselves in a Vizor Mask. (*DD*, III.i, p. 158)

When skin is most naked it is most disguised, just like Maskwell's words. A woman is more natural masked because her true mind shows through disguise. Not only is art, or the mask, the most natural state. Psychological nature, or the true mind of a woman (in particular), will inevitably dominate the physical mask. The mask allows sufficient distance for truth to emerge and at the same time offers women the sense that they have sanctity from the assault of physical incarnation, which allows them to be "truly themselves."

The mask offers the wearer a kind of sanctity that is equivalent to the insularity of solitude (a solitude that must be earned in the theater, but that is a necessary given in reading). Throughout *The Way of the World*, Millamant seeks her own forms of solitude in order to preserve her self from the ways of the world (although she uses them). She clings to her closet, reading, through much of the play. She longs to keep "My dear Liberty . . . My faithful Solitude," to "have my Closet Inviolate; to be sole Empress of my Tea-table." She is coyly horrified at the thought of "Breeding" ("Name it not") and its accompanying "endeavours" (IV.i, pp. 449–51), both the most social of actions. (An "other" is necessary to the latter, and the other produces another other.) She fights the way that Mirabell's words reinvent her in the contract scene.

Through Millamant, Congreve tries to understand exactly the nature of the self that is left when one is sequestered in the solitary closet, the nature of the sense of personal identity that the late seventeenth century had inherited from, among others, Montaigne and Descartes, and that continued to be transformed by solitary reading. The period's concern for personal identity was connected to the interest in nature, through the urgency to identify the sincere self, beneath the arts of dissimulation and learning.[33] Congreve makes the usual identification of sincerity with nature when he writes to Sir Richard Temple that Temple is perfect in "the Pleasing Art,"

> If Art it may be call'd in you, who seem,
> By Nature, form'd for Love, and for Esteem.
> Affecting none, all Virtues you possess,
> And really are what others but profess. (S: pp. 149–50)

The concern for personal identity is reflected not only in Locke's explorations of the self as a series of continuous remembered moments, but also in such forms as Puritan autobiography.[34] Dryden seems to touch on a more philosophical version of this concern in *Amphitryon*, when he stresses Sosia's confusion about whether he is different from the other (identical) Sosia: "What am I then? for my Mind gives me, I am some body still, if I knew but who I were."[35] Congreve, too, suggests a philosophical exploration of personal identity in Witwoud's description of Petulant's activities:

> Why he wou'd slip you out of this Chocolate-house, just when your Back was turn'd—Whip he was gone;—Then trip to his Lodging, clap on a Hood and Scarf, and Mask, slap into a Hackney-Coach, and drive hither to the Door again in a trice; where he wou'd send in for himself, that I mean, call for himself, wait for himself, nay and what's more, not finding himself, sometimes leave a Letter for himself. (*WW*, I.i, p. 405)

Petulant's hood, scarf, and mask, his theatrical protection from the banality of his naked identity, allow him the privacy to retreat into a world, like Sosia's, of reduplicating selves. The other is unnecessary here, for Petulant (like Bottom) can play all the roles himself. After he has tried different ways of defining himself through voice and presence (calling and waiting for himself), Petulant leaves a letter for himself, the final retreat into a self defined by its isolation. (Sir Wilfull Witwoud's odd syntactical construction, in which he "writes himself," similarly suggests the interest in the creation and identification of the self.)

The period's discomfort with the prioritizing of the self, particularly noticeable in the writer's obsessive insistence that "I hope I will not be accused of vanity," shows not only in Petulant's bizarre descent into a self-contained world, but also in Congreve's treatment of Millamant.[36] One of the developments of *The Way of the World* is Millamant's education in community, her education in the other. By the end of the contract scene, she has come to the brink of affirming a community with Mirabell: "Well, you ridiculous thing you, I'll have you" (IV.i, p. 452). If the solipsism of the desire to define and preserve the self is increasingly insistent, that solipsism must be coaxed into the public, into the theatrical mode of shared experience.[37] That public mode, however, remains in many ways a solitary one for Congreve. For public experience is, for him, merely a set of norms (like language), on which the social animal has chosen to agree. Those norms are formed not by the external world, but by the mind, which uses its artistry to create nature. Mirabell tells Millamant:

> You are no longer handsome when you've lost your Lover; your Beauty dies upon the Instant: For Beauty is the Lover's Gift; 'tis he bestows your Charms—Your Glass is all a Cheat. The Ugly and the Old, whom the Looking-glass mortifies, yet after Commendation can be flatter'd by it, and discover Beauties in it: For that reflects our Praises, rather than your Face. (*WW*, II.i, p. 420)

Mirabell connects this subjective and psychological determination of nature to the verbal determination of the world, which modifies it by offering public verification of subjective "truth," thus socializing it. For him, the subjective reality of others (Millamant, in this case) can be determined by his language ("Praises"), produced out of his own subjective knowledge, but forming the objective state of beauty or ugliness. This is another version of Bellmour's ironic claim that

> No Husband, by his Wife, can be deceiv'd:
> She still is Vertuous, if she's so believ'd. (*OB*, V.i, p. 96)

The claim grows less ironic with each play. For Cynthia, the verbal identification that the outside world has given to what she perceives as foolishness almost convinces her that such foolishness is wisdom:

> Why should I call 'em Fools? The World thinks better of 'em; for these have Quality and Education, Wit and fine Conversa-

tion are receiv'd and admir'd by the World—If not, they like and admire themselves—And why is not that true Wisdom, for 'tis Happiness: And for ought I know, we have misapply'd the Name all this while, and mistaken the thing. (*DD*, IV.i, p. 167)

Cynthia knows that the misapplication of a name can cause one to "mistake" the thing and, further, that the quality of the thing can be altered by the word one uses to identify it. She might have added that the other associations of the name, socially determined, are what help alter the thing. She identifies this verbal and psychological subjectivism with the admiration of the self, although her failure to feel a community with the social group doing the naming leaves her doubts. Osmyn, in his recognition that he can know nothing about emotions without identifying them with names, is more willing to accept Zara's verbal identifications:

ZARA   O, give that Madness yet a milder Name,
         And call it Passion; then, be still more kind,
         And call that Passion Love.

OSMYN   Give it a Name,
         Or Being as you please, such I will think it. (*MB*, III.i, p. 354)

Congreve's invocation of the name as a psychologically determining mask and of psychological resolutions of the dichotomy between art and nature is a way of charting what seemed to the period to be new territory: the territory of the mind. Explorations of the nature of language as an epistemological function, explorations of the individual and of empiricism, had turned inward by the 1690's (although the interest in the external linguistic, social, and natural worlds had not disappeared). Locke, like Hobbes, is interested in words as signs that serve human communication and in distinctions between wit and judgment. But he is equally interested in (and wary of) language as the secondary structure (after perceptions) around which we build ideas.[38] Locke, like Hobbes, is interested in the relation of the individual to the power structure. But he is equally interested in the construction of the interior spaces of the mind. He is interested in the way in which bodies exist both in the world and in the mind. He is interested in investigating the constitution of the individual and of personal identity and in the things this constitution says about the individual's rights in such a structure.[39] Locke, like the empiricist scientists, may believe that all knowledge comes from sensory perception and may be interested in the external world that the senses reveal. But his epistemology equally concerns itself with the operations the mind plays on the simple ideas of the senses (comparing, compounding, naming, and abstracting, for instance), and how these operations create the world as we know it (through perception and understanding).[40]

Mirabell demonstrates a miniature and conscious version of Locke's more passive epistemology when he catalogs Millamant's failings in order to learn to hate her:

> I took her to pieces; sifted her and separated her Failings; I study'd 'em, and got 'em by rote. The Catalogue was so large, that I was not without hopes, one Day or other to hate her heartily: To which end I so us'd my self to think of 'em, that at length, contrary to my Design and Expectation, they gave me every Hour less and less disturbance; 'till in a few Days it became habitual to me, to remember 'em without being displeas'd. They are now grown as familiar to me as my own Frailties; and in all probability in a little time longer, I shall like 'em as well. (I.i, p. 399)

As in Locke's epistemology, Mirabell's knowledge comes first from empirical observations, which he must separate in order to identify them as discrete entities and to understand them. Then knowledge comes from the operations performed on those discrete entities. They are separated, studied, and cataloged (the operations follow not only those of the mind, but also those of philosophical and scientific investigation), and finally they are memorized. For Locke, memory is essential in at least two ways: it allows us to preserve the simple ideas in order to build complex ideas, and to preserve those complex ideas in order to build more complex ideas; and it is the foundation of personal identity, for personal identity consists in consciousness, "And as far as this consciousness can be extended backwards to any past Action or Thought, so far reaches the Identity of that *Person*."[41] The self consists in the idea of the continuity of moments in a single body, and only memory allows us that idea of continuity. Self is the capacity, through memory, for the identification of one idea of consciousness with a past idea of consciousness, and the combination of different ideas of consciousness in a single body. Thus, Mirabell builds the foundations of his knowledge on an increasingly large store of perceptions, which he saves through memory and retrieves for use through habit, and with which he grows increasingly comfortable; but he also constitutes his "self" through the memories of his sensations (of Millamant's failings) and in fact begins to identify himself with those perceptions, which are as familiar to him as his own frailties (his other memories of his self). He has created his world and himself through perception, consciousness, and the association of ideas.

There is, of course, much more going on here than a Lockean association of ideas of consciousness, for the passage shows one of the intersections among Lockean psychology, the old topos of art as nature, and the problem of orality and literacy. Like Millamant in her poetic recitations, Mirabell combines the artful forms of literacy (or the formal structures of print) with some of the effects of orality. He is full of the sententious phrases and grammatically completed sentences of print, which are overlaid with the aural grace valued by oral culture. Here the initial impulse is to control by the oral methods of artful literacy akin to the learning of Latin in school: he sifts, separates, studies, and memorizes in order to be able to recite by rote. This is orality turned backwards on literacy. As in orality, the repetition becomes habit, and familiarity increases the pleasant effects rather than decreases them. The artificial catalog, sifted and sorted, is naturalized in the mind and made into the oral formula of repetition.

And yet there is a self-consciousness about oral functions that suggests a backwards glance toward the declining oral. Mirabell's use of rhetorical habits akin to the oral formula remains private and uses material on which literacy has left its mark. Millamant's failings consist in her affectations, her art of formulating her self. As much as the literary artifices of Waller or Suckling (or Congreve, for that matter) imitate the world, Millamant imitates the books she has read and the heroines she has discovered, the coy Daphne, for instance. Mirabell has tried to impose orality on a literate universe as a way of controlling, by art, the artificial. But the list itself begins to control him, comes to be familiar to him, part of the structure of his mode of perceiving. Mirabell's sifting and sorting has had its effects on his mind. Millamant's literate and artful self has imprinted itself on his consciousness, a consciousness that through its solitude defines the nature of the world for Mirabell.

Locke's epistemology indirectly suggested to many a world constructed on the association of ideas, on private consciousness itself. Although he insisted repeatedly on the reality of the material world and its connection to perception, he found it hard to reconcile this notion with his strictly empirical methodology (which could offer no proof of such material reality). Empiricism's elimination of innate (natural) ideas would lead through Locke, in the century to come, to a notion of the mind (formed by habit, culture, art) as the container and shaper of sensory (natural) data. When some—who, like Locke, had sought an unadulterated empiricism—began to find it difficult to uphold proof of the material world with purely empirical evidence, there seemed to be no choice but the renunciation of any certainty of material existence and the embrace of an idealist model. This rejection of the material (and thus of a traditional notion of nature) suggested a location of nature in consciousness alone. In fact, it had been the playful manipulation and inversion of the idea of mimesis during the seventeenth century (Congreve's, for instance) that had encouraged the coherent formulation of these central challenges to conventional epistemology and metaphysics in the eighteenth century. These philosophical inquiries had quietly interiorized the literary modification of the topos of art and nature (which the multiplication of artificial ways of learning—of books—had put under pressure): not only does art imitate nature, not only does nature imitate art, not only are nature and art indistinguishable, but the arts of psychological perception determine all nature.

Millamant's objection to Mirabell's claim that "Beauty is the Lover's Gift" underlines their fundamental accord, their mutual belief in a psychological subjectivism (which contains echoes of Cynthia's "If not, they like and admire themselves"). It is not his subjectivism to which Millamant objects, nor is it simply a case of two subjectivities at war (although it is also that). Rather, she suggests that his psychological understanding of reality is too shallow:

> Beauty the Lover's Gift—Lord, what is a Lover, that it can give? Why one makes Lovers as fast as one pleases, and they live as long as one pleases, and they die as soon as one pleases: And then if one pleases, one makes more. (*WW*, II.i, p. 420)

In Millamant's view, Mirabell's notion of "Praises" as determining, his understanding of the "social construction of reality" (to borrow a phrase), is inadequate to describe the actual nature of the solitary psychological structuring of the world.[42] The world is not defined only by social and verbal agreement on psychological perception, but by the self, a self isolated from others. She continues:

> One no more owes one's Beauty to a Lover, than one's Wit to an Eccho: They can but reflect what we look and say; vain empty Things if we are silent or unseen, and want a being. (II.i, pp. 420–21)

Nothing, in fact, happens in the physical world if the agent of perception, the self, "wants a being." The echo, the other in the external world, neither defines the world nor acts on the self. The self alone, and the worlds of the self, define all.

The notion of a psychologically constructed world, a world

in which the individual is essentially solitary in the private and silent space of the mind, is encouraged only by the book. The book is read in solitude, silently (increasingly) in the space of an isolated room far from the models the words are meant to represent.[43] In *Incognita*, Congreve attempted to overcome the solitude of novelistic reading by giving the novel a theatrical form. It would hardly be necessary to point out the wealth of theatrical detail in the novel, not only in the mistaken identity plot but also in the dialogues and description of physical motion that emerges from the containment of the stage. The very title of the novel suggests its connection to the theatrical world of the mask. This desire to experiment with the theatrical in novelistic form is further emphasized by the narrator's attempts to invoke the physical presence that the theater comes by naturally. Congreve's repeated apostrophes to the reader in the novel, for instance, can be understood as attempts to invoke through novelistic means the theater's intimacy between author and audience. This intimacy, however, was beginning to disintegrate with the rise of increasingly large theaters in the eighteenth century and with the increasing relegation of the audience to darkness on the other side of the proscenium arch.[44] Apostrophes to the reader would grow more insistent in eighteenth-century novelists like Fielding and Sterne, in an attempt to personalize the increasingly large reading public.[45] (When nineteenth-century writers ceased to remember what it meant to have an intimate reading public, such apostrophes began to fade.) Many of Congreve's narratorial interventions also serve to invoke immediacy, mingling other forms of presence with authorial/audience presence. For instance, the unseen author's desire for intimacy with an audience combines with the historian's claims for authority through a firsthand encounter with the subjects of inquiry: "But scarce had [Aurelian] acquitted himself of a preliminary bow (and which, I have heard him say, was the lowest that ever he made)" (*I*: p. 15). Such a struggle for presence is a struggle for nature, the naturalness of the live voice, "beyond the reach of art," beyond the art of the novelistic page.

But the title of Congreve's novel also suggests the insufficiency of the theatrical to novelistic form. Incognita is the heroine whose *cognition* of her identity is far more important than
her final unveiling at the end.[46] Despite the novel's attachment
to the theater and to the burlesque romance, it provides a narrator full of insights into the minds of the characters and interpretations of psychological function.[47] Leonora reads Hippolito's letter and then wanders in a dizzy "maze of Thought" to
which the reader is privy in all its details: "This thought was
parent to another of the same kind, till a long Chain successively
had Birth . . . when she started to find her self so lost to her
Reason" (*I*: p. 38). The "Difficulties which [Hippolito] saw in
his Friend's Circumstances, put him upon finding out a great
many more in his own, than really there were" (*I*: p. 35). Leonora "knew it was in vain to deny a Passion, which [Hippolito]
had heard her so frankly own; (and no doubt was very glad it
was past and done;) besides . . . having some little Jealousies
and Fears of what Effect might be produced between the Com-
mands of his Father and the Beauties of *Juliana*" (*I*: p. 64).
When Aurelian is roused from his thought by "a profound Silence," the narrator explains the perplexing fact that "Silence
should make a Man start," with the analogy of light: "Which
though it does chiefly entertain the Eyes, and is indeed the
prime Object of the Sight, yet should it immediately cease, to
have a Man left in the Dark by a suddain deficiency of it, would
make him stare with his Eyes, and though he could not see,
endeavour to look about him" (*I*: p. 51).

Such psychological meanderings and analysis, even when
parody, crucially differentiate the novel from the purely theatrical mode it claims. Like the heroine to whom the title is devoted, the author of the novel is incognito (unseen by his readers). He does not have the live presence that is the prerogative
of playwrights, who see their audiences. Instead, he is "Cleophil" (Cliophil), a lover of history, a lover of truth, one who
observes and records (far from an audience) in order to make
truth more transparent, in order to render it more naturally. He

is one who tries to overcome the mask of time and of the page in order to give the "bare facts," in order to lift the mask of art to reveal true nature. Congreve playfully contrasts poetic diction with the diction of "*natural* history" as a way of emphasizing this claim to natural truth: "Madam Night was no more to be seen . . . and the chymists were of opinion, That her fuliginous damps rarefy'd by the abundance of flame, were evaporated" (*I*: p. 16). The natural can be redeemed through the art of scientific investigation or historical scholarship (albeit ironic historical scholarship), a scholarship that, by its function, shows the limits of the theatrical.

These limits are further emphasized by the meanderings of the narratorial voice, meanderings that suggest a desire to break from the constraints of theatrical plot:

Now the reader I suppose to be upon thorns at this and the like impertinent digressions, but let him alone and he'll come to himself; at which time I think fit to acquaint him, that when I digress, I am at that time writing to please my self; when I continue the thread of the story, I write to please him; supposing him a reasonable man, I conclude him satisfied to allow me in this liberty, and so I proceed. (*I*: p. 16)

It is interesting to note that Congreve's "reader" is most emphatically male, and thus the relation between narrator and reader retains some of the elements of male combative disputation (elements on which the theater's wit wars are founded). The "thread of the story" is here the result of the public (theatrical) contract with the reader. Digression is the private activity in which the narrator engages to please his impertinent "self." It is the self-serving and solitary activity of the closet, the novelistic activity itself, that is identified with "liberty" from the constraint of the public. (Fielding and Sterne would revel in the privilege of digression that solitary writing permits, and in Sterne it would be even more fully linked with contemporary notions of freedom and personal rights.) This liberty is not only the liberty to write as one pleases. It is also the liberty to imagine the ideal reader (the "reasonable man," for Congreve) and to invoke an idealized form of theatrical presence of which the theater is incapable.

Incognita may seem artful, with all its scholarly devices. It may seem to be invoking an artful narratorial voice in gentle mockery of historical pedantry. But such an invocation is actually a naturalistic technique in two seemingly contradictory (but related) senses: it promotes the novel's "historical" pretense, thus validating its claim to represent true nature; it promotes a notion of writing as a natural activity itself, in which the writer is at liberty to digress, in the same way that the solitary stroller is at liberty to meander as fancy dictates through the "natural" garden of the period.[48] The novel provides a space in which the arts of literacy, even of pedantry, can be used naturally (with the liberty of digression from form) to reach nature by validating claims to truth.

Congreve's attempt to write a theatrical novel by using the arts of literacy to invoke presence and nature is a gesture analogous to the book's attempt, as a manifest form of art, to overcome its artfulness in order to reach nature. The book, like the reader who is masked by the enclosure of the closet, is already inherently masked. The page itself, and the words on the page (words that, the era had come to recognize, only hide the nature of things), serve as concealment. The novel itself replaces the mask represented in the theater, acting as the protector and the shield of solitude that allows the "self" to emerge fearlessly.[49] The way that nature forces itself to view by breaking the bounds of art is a model for the theater's traditional mode of presentation, which conceals its own nature with abstraction in order to reveal its own nature. The theater assumes the mask because the ruptures in the mask are the only means of showing nature.[50] It assumes the mask because there is either too much inherent violence or too much absurd fleshiness in the naked physical incarnations of a stage of maskless presence, a stage that steps over its threshold (the threshold being a form of the mask). A stage that self-consciously uses the mask recognizes

the violence of the physical and knows that such physical incarnations must be controlled through the mask if they are not
to become either cataclysmic or ridiculous.[51] The stage needs
masks in order not to be naked. Print is art in that it is distant
from nature. Theater needs art in that it is too natural. Similarly, if paradoxically, print needs naturalism in that it is too
artful. The paradox of abstracted theater is that it tries to overcome the inherently naturalistic quality of the stage. The paradox of literary naturalism is that it tries to overcome the inherently artificial quality of the printed word.

Congreve found that theatrical techniques are not altogether
sufficient or appropriate to the novelistic form, for the masks
and disguises of theater are appropriate to a form that must protect itself from too much naturalism. Like *Incognita*, fiction during the eighteenth century would struggle to find an approach
to nature (whether through truth claims, assumption of historicist technique, or various other attempts at naturalism) that
could overcome the artifice of the book. The forms of the novel,
in particular, increasingly came to suggest that the printed text
did not need the explicit evocations of disguise on which the
theater had always depended, although it may refer to them as
subject matter. Many novels, like *Incognita*, invoke theatrical
technique, but many, also like *Incognita*, strive to find forms of
naturalism that will overcome the mask of art that is the book.
Swift and Pope, in their use of print as a way of struggling
against Grub Street's impositions, deliberately use antinatu-
ralistic techniques to counter what they see as the plodding naturalism and "dullness" of much prose narrative or the sentimental drama's psychological naturalism, which was not copied
from Homer and thus not copied from nature.[52] (The change
from Theobald to Cibber in *The Dunciad* is a telling one, suggesting that rejection of print had moved from satire of scholarship to satire of theatrical psychological naturalism.)

But a great part of Swift and Pope's formal experimentation,
particularly in prose, is a way of attempting to achieve a more
naked voice. Pope's "easy style" in such poems as the "Epistle

to Arbuthnot" may be far closer to "the real language of men" (if there is, in fact, such a thing) than Wordsworth's voice in the lyrical ballads, for instance.[53] Not only Swift's dressing-room poems, not only the poems of urban enumeration, but also the truth claims of even such fantasies as *Gulliver's Travels* can be seen as attempts to lift the page and lay bare things as they are. If such novelists as Defoe, who can be seen as exemplary here, employ versions of the mask—for instance, through narrative irony—Defoe's descriptive intimacy with the things and thoughts of his characters shows more strongly a desire to remove the veil of the page, to overcome the distance between referents and the unseen reader, to offer the plenitude of the world without the air of external narratorial intervention. Similarly, the desire for psychological naturalism was the logical extension of the lifting of the mask (beneath the mask is the face, and beneath the face is the mind). In Defoe and Richardson, the interloping narrator is absorbed into the prolific heros or heroines themselves in a gesture that reclaims the immediacy of the theater, but in which that immediacy presents itself through the mind/pen of the character/author. Richardson and Sterne wish to reveal the exact and to-the-moment motions of the mind, whatever dizzying games that mind itself may play, whatever obliqueness it may hold in its meanderings. In Sterne, the erratic gestures and notations—theatrical in the sense that they look to motion beyond language, novelistic in that they assume the privacy linked to the privilege of digression—attempt to defy the unnaturalness of the page and to crack its surfaces.

Thus, the early novel did not altogether avoid the forms of masquerade it had learned from the theater: irony, dialogue, mistaken identity. In fact, it even invented new forms of its own: the unreliable narrator; the epistolary form, which layers text upon text; the pseudohistorical narrator, who is at once a mask and a validator of naturalism. But its ultimate goal in most cases was sincerity, the revelation of the folds of the inner self, not the anatomy of the layers of external and corporeal ex-

perience. By treating "lower," or more "natural" characters, it
could eliminate the mask of artifice associated with the aristocracy (whose lavish belongings become a form of concealment).
Ultimately, the self would show itself to be just as masked as
the physical world, the anatomy of the mind's masks culminating in the work of late-nineteenth-century psychology. But
the early novel, although it borrowed from the theater, chose
more often to model itself on the unmasking self-explorations
of Christian autobiography (for instance, that of Augustine) or
on the sincere Puritan's understanding of the self (for instance,
that of Bunyan). In the eighteenth-century novel, the mask of
allegory drops off, and Christian's self-flagellations, for instance, are replaced by, and yet not so far distant from, Clarissa's
intricate self-explorations.

Neither the theater's obsessive contrasts between nature and
art nor the implication that the book and art were separate from
the true nature of things was to remain stable. The same physical circumstances (the growth of print) that had strengthened
the emphatic nature of this contrast would help alter it over the
course of the eighteenth century, and in fact some of these al-
terations were already beginning to show in the last decades of
the seventeenth century. Congreve hints at this future instability in his own theatrical explorations of the nature of the self
and the solitude of psychological subjectivism. If the theater
had suggested modes for the novel, the novel also suggested new
modes for the theater, which would grow stronger on the
eighteenth-century stage, not only in the psychological explorations of Vanbrugh, Cibber, and Steele, but also in the bourgeois settings of the sentimental comedy, and the prose articulations and lower-class themes of such tragedy as Lillo's.

Although the theater would continue to articulate the masks
of the world and of human experience, in the eighteenth century it would increasingly incorporate novelistic conceptions of
experience. The eighteenth-century theater would focus more
and more on the vicissitudes of the sincere heart—for instance,
Jane's in Rowe's *Jane Shore* (1714) or Indiana's in Steele's *The*

Conscious Lovers (1722). It would, more and more, imitate the novel's distance between reader and stage of action, in increasingly large theaters divided by the proscenium arch, relegating the audience to darkness, to hear and see but not to be heard or seen. At the same time, it would imitate the novel's manner of bridging that distance with emotional sympathy, for instance, the sympathy to which Steele lays claim in his preface to *The Conscious Lovers*, when he writes that the object of comedy is "to introduce a joy too exquisite for laughter" and that "To be apt to give way to the impressions of humanity is the excellence of a right disposition."[54] The drama would attempt an increasingly literal naturalism throughout the eighteenth and nineteenth centuries, culminating (on the Continent) in Zola's call for a theater of perfect naturalism, "Le Naturalisme au théâtre" (1878), and in Ibsen's and Strindberg's attempts to make the stage a room missing only the fourth wall. In Ibsen's and Strindberg's later rejection of this literalism, and in Shaw's insistence that he was never a "realist,"[55] the theater had already begun to rebel against the naturalism that the twentieth-century theater would come to identify as an inappropriate usurpation of the page.

If the late-seventeenth-century theater still concentrated heavily on the problem of disguise, some changes were beginning to show in Congreve and elsewhere. Perhaps the novel, with its claim for a naturalistic reality but with its disturbing remoteness from that reality, gave the dramatists the uneasy sense that their model of the relation between nature and art had been too simplistic and that even to invert the terms could not describe a nature and art now interpenetrated with such complexity. Congreve's fusion of the physicality of the mask tradition with the psychological solitudes of print narrative, in which the incarnation of artifice finally permits the sincerity of the natural, is paradigmatic of the way he resolves the topos of art and nature. Those who wish for sincerity, those who wish men and women to be what they are, are misguided. For as Heartwell knows, the greatest hope is merely that people might

"be what they pretend to be" (*OB*, I.i, p. 43). Even metaphysical truth is irrelevant. When Lady Froth defends her poetic
line, "For as the Sun shines every day," by arguing that the sun
"does shine all the day too, you know, tho' we don't see him"
(*DD*, III.i, p. 164), she offers the absurdities not only of lit-
eralist versifying, not only of scientific literalism, but also of
claims for a natural world beyond the art of the mind's perceptions.

Cynthia finds in science a more appropriate model for perception, that of the adjustable tools of empiricism, when she
says to Mellefont: "Why have you look'd through the wrong end
of the Perspective all this while; for nothing has been between
us but our fears" (*DD*, IV.i, p. 168). Millamant expresses something of the same thing when she asserts that she makes lovers
and kills them at will, and Valentine states it most clearly when
he says, "I know no effectual Difference between continued Affectation and Reality" (*LL*, III.i, p. 254). "Continued Affectation," or sustained art, determines what we see, and what we
see is the reality that exists for us, the only reality we can know.
In one sentence, Congreve articulates the essential logical implication of Locke's point of view (although one that Locke
would not have accepted), which would be elaborated by
eighteenth-century rejections of materialism, by explorations
of habit, and which would be essential to the novel's understanding of empiricism and consciousness. If there is no difference between perception and reality, then there is little difference after all between the world and the book or between the
book and the mind. The world exists only insofar as we perceive
and express it through language, and the language we have is a
literary language, first saturated and finally fully defined by the
printed text.

Conclusion

Congreve's fusion of print and the theater, like his life, finally led him away from the theater into the solitary spaces of the library, the solitary spaces of the mind, where he did not need to "conform . . . to the manners of [his] court or chocolate-house acquaintance."[1] He grew more interested in the beautiful editions in his library than in the live Minerva on the stage and eventually nearly ceased to attend the theater, spending much of his time collecting and cataloging books for his library. His plays may be less explicit about their connection to print than those of later dramatists would be. But Congreve promoted his notion of the ideal drama by drawing on an alliance between print and the theater; his drama finally absorbed into itself the consciousness that can belong only to a print culture.

Through the Renaissance and even more fully by the late seventeenth century, print was the purveyor of the classical. The ideas of indestructibility and permanence that could be identified imaginatively with the classical and materially with print heightened the prestige of a theater tied to the printed text. Even if the drama, partly thanks to Aristotle, had prestige as the foremost locus of poetry, Aristotle was identified by the late seventeenth century not only with literacy, but with print. If the Renaissance theater showed signs of responding to the new technology of literary mass reproduction, the late-seventeenth-century theater responded in a more fully articulated manner.

Congreve's careful choice of publishers and compilation of the 1710 *Works* suggest the degree to which he identified himself with the material world of print. The physically manifested dramatic lineage created by Congreve's *Works* and his arrangement of his library shelves was not, like the live theater, temporally fleeting. In devoting his energies to the published versions of his plays and to his library, Congreve was both devoting himself to an enterprise over which he could maintain control, far from the interference of managers and actors, and making a permanent place for himself as a dramatic poet.

Like many playwrights of the period, Congreve showed an increasing consciousness that performance and text would have to work out some kind of alliance in order for the theater to achieve and maintain the elevated status he wished to give it. The theater would have to use and assimilate the values of print in order not to lose its place entirely to prose fiction and in order to preserve its own special territory. This meant not only stylistic changes, as Congreve and other playwrights began to replace such oral stylistic habits as "copia" and additive syntactical structures with conciseness and periodic, subordinating syntax; it also meant a heightened attention to plot and formal principles, in part because formal regularity could be checked in published editions. Other specifically theatrical elements yielded to the textual supremacy that surrounded them. If Congreve's visual sense drew on the printed engravings sold everywhere by print shops, he learned from them that vision needed textual explanation. If he understood gesture as a stay against linguistic uncertainty, gesture could never be self-sufficient: it would always be identified with the vulgarities of farce and would need the inscriptions of the textual. Language, it was true, might always be mediation; it might always fail to represent. The printed word might always be art. But it was art as proximate to consciousness as it was possible to get and was finally indistinguishable from experience. It was art that, like "continued Affectation," was indistinguishable from "Reality."

Congreve's understanding of the old dichotomy between nature and art led him to affirm private experience in the face of the erosion of linguistic referentiality and of the wholly theatrical. His belief that nature is only sustained art, the art of the mind, brought him a recognition of subjectivity and of the primacy of the solitary self, a self that could be most fully explored on the printed page. Increasingly, Congreve could find certitude only in the workings of the mind, a mind trained by the detailed psychological investigations of prose fiction and by the solitude necessary to reading and impossible in the theater. In acknowledging immateriality, and in yielding to the certitude of the mind alone, he retreated from the ways of the world and from the theater of the world into the library. The acknowledgment of an essential solitude in the face of immateriality, an immateriality that is a version of the absorption of the theatrical by the literate, was the price that Congreve and other playwrights paid for the control over their work that print offered. Such control, promotion of the individual author-celebrity, the solitude of a psychologically determined reality, and the displacement of the live theater by the reading text were all parts of the same motion. It was a motion toward an atomism that, if fundamentally solipsistic, was perfectly suited to a culture whose primary means of communication was through the printed word.

Congreve's retreat from the theater can be seen as a paradigm for the literary drama of the centuries that followed. The thriving activity of the nineteenth-century theater, with all its spectacular effects, had little to do with the efforts serious poets were making to create a drama equal to their notion of the literary. When Shelley wrote *The Cenci* (1819) and when Byron wrote *Manfred* (ca. 1820), they no longer knew how or no longer chose to write for the live stage, for their notion of the true poetic drama had been fully formed by the ideals of print. Hazlitt, in recognizing "how far asunder the closet and the stage are," imagined the true drama as so page-bound that performance could only violate it: "Poetry and the stage do not agree to-gether. The attempt to reconcile them fails not only of effect, but of decorum. The *ideal* has no place upon the stage, which is a picture without perspective; every thing there is in the fore-ground. That which is merely an airy shape, a dream, a passing thought, immediately becomes an unmanageable reality."[2] Even Shaw, interested as he ostensibly was in unifying the lit-erary and the theatrical, wrote plays that were wrapped in their elaborate prefaces, as if for fear that the theatrical might still betray the seriousness of the rhetorical drama of ideas, which could be conveyed only through print. Yet perhaps one can see in Shaw some of the first genuine struggles to reclaim the the-atrical for the literary, struggles that would dominate the twen-tieth century. Stanislavsky, Artaud, and Brecht—reacting to the culture of excess print, to the culture of the masterpiece, and rebelling against the dominance of the text (even while they used the text)—would try to reclaim a fully physical and ma-terialized stage. But the theater had been forever changed by print.

Reference Matter

Notes

Introduction

1. Peter Blayney and others have recently thrown more than serious doubt on the "romantic tale of piracy" established by Alfred W. Pollard in the first decade of this century, that "bad quartos" like those of *Romeo and Juliet* or *Hamlet* were pirated by disgruntled players and sneaky publishers. Blayney argues, rather, that most of the plays were acquired perfectly legitimately and amicably, probably from manuscripts copied by actors for friends. See Blayney, "Shakespeare's Fight." Whether or not we accept that most of the plays were published legitimately, no one would claim that Shakespeare paid much attention to the survival of his plays.

2. On his editing of Dryden, see Congreve's dedication to Dryden's 1717 *Dramatick Works*, published by Tonson. Evidence of Congreve's actual editorial work on this edition may be scanty, but Congreve's phrasing suggests that he did more than simply write the dedication. Dryden "recommended it to me to *be kind to his Remains*," writes Congreve. "I was then, and have been ever since most sensibly touched with that Expression: and the more so, because I could not find in my self the Means of satisfying the Passion which I felt in me, to do something answerable" until the publication of the *Works* (Congreve, *Letters*, p. 126).

3. See my Bibliographical Note, pp. 257–59, for many of the sources on which I rely for general information about publishing history.

4. See Belanger, "Publishers and Writers," p. 6.

5. There has been much work in the past decades on the cultural distinction between orality and literacy (see my Bibliographical Note, pp. 257–59). Here, I am conflating literacy and print for simplicity, although I will make many distinctions between the two in specific instances. Walter Ong, in "Print, Space and Closure" (in *Orality and Literacy*, pp. 117–35), argues that print merely intensifies literacy, but Elizabeth Eisenstein (*Printing Press*) justly points out significant differences between the effects of each. I have resisted Marshall McLuhan's terms "chirographic" and "typographic" (which Ong uses sporadically) as unnecessarily technical.

6. The distinction between oral effects (such as conversation and dialogue) and oral residue ("habits of thought tracing back to preliterate situations") is Ong's, and is a useful one. See Ong, *Rhetoric*, p. 25.

7. I almost always use *theater* to indicate the idea of a live theater, conceived in terms of performance, and *drama* to indicate the idea of a written drama, conceived in terms of solitary reading. I often, however, wish to convey both ideas simultaneously, so I use the terms (and their adjectival forms) fluidly.

8. There is a reason that Eisenstein ends her study with the eighteenth century, the period that brings to full development some features of the interaction I am describing. But by the end of the eighteenth century, reactions to print are dominant and largely reflect values exactly opposite to those that emerge more directly from print. Thus, it is often difficult to distinguish preprint values from a reaction to postprint values.

9. For the mid-eighteenth century and after, such a presupposition cannot hold, for print results in even greater changes: an increased reading public, which gives writers a sense that oral communication is a source far distant from the written, and the yielding of educational disputation and dialogue to monologue, increasingly impersonal modes, and reading. See Ong, *Ramus*, pp. 149–67. By then, nearly all plays performed were printed, and it was impossible to write a play without thinking of the "readers in the closet." Garrick, for instance, repeatedly uses the phrase.

10. Ong, *Orality and Literacy*, p. 152, classifies the drama as a literate form, in its "roundness" of character and plot closure, but the fact that it is performed rather than read and has its origin in spontaneous ritual connects it far more fundamentally to orality. Eric Havelock, in "Oral Composition," stresses the drama's essential oral-

ity, which is partly due to the nonliteracy of the early playwrights and partly due to its connection with the Homeric epic.

11. The lively late-seventeenth-century discussion of genre—for instance, in Dryden's "Essay of Dramatic Poesy" (1668) or Rymer's "Tragedies of the Last Age Considered" (1678)—suggests both the repetitive, formulaic quality of the drama (plays can be classified according to predictable types) and the strain on this quality (the clear distinctions between the types are breaking down and must be re-identified). Hume, in *Development of English Drama*, subtly registers such formalism and the strain it was undergoing, in the difficulty he has classifying the plays into limited categories.

12. This transformation could serve as an example of a more general pattern of historical change: a revolution in material culture produces, after a time lapse, a revolution in cultural consciousness that is largely interiorized; only after the full interiorization of the material change has occurred does a culture begin to call attention in vivid, deliberate, and expressive ways to that change. Usually that attention is a form of reaction, the culture's way of saying that it must step back from this radical change, which happened in the recesses of its consciousness and which it has only begun to notice.

13. If I avoid causal historicism where possible, I also resist the conceptual inversions of cause and effect and the use of *écriture* as cosmic metaphor, which serve the thinking on speech and writing of Derrida and others. In fact, Derrida might be seen as himself a product of print, in his identification of all forms of communication (verbal and nonverbal, spoken and written) with an inscription that he calls writing, as well as in his ahistoricism (the privilege of a print culture that does not value the easy recording of history). Nonetheless, his distinctions might be useful here in describing Congreve's (and the period's) conscious prioritization of speech and Congreve's notion (confused, according to Derrida) that speech is prior to and the foundation of writing.

14. I have borrowed the phrase "organized network of obsessions" from Barthes, who uses it to describe his recovery "of the structure of an existence" in his *Michelet* (p. 3).

Chapter One

1. Jane P. Tompkins rephrases Plato's theoretical complaint about the written when she writes: "Once frozen into letters, speech can no longer defend itself against abuse or suit its terms to the various

people it wishes to address. It cannot take advantage of opportunities or forestall misprision; in short, because it lacks the power of accommodation to circumstance, it loses its power to mold circumstance in its own image" ("Reader," pp. 204–5).

2. Ong writes that Latin, which "was permanently aligned with the primary oral and rhetorical tradition . . . paradoxically also built up an extreme deference for the written word which verged on superstition and was to affect the aims of lexicography down to our present day" (*Rhetoric*, p. 17). See also *Orality and Literacy*, p. 113.

3. On the literacy of the drama, see Ong: "Greek drama, though orally performed, was composed as a written text and in the west was the first verbal genre, and for centuries was the only verbal genre, to be controlled completely by writing" (*Orality and Literacy*, p. 142). Havelock, however, argues forcefully for the strong orality of the early-Greek drama in "Oral Composition." On the orality of the drama, see also Bertrand Bronson: "Drama was an *oral* art. Play *printing* was an art of embalming" (*Facets*, p. 301); and D. F. McKenzie: "Plays belonged to a totally different sphere from print. . . . We just misconceive the nature of drama as it was so wholly accepted then when we harden performance into text" ("London Book Trade," p. 2).

4. See McKenzie, "Poetry, Politics and Press," in "London Book Trade," pp. 1–15, for a discussion of this play and its relation to London publishing.

5. As McKenzie writes, it was "the end of the theatre as the only secular mass-medium, the end of the playhouse as the principal forum of public debate, the end of the actors' popular function as the abstracts and brief chronicles of the time. It was a confession that the dramatic poet had lost his vocation to a journalist" ("London Book Trade," p. 10).

6. See Blagden, *Stationers' Company*, pp. 153–55. Unless otherwise noted, I use the word *publisher* (or *publishing*) in the modern sense, not in the seventeenth-century sense of one who makes public (usually an author or editor). The trade was generally divided between printers and booksellers (who combined the services of the modern publisher and bookseller), although often one person would act as both printer and bookseller, especially in illicit publishing. The printers had dominated the sixteenth-century trade, but over the course of the seventeenth century, they increasingly lost power to the booksellers.

7. Dryden and Tate celebrated L'Estrange's zeal in the character of Sheva in *Absalom and Achitophel*, part 2:

> In vain our factious Priests the Cant revive,
> In vain seditious Scribes with Libels strive
> T'enflame the Crowd, while He with watchfull Eye
> Observes, and shoots their Treasons as They fly.
>   (Dryden, *Works* [ed. Hooker and
>   Swedenberg], vol. 2, p. 92)

8. Evelyn, *Diary*, p. 627.

9. Sutherland, *English Literature*, p. 235. For a more complete history of the Restoration newspaper, see Sutherland, *Restoration Newspaper*.

10. This was enacted on April 10, 1710. The phrasing of the act, "An Act for the Encouragement of Learning by Vesting copies of Printed Books in the Authors or Purchasers of such Copies, during the Times therein mentioned," suggests the concern for the "learned" authors themselves. See Blagden, *Stationers' Company*, pp. 175–77.

11. For instance, as McKenzie notes, even quartos as late as Congreve's "follow the seventeenth-century trade stereotype, reflecting the lack of any sympathetic relationship between writer or theatre company, bookseller and printer" ("London Book Trade," p. 37).

12. See Peter Holland, *Ornament*, pp. 99–137, for a more-detailed discussion of the relationship between text and performance. Holland suggests the way in which playwrights became increasingly concerned with texts.

13. See Belanger, "Publishers and Writers," pp. 17–18.

14. John Downes (*Roscius Anglicanus*, p. 78) writes that it "produc'd vast Profit to the Company," and it was given at least eight different productions between 1681 and 1700, despite the fact that it was periodically prohibited. See *London Stage*, vol. 1.

15. Plant, *English Book Trade*, pp. 74–75.

16. Blagden, *Stationers' Company*, pp. 175–76; Mumby, *Publishing*, p. 127.

17. Quoted in Plant, *English Book Trade*, p. 117.

18. Shakespeare, *As You Like It*, p. 30 (II.i.16). To follow the *Oxford English Dictionary* (*OED*) entries for *book* and *print*, although they have provided me with several of the instances I cite here, is misleading, since the *OED* attempts to give instances of each usage throughout the history of the language, rather than to identify the frequency

or dominance of a usage. Tennyson, for instance, can almost invariably offer a nineteenth-century instance of phrases otherwise largely restricted to Elizabethan usage; official records invariably offer early instances of usages that have no relation to a period's way of imagining the world.

19. Bacon, *The Advancement of Learning* (book 1), in *Works*, vol. 3, p. 301.

20. Milton, *Paradise Lost* (book 3, ll. 47–48), in *Complete Poems*, p. 259.

21. In Charles Butler's *The Feminine Monarchie: or, the Historie of Bees* (1623). Cited in the *OED*, s.v. print.

22. John Suckling, *Aglaura*, p. 14 (I.i).

23. John Evelyn, *Sculptura*, p. 15.

24. Carew, *Poems*, p. 15.

25. Although this poem was first printed in Congreve's 1710 *Works*, it was probably written significantly earlier. No scholar has attempted to date the poems with any accuracy.

26. Molière, *Œuvres complètes*, vol. 2, p. 791 (III.iii).

27. Wycherley, *Country Wife*, p. 13 (I.i).

28. Thomas Hearne, *Collections* (1716). Cited in the *OED*.

29. Pope, "First Satire of the Second Book of Horace Imitated" (1733; ll. 99–100), in *Poems*, vol. 4, p. 15.

30. Congreve, prologue to *The Mourning Bride*, p. 323.

31. Evidence for literacy remains sparse, and there is still much disagreement among scholars about who was reading, how much, when, and where. Most studies suggest that literacy was not widespread in England until the last decade of the seventeenth century and that it remained (and remains) a function of class. See Stone, "Literacy and Education"; Laqueur, "Popular Literacy"; and Cressy, *Literacy*. These studies correct the earlier claim of Altick, *English Common Reader*, that literacy rose during the Commonwealth but declined again after the Restoration, not to rise again until "the time of Addison and Steele" (p. 30).

32. The list of libraries extensive enough to require cataloging during this period is vast. See De Ricci, *English Collectors*. See Mumby, *Publishing*, p. 123, on book auctions; and Feather, *Provincial Book Trade*, on the spread of provincial printing.

33. *The Post Man*, 920 (January 8–10, 1702).

34. McKenzie, "London Book Trade," pp. 25–26.

35. The act was intended to encourage the "bringing of plate and hammered money into the Mints to be coined" and placed a 25 percent duty on imported books, a 20 percent duty on paper and parchment made, and a 17½ percent duty on stock-in-trade. In addition to encouraging foreign piracy, it was also partly responsible for the increase in collective publishing and stock sharing during the period and for the campaign for a copyright law. See Plomer, *Dictionary of Printers*, p. vii.

36. Mumby, *Publishing*, pp. 119–20.

37. See Blagden, *Stationers' Company*, chs. 8 and 9.

38. See Steinberg, *Five Hundred Years*, pp. 142–44. As newspaper advertisements show, the bookseller of the first decade of the eighteenth century still had many other functions, from selling medicine to serving as a lost-and-found agent, to posting information on runaway servants or army deserters.

39. Mumby, *Publishing*, p. 129.

40. Dryden wrote, "The printing an Authours name, in a Play bill, is a new manner of proceeding, at least in England" (Congreve, *Letters*, p. 102).

41. For a complete discussion of Dryden's relation with Herringman, see Osborn, *Dryden*, pp. 184–93; and Winn, *Dryden*, pp. 95–96.

42. Milton's political position after the Restoration and Dryden's youth when he might have been working for Herringman naturally temper such figures. The debasement of coinage may also be partly accountable, but the change remains enormous. Winn describes the state of "commercial publication," which was "still in its infancy and not yet the viable system" in the 1660's and 1670's that it would later become: "Lest we imagine that Herringman's business operated on the scale of later publishers, however, we should recall that literacy remained appallingly low; books were a luxury, and Herringman's customers, virtually without exception, were 'gentlemen.' Without hope for a sustaining public, young writers like Dryden had to hope for patronage" (Winn, *Dryden*, pp. 95–96). Hepburn, in *Author's Empty Purse*, lists the causes of improvement in the writer's condition in the late seventeenth century as "rises in population, literacy, leisure, and wealth; the physical and cultural unification of the populace; inevitable refinements in legal doctrine; the increasing dependence of society upon the written word; the accumulating weight of

England's literary genius and the painfully acquired business-sense of her geniuses" (p. 6).

43. Dryden, *Works* (ed. Hooker and Swedenberg), vol. 13, p. 98. On Dryden's interest in an English academy, see Emerson, "Dryden."

44. Congreve did both in the quarto of *Love for Love*: "Here are some Lines in the Print, (and which your Lordship read before this Play was Acted) that were omitted on the Stage; and particularly one whole Scene in the Third Act, which not only helps the Design forward with less Precipitation, but also heightens the ridiculous Character of *Foresight*, which indeed seems to be maim'd without it" (p. 210).

45. See McKenzie, "London Book Trade," for Jonson, Congreve, and Tonson in particular.

46. Even Hume's *Development of English Drama* rightly describes the plays more in terms of types and trends than in terms of uniform development.

47. Although some critics reject the usual claim for an increase in "sentimentalism," and although Scouten and Hume reject the notion that there was any change in the audiences, all seem to identify a shift toward what Novak aptly calls "douceur." See Scouten and Hume, "Restoration Comedy"; Novak, *Congreve*, p. 25; Fujimura, *Restoration Comedy*, pp. 156–96; and Holland, *Ornament*, p. 229.

48. Holland, *Ornament*, p. 238, writes of the contrast between "fixity and flux" in the play but does not identify these qualities with either character.

49. I use the phrase "revelation of internal complexity" only with a great deal of hesitation and as shorthand for a quality I am not alone in having difficulty describing. The twentieth-century critical topos of Shakespeare's characters' depth and complexity, originating with A. C. Bradley's judgment in *Shakespearean Tragedy* (1904) that the central interest of Shakespeare is in character issuing in action, has not come very far. Critics like Goldman (*Acting and Action*) and Bayley (*Shakespeare and Tragedy*) are still arguing about whether consciousness replaces action or is inseparable from action. However influential the quasi-structuralist critique that the reduction of the dramas to "realistic" portraits annihilates their emblematic and mythic power, such arguments still often cling to a notion that there is a simple dichotomy between the realistic and the nonrealistic. As Goldman quite accurately describes matters, "The implication in the typical

debate . . . is that the psychological discourse of novels and novelizing psychology is the most accurate form for describing character in what we helplessly refer to as real life" (p. 141). If such debates fail to take into account the impact of the nineteenth-century novel's discursive analysis of character on their own assumptions, a more complex form of historical predetermination underlies psychoanalytic notions of character, whose assumptions have been formed partly by the strange crossbreeding of the nineteenth-century novelistic and the twentieth-century mytho-symbolic (filtered, most recently, through structural linguistics). Despite the fact that psychoanalytic readings like those of Harry Berger Jr., Janet Adelman, or Joseph Westlund have been able to offer some suggestive ways of playing with textures of contradiction, they have not brought us any closer to a historical account of shifting notions of character.

Goldman (p. 142) does offer a distinction between the implicit and the explicit identification of character depth that might be useful for distinguishing the tendencies of the early part of the seventeenth century from those of the later part: in *Hamlet,* lines that seem to be about character depth almost always mean "either that something is bothering Hamlet or that he is up to something which, like love or ambition, is capable of simple definition and explicable as the product of an external situation"; in *Coriolanus* (as in so many late-seventeenth-century plays), there is an explicit debate about the complexity of Coriolanus's character.

The history of the debate itself might prove an interesting measure of the fluctuations of twentieth-century American criticism. For instance, the periodic appearance of the Marxist critique of the notion of personality as history, the various attacks on the privileging of character over action (which came to the aid of the theater historians' attempts to reclaim the plays as performances), or the rhetoricians' desire to see character as a function of linguistic incoherence (both in New Criticism and in deconstruction) each serves to define quite precisely some of the conflicting impulses that have made up the history of English studies since its institutionalization at the beginning of the century.

50. Vanbrugh, *Provoked Wife*, p. 7 (I.i).
51. Southerne, *Fatal Marriage*, p. 65 (V.i).
52. Manley, *Royal Mischief*, p. 19 (III.i).
53. Shakespeare, *Richard II*, p. 169 (V.v.9).

54. Granville, *Heroick Love* (preface).

55. *The Rehearsal* was written over several years, with the help of several hands, and satirized several playwrights, although by 1671, Dryden and his rhymed heroic tragedy had become the principal target.

56. Buckingham, *The Rehearsal* (prologue).

57. Ibid., p. 8 (I.i).

58. Benjamin, in his "Work of Art in an Age of Mechanical Reproduction" (in *Illuminations*) wrote of a related phenomenon in twentieth-century society: "With the increasing extension of the press, which kept placing new political, religious, scientific, professional, and local organs before the readers, an increasing number of readers became writers. . . . And today there is hardly a gainfully employed European who could not, in principle, find opportunity to publish somewhere or other. . . . Thus, the distinction between author and public is about to lose its basic character" (pp. 233–34).

59. Rymer (preface).

60. The London 1704 edition, the first, was not printed until eight years after the first performance.

61. See Saunders, *Profession*, especially chs. 6 and 7.

62. Buckingham, *The Rehearsal*, p. 31 (III.ii).

63. Oldmixon, *Grove* (dedication).

64. *Female Wits*, pp. 15–16 (I.i).

65. As Ong writes, the romantic, literate, print-era mind is "subconsciously convinced that what is known is stored in books, whereas art is necessarily a venture into the unknown" (*Rhetoric*, p. 21).

66. In the late seventeenth century, the use of the word *original* increases substantially and begins to refer to works of art that are not copies or imitations, although it is not until the early eighteenth century that it becomes a word of praise that needs no other modifiers. See the *OED* entry.

67. Buckingham, *The Rehearsal*, p. 11 (II.i).

68. Ong writes: "In the earlier oral or residually oral ages of mankind, when knowledge was in short supply and in constant danger of being lost, the romantic celebration of the mysterious and the unknown was at best a luxury and could prove a serious psychological threat. Hence earlier ages show only limited traces of romanticism, which can break out as a large movement only when vast supplies of

knowledge have been stored in the readily retrievable form made possible by print" (*Rhetoric*, pp. 19–20).

69. Buckingham, *The Rehearsal*, p. 11 (II.i).

70. Ibid., p. 45 (V.i).

71. Quoted in Daiches, "Presenting Shakespeare," p. 63.

72. Saunders, *Profession*, p. 96.

73. The explosion of antitheatrical pamphleteering is as much a part of this evaluation as the theater histories. The increased volume of the old reformers' defiance of the Image in favor of the Word during this period may be partially due to the increase in printing. Not only could reformers' tracts have a much wider circulation, but one might perhaps also think of them as the print world's reaction to the theater's abuse of it during the early Restoration. For the stage-reform movement, see Barish, *Antitheatrical Prejudice*, especially chs. 6–8.

74. In Congreve, *Complete Plays*, p. 124. For a perceptive reading of Dryden's poem to Congreve, see Winn, *Dryden*, pp. 465–67.

75. Congreve, preface to the reader, *Incognita*, in *Letters*, p. 159.

76. Congreve mocks the pretentious use of asterisms (as a means of concealing true—aural and logical—poetic weakness) in *The Double Dealer* (III.i).

Chapter Two

1. Congreve, "Poem in Praise of the Author" (S: p. 61).

2. The standard biography is still John Hodges's *William Congreve*, which is mostly careful and well documented, if extremely limited in scope and not up-to-date. I have confirmed most of Hodges's London and Oxford manuscript sources and all of the material specifically relating to publishers.

3. Congreve, *Letters*, p. 243. He repeatedly refers to his works as "trifles" and insists that he prefers retirement, away from the bustle of the commercial realm (pp. 12, 53, 157–58, 172, 230). The writer's gentlemanly stance in a period when the decline of noble patronage and the rise of public "patronage" were putting pressure on such a stance has been more fully explored by, among others, Folkenflik, "Patronage"; Winn, *Dryden*, pp. 95–103; and Kernan, *Printing Technology*, pp. 24–47.

4. I have been unable to find either a record of Peter Buck's birth or a will for John Buck. I rely here (and for most of my information

on dates of apprenticeship and paternity) on the two volumes by McKenzie (ed.), *Stationers' Company Apprentices*. A majority of the apprentices at the end of the century had fathers who were clergymen, as the prestige of the trade increased. See Blagden, *Stationers' Company*, p. 117.

5. The minimum age for freedom for an apprentice changed over the seventeenth century from twenty-four to twenty-one. See Blagden, *Stationers' Company*, pp. 78, 248. See pp. 78–88 for an example of a typical bookseller's career during a slightly earlier period and for the regulations governing apprentices. Such rules remained largely unchanged from the sixteenth to the eighteenth century.

6. Roper had originally come as an apprentice to his uncle, who died soon after, so Roper was turned over to Wilkinson. Roper was brought before the Stationers' Company for numerous offenses, from failure to license to political misdemeanor to obscenity, but nonetheless (or perhaps as a result) had a very successful career. Although Buck collaborated with a vast number of publishers in his short career, there is no sign that he and Roper ever worked together afterwards. Roper must have been a difficult co-worker, and his manner of handling his business was probably not to Buck's taste. See the more lively than accurate biography of Roper by "Dr. Andrew Tripe" (William Wagstaffe, *Some Memoirs*).

7. The name Buck was common enough, and neither the apprenticeship records nor the imprints suggest a connection. I have relied principally on Wing's *Short Title Catalogue*, Plomer's *Dictionary of Printers*, and my own examination of imprints for my bibliographical information.

8. In his dedication to *The Old Batchelour*, Congreve writes that "had it been Acted, when it was first written, more might have been said in its behalf . . . which now, almost four Years Experience, will scarce allow of." This suggests that it was written in 1689, perhaps under the oak tree at Stretton, where nineteenth-century tradition placed the composition (Congreve, *Letters*, p. 162). See also Hodges's comments, pp. 9, 164. If so, Congreve composed it before having arrived in London. *Incognita* was written, according to him, "in the idler hours of a fortnight's time" (preface to the reader, *Incognita*, in *Letters*, p. 160), sometime before its licensing in December 1691.

9. In his dedication to Katharine Leveson, he wishes to avoid her "Censure of this Trifle," and in his preface he thinks it necessary that

a few words "be prefix'd to this Trifle" (*Letters*, pp. 157–58), although the carefulness of the preface and his habitual use of the phrase suggest that he does not regard his work as entirely trifling.

10. Congreve, *Letters*, p. 160.

11. Lady Mary told Joseph Spence, "I never knew anybody that had so much wit as Congreve" (Spence, *Observations*, vol. 1, p. 304, no. 744).

12. Gildon (ed.), *Miscellany Poems* (1692).

13. Congreve's later description of Dryden's reticence suggests that the meeting was more probably at Congreve's own initiative: "He was of very easy, I may say of very pleasing Access: But something slow, and as it were diffident in his Advances to others. He had something in his Nature that abhorr'd Intrusion into any Society whatsoever" (in Dryden, *Dramatick Works*, vol. 1 [epistle dedicatory]).

14. See Southerne's short biographical note on Congreve, in Congreve, *Letters*, p. 151.

15. Congreve, *Letters*, pp. 89–90.

16. See Treadwell, "Congreve," pp. 265–69. An anonymous laudatory epistle to Congreve, which Treadwell does not mention, may also refer to the period during which Congreve lodged with Tonson, although the "Judges Head" of Tonson's shop may be a cradle only in that it gives birth to Congreve's poetry. An admiring poet seeks Congreve's praise:

> [He has] Waited like Dun, or Court depender
> On Nobleman, or Fortune Mender
> At the great Mid-Wife of the Muses,
> Who Judges Head for Cradle Uses.
>   ("A Letter to Mr. Congreve,"
> in Gildon [ed.], *New Miscellany*, p. 299)

17. McKenzie, "London Book Trade," discusses in great detail the collaboration of Congreve, Tonson, and Tonson's printer, John Watts, so I have condensed my discussion as much as possible.

18. The most detailed account of publishers' financial dealings of the period is McKenzie's *Cambridge University Press*, which treats the press in the context of other presses of the period. Congreve's financial situation was insecure enough until he received his post as Commissioner for Licensing of Hackney and Stage-coaches in 1695 at £100 per year, and in 1693 he would have needed the extra income. Not

until he was appointed Undersearcher of Customs and Secretary to Jamaica, at the end of 1714, did his income allow him to live in relative comfort. See Congreve, *Letters*, pp. 83–88.

19. Tonson paid Dryden £200 and any subscription money exceeding £5 per subscriber for his Virgil translation, and 250 guineas (to be increased to £300 at the second impression) for the *Fables*. Many specifications as to illustrations, paper size, and ink quality were included in the contracts and the subscription advertisements. Congreve received £157 from Tonson in June 1709, probably simply for the edition of the *Works* that they were planning, although Tonson had already printed most of the material it contained. Tonson agreed to pay him another 20 guineas for the second edition of his poems (the third volume of the *Works*). See Congreve, *Letters*, pp. 96–99, 103–4, 116–17.

20. Quoted in Simpson, *Proof-Reading*, p. 44.

21. The lines are:

> Of common Bone, the Handles of my Knives
> Are made, yet no ill Taste it gives
> To what I carve, nor is there ever left
> Any unsav'ry haut-gust, from the Hast.
> (Dryden et al. [trans.], *Juvenal and
> Persius*, p. 227 [ll. 220–23])

The erratum reads: "In the Eleventh SATIRE, *Page* 227. *Line* 221. Read for *ill*, *unpleasant*."

22. It seems highly unlikely that Wellington simply pirated the novel, since he and Buck continued to collaborate occasionally and since his list began to contain many Buck imprints at this time. He may have bought the copyright or come to some other agreement, for instance a profit-sharing or stock-sharing arrangement. Perhaps Buck was trying to concentrate more on the sales side of the business by 1700.

23. For instance, John Dennis published his first play, *A Plot and No Plot*, with Buck, Richard Parker, and Richard Wellington but went to other publishers afterwards. Rowe published his *Ambitious Stepmother* with Buck in 1701 but then went to Wellington and Thomas Osborne for the second edition in 1702. In 1703 Rowe published *The Fair Penitent* with Tonson.

24. Wotton, *Reflections*, pp. xxxvi–xxxviii.

25. *The Post Man*, 943 (March 14–17, 1702).

26. For an example of a notice of retirement into the country and stock sale, see *The Post Man*, 945 (March 19–21, 1702). For a bookseller leaving the trade, see *The Post Man*, 950 (March 31–April 2, 1703).

27. I have been unable to find any trace of him in wills or death and sale-of-stock notices. Although several Peter Bucks appear in birth and marriage records, they seem to be neither unquestionably tied to the bookseller nor to offer strong evidence of his whereabouts.

28. An article by Michael Harris, "Moses Pitt and Insolvency," has provided me general information on publishers and insolvency in the late seventeenth century. Dunton, *Life and Errors*, has many anecdotes on the struggles of impoverished booksellers during the period, and the Stationers' Company had special provisions for helping its poorer members.

29. For the most accurate account of the Hills family, see Velz, "Pirate Hills." Velz clears up many contradictions that plagued earlier bibliographers.

30. P.C.C., 6 Dyke, PROB 11, 398 (P.R.O., Chancery Lane).

31. I have relied largely on the Mormon genealogical index of parish registers and on Hills Sr.'s will for my information about Hills's family. Perhaps Hills Sr. was nervous about the anti-Catholicism that accompanied the Popish Plot and Exclusion Crisis. On August 23, 1681, he christened in the Anglican church all three of his children (by his first wife, Dorothy): Henry Jr., Gilham, and Dorothy (London, St. Martin Outwich, Baptismal Record, Guildhall Ms. 6837). Hills Jr. began christening children with his wife, Anne, at Saint Ann, Blackfriars, in the same year: Henry in 1681; Peter in 1682; James in 1685; Elisabeth in 1687; Christopher in 1692; Thomas in 1695; and William Henry in 1700. The fact that the names do not repeat suggests that all may have survived.

32. The numerous editions and reissues of the works he printed suggest a high turnover, although he may have simply printed small editions to encourage sales.

33. Congreve, *Works* (1710), vol. 1 (preface).

34. Congreve, *Five Plays*, pp. 4–5.

35. I have been unable to find a will for Hills. Both Plomer and Velz write that he died in 1713, but neither gives any evidence other than the *Evening Post* advertisement.

36. Lintott (ed.), *Miscellaneous Poems*, pp. 173–74.

37. Congreve, interestingly enough, included few play quartos, his own or those of others, in the library catalog made for him in the 1720's. Although it seems unlikely that he owned so few, he considered them more closely related to the cheap pamphlets and broadsides that George Thomason and Pepys collected, but which Congreve did not find worthy of his library.

38. Congreve to Tonson, July 1, 1703, in Congreve, *Letters*, p. 108.

39. In the eighteenth century, Pope constructed an even more elaborate version of this gentlemanly stance to shield his sophisticated professionalism, having conveyed an imperfect version of his correspondence to Edmund Curll so that he would be "forced" to publish the "true" version (much of which was actually fabricated) with Lintott. See Winn, "On Pope."

40. Two examples from the period show the range of tone. In 1663, Cowley complained not only that a collection of poems had been published under his name during his absence from England, but that some of his own pieces had been published without his permission: "It was in vain for me, that I avoided censure by the concealment of my own writings, if my reputation could be thus *Executed in Effigie.* . . . I esteem my self less prejudiced by it, then by . . . the publication of some things of mine without my consent or knowledge, and those so mangled and imperfect, that I could neither with honour acknowledge, nor with honesty quite disavow them" (*Poems*, pp. 4–5). John Oldham's "Satire Upon a Printer That exposed Him, by Printing a Piece of his, grosly mangled and faulty" shows a more violent version of the common complaint:

> Dull, and Unthinking! hadst thou none but me
> To plague, and urge, to thine own Infamy?
> Had I some tame, and sneaking Author been,
> Whose Muse to Love, and Softness did incline,
> Some small Adventurer in Song, that whines
> *Chloris* and *Phyllis* out, in charming Lines . . .
> Perhaps, I might have then forgiven Thee,
> And thou hadst scap'd from my Resentment free.
> (Works, vol. 1, pp. 248–49)

41. Ward, *Sot's Paradise*. "Grub Street" would not become a cliché until the early eighteenth century.

42. The Copyright Act went into effect April 10, 1710. Congreve's 1710 edition was advertised in the *London Gazette* for December 5–7, 1710.

43. For more extensive discussions of the changes, see McKenzie, "When Congreve Made a Scene" and "Typography and Meaning"; and Peter Holland, *Ornament*, pp. 125–37. For bibliographical essays on the changes in *Love for Love* and *The Mourning Bride*, see Eaves and Kimpel, "Text of Congreve's *Love for Love*"; and Mann, "Congreve's Revisions."

44. The phrase "imaginary library" is Alvin Kernan's, which he uses to refer, in the words of Shelley, to "that great poem" that "all poets, like the cooperating thoughts of one great mind, have built up since the beginning of the world" (Shelley, *A Defense of Poetry*, in Adams, *Critical Theory*, p. 506). With print, the nature of the library changed: "A vast body of earlier poetry and prose originally conceived of as primarily in the service of morality and society had already been slowly assembled to create the older conception of poetry. Now these works all became available in actual libraries by the power of print. . . . Not only were works of the past assembled in this way but contemporary works were, as they continue to be, constantly sifted and tested to establish which are canonical and which belong to apocrypha" (Kernan, *Imaginary Library*, pp. 8, 22).

45. Milton, "To John Rouse, Librarian of Oxford University," in *Complete Poems*, p. 148.

46. Bacon, *The Advancement of Learning* (book 2, "To the King"), in *Works*, vol. 4, p. 285.

47. Cowley, "Ode. Mr. *Cowley*'s Book presenting it self to the University Library of *Oxford*," in *Poems*, p. 410.

48. Pope, *The Dunciad* (book 1, ll. 127–30), in *Poems*, vol. 5, pp. 278–79. The library conceit is already part of the *Dunciad Variorum*, but it does not include these lines.

49. The list is in the handwriting of three different clerks, each cataloging at different periods. The shelf indications reflect, at the very least, the state of Congreve's shelves at the periods the catalog was made and expanded, and seem to indicate the way that Congreve intended his books to remain. A consistency of mind (although not a rigidity of principle) informs the entries of the first two hands, but not those of the third hand, which were made either when Congreve was very ill or after his death, and which are spare and confused, failing to indicate shelf numbers. The consistency of the first hands and

the irregularity of the third suggest that Congreve himself supplied the first two hands with the bibliographical principles of the list, and perhaps even dictated it, although there is no proof of either. The scholarly and bibliographical knowledge of the entries and cross-references also suggests Congreve's extensive involvement. (See Congreve, *Library*.)

50. Jacob Tonson to Jacob Tonson II, in Congreve, *Letters*, p. 147.

51. Foucault, in *Order of Things*, p. 128, chooses 1657 as the symbolic date marking the beginning of the classical age of taxonomic order. The schema he discusses for a "natural history" reflects the period's overall uncertainty about the older forms. On the movement from virtuoso to catalog, see his "Classifying" (in *Order of Things*, pp. 125–65); and Holdengräber, "Visible History."

52. Williams does not mention Congreve's library in his *Approach to Congreve*, but the contents of the shelf might seem to support his claim that the plays rely more on traditional Christian argument and imagery than, for instance, on Epicurean or Hobbesian theory. I would be more inclined to see the shelf arrangement here as a reflection of Congreve's state of mind well into the eighteenth century, after he had done his best to eliminate the "impieties" from his works (in the 1710 edition)—a retrospective look at the role of the theater after he had left it. Williams's reading does suggest the necessity of a corrective to the usual clichés about Hobbes and libertinism during the period, the necessity of remembering the shared Christian education of playwrights and audience. But rather than offering a corrective, he offers a reversal, ignoring irony and parody, for instance, where they are inconvenient to the Christian frame he claims. In this, he follows the example of both Collier and Congreve, who, in the 1698 debate, chose to ignore what they both understood perfectly: that a word is only a function of its syntactic and semantic relations. (Congreve, in fact, points out this precise method of misconstruction in Collier, even while he himself is using it.) Williams often simply repeats Congreve's defense against Collier, allowing some of the distortions that Congreve had put forth in his own eagerness to prove his "innocence" against Collier's accusations to stand as "demonstration" of Congreve's orthodoxy. For instance, Bellmour's claim that he is not content to "go to Heaven" immediately (by marrying, is the implication) because he would "do a little more good in my generation first" (one can almost hear the moan in "good") gets from Williams,

as commentary, only Congreve's desperate explanation that Bellmour "does not think himself worthy, till he is better prepared" and Old- mixon's simpering "who knows but *Bellmour* might mean he would live and grow better" (Williams, *Approach to Congreve*, pp. 86–87).

For more measured approaches to the problem, see Novak, *Con- greve*, pp. 41–51; and Scouten and Hume, "Restoration Comedy." I would argue (and perhaps Williams would accept this description) that Congreve saw his plays as compatible both with the volatile im- pulses of contemporary Anglicanism (there *still* wasn't anyone who had figured out what to do with evil, and do you throw out faith just because the dissenters have got the monopoly on it?) and with popular libertinism, just as he could see his plays as compatible both with popular Epicureanism and with popular stoicism. The mind is quite capable of holding contradictory ideas at once, the drama even more so. Like most dramatists worth watching, Congreve uses all available cultural material to try to work out conflicting cultural impulses in a theatrical (rather than an argumentative) way, the way that is, in fact, closest to the way we live internal contradiction, as Congreve knew.

53. Item 302 is Nicholas Baudot de Juilly, *Relation historique et galante, de l'invasion de l'Espagne par les Maures* (1699). Item 309 is Jean Baptiste de Rocoles, *The history of infamous imposters. Or, The lives & actions of several notorious counterfeits* (1683). Item 19 is Jean de La Fon- taine, *Les amours de Psiché et de Cupidon* (1700). Item 21 is Roger de Bussy-Rabutin and others, *Amours des dames illustres de notre siecle* (1700).

54. In a manuscript culture, a book is an object worth great at- tention and care. In a print culture, a book may cease to be an object and become only its contents, or its status as an object may alter. In moving from the sacred to the bibliographical, a book becomes cat- egorized by a system linked essentially to a commercial sphere, the "book trade," and by the discourse that system creates. On the sa- credness of the manuscript book, see Curtius, *European Literature*, pp. 302–47. On the commercialization of the book, see Hepburn, *Author's Empty Purse*.

55. A copy of the small-paper version was sold at the 1930 Leeds auction at which many other books were sold that had probably be- longed to Congreve's library. The library had descended through the daughter of Henrietta Duchess of Marlborough and Congreve (Mary,

later Duchess of Leeds) into the Leeds family library. (See Hodges's introduction to Congreve's *Library*, pp. 5–9.) Thus, it is likely that the book stayed in Congreve's library, unless he gave it to the Duchess of Marlborough.

56. See Treadwell, "Congreve."

57. On the link between the decline of patronage and the heroism of the poet-celebrity, see Folkenflik, "Patronage."

58. For further discussion of portraits and frontispieces, see ch. 5.

59. Congreve to Joseph Keally, December 15, 1710, in Congreve, *Letters*, p. 61.

60. Congreve to Keally, October 9, 1708, in Congreve, *Letters*, p. 51.

61. See Doody, *Daring Muse*, pp. 19–22, for a discussion and reproductions of Francis Hayman and Charles Grignion's portrait illustrations to Pope's *Works* of 1751. For a full discussion of Pope's iconology, see Wimsatt, *Portraits*.

62. "A Letter to Mr. Congreve," in Gildon (ed.), *New Miscellany*, p. 299.

63. *Mourning Poets*, pp. 4–5.

64. As Coburn Freer writes: "After the Restoration, *poem* and *poet* seem to have undergone some subtle shifts in meaning, in the context of drama if no other. Toward the end of the seventeenth century, plays are described ever more consistently as *poems*, but the term now becomes inseparable from its narrower denotation of a logical and rhetorical structure" (*Poetics*, p. 50).

65. Dryden, *Works* (ed. Hooker and Swedenberg), vol. 17, p. 55.

66. Winstanley writes that Shakespeare "attained to an extraordinary height in all strains of Dramatick Poetry. . . . [He] had excursious [*sic*] into other kinds of Poetry" (*Lives*, p. 131).

67. Brian Corman writes about Congreve's response to the debate about genre in "Mixed Way of Comedy." Doody, in "Generic Self-Consciousness" (in *Daring Muse*, pp. 57–83), discusses the importance of poetic genre during the period. Raymond Williams, in *Keywords*, identifies some generic shifts that took place primarily in the eighteenth century by tracing the changing meanings of *art*, *fiction/novel*, *history*, *literature*. He notes a late-eighteenth-century usage, *dramatic fiction* (p. 134), which may have replaced the earlier *dramatic po-*

etry. McKeon discusses extensively the "destabilization of generic categories" in seventeenth-century prose fiction, identifying print as an important agent (in *Origins*, pp. 25–64).

Chapter Three

1. There is no comprehensive study of Congreve's relation to his predecessors, and few essays even touch on the subject. But see Waith, "Aristophanes"; and Ellehauge, *English Restoration*, pp. 185–310. I have gained much of my sense of the history of scholarship from Reynolds and Wilson, *Scribes and Scholars*; and Pfeiffer, *Classical Scholarship*. Although the absorption, interpretation, rejection, and acceptance of the classics during the period is under constant reevaluation, the specific relation of English "neoclassicism" and print during the period has been touched on only parenthetically. Relations on the Continent among print, classical revival, and scholarly comparison have been discussed more extensively. See especially Febvre and Martin, *Coming of the Book*, ch. 8, part 2; and Eisenstein, *Printing Press*, pp. 163–302. Some studies on the more general problem of late-seventeenth- and early-eighteenth-century neoclassicism are Weinbrot, *Augustus Caesar* and *Formal Strain*; Trickett, *Honest Muse*; Doody, "The New Augustans and the Roman Poets" (in *Daring Muse*, pp. 84–118); and Rothstein, "The Uses of the Past" (in *Restoration*, pp. 84–118).

2. Dryden had admired the learning of the twenty-three-year-old Congreve. See Congreve, *Letters*, p. 245. On Congreve's lecture attendance, see Hodges, *William Congreve*, p. 25.

3. The *Journal des Sçavans* and the Royal Society's *Philosophical Transactions* both began publication in 1665. Eisenstein (*Printing Press*, pp. 460–63) discusses the radical change that the printing of learned periodicals brought about.

4. For discussions of the "quarrel," see Jones, *Ancients and Moderns*, especially pp. 183–267; Baron, *"Querelle"*; and Levine, *Humanism and History*.

5. Levine, for instance, writes that the quarrel of the ancients and moderns "holds interest . . . for the . . . underlying agreement between the rivals, which was so much more extensive than they realized" (*Humanism and History*, p. 156). Dryden accepts as fully as any that the ancients are necessary to any conception of modernity. In

Restoration Mode, Miner notes that Dryden recognizes, in the poem to Congreve in particular, "that if there is to be something new, then the pastness of the past must be equally a reality" (p. 30).

6. See Curtius, *European Literature*, pp. 251–56.

7. Swift, *Prose*, vol. 1 (*Tale of a Tub*), p. 143.

8. Ibid., p. 139. Though the comic effect of the entire battle relies on the notion that both ancients and moderns are material books, the ancients are identified more with orality, the moderns with print. The strength of the ancients lies in their resolution and in the "Courage of certain Leaders and Allies," qualities that might be associated with virtues necessary to oral performance. The strength of the moderns lies in "the greatness of their Number," a quality more explicitly linked to the mass production of the press (ibid., p. 143).

9. Congreve, "Amendments of Mr. Collier's False and Imperfect Citations," in *Complete Works* (Summers ed.), vol. 3, p. 173.

10. Congreve, "A Discourse on the Pindarique Ode," in *Letters*, pp. 213–14.

11. Ibid., p. 216.

12. Congreve, *Complete Works* (Summers ed.), vol. 3, p. 1.

13. On the pastoral and georgic in England during the period, see Congleton, *Theories*, pp. 13–95; Chalker, *English Georgic*; and Low, *Georgic Revolution*. Low identifies the idealization of labor in the georgic (as opposed to the idealization of leisure in the pastoral) with the Protestant work ethic. On the idea of the golden age, see Levin, *Myth of the Golden Age*. For the relationship between such primitivism and important eighteenth-century notions of benevolence, see Whitney, *Primitivism*. Classical pastoral, of course, shows as much nostalgia for a pretechnological age as seventeenth-century pastoral does.

14. Both Eisenstein and McLuhan refer repeatedly to the links between historicism and print (the preservation of evidence and the possibility of comparing numerous sources). McLuhan, for instance, writes: "A historical 'point of view' is . . . closely related to typography, and flourishes where the unconscious effects of literacy flourish without countervailing cultural forces" (*Gutenberg*, p. 6). He acknowledges the "countervailing cultural forces," a reaction to typographical historicism resulting in romantic antihistoricism (which certain forms of ahistorical criticism have continued in the late twentieth century). But neither he nor Eisenstein discusses the peculiar linkage of scholarship and utopian ahistoricism inherent in neoclas-

sical pastoralism, a linkage that later would express itself in a fascination with the origin of language (during the eighteenth century) and in romantic philology and folklore.

15. Chalker, *English Georgic*, discusses the English use of the georgic as a means of measuring distances between the golden age and seventeenth- and eighteenth-century England.

16. Congreve, "Letter to Viscount Cobham" (1729; S: p. 178).

17. See Summers's notes to Congreve's translation of the "Hymn to Venus," in *Complete Works* (Summers ed.), vol. 4, p. 218.

18. Cited in Ong, *Orality and Literacy*, pp. 18–19.

19. John Hollander, in his suggestive essay on Echo, writes: "From the mid-seventeenth century on, the acoustical phenomenon itself, with or without the decorative application of the moralized nymph, inhabits a realm of figurative language as dense as any literal wood." Hollander notes that "by 1657, the poetic cliches about echo listed in Joshua Poole's *The English Parnassus* have 'pratling, twatling, babling, tearing, loud, resounding, shrill, vocal, heavy, cavy, talking, solitary, wood-haunting, wandering, roving, piercing' as epithets" (in *Figure of Echo*, p. 18n).

20. Ong's essay "Oral Residue in Tudor Prose Style" (in *Rhetoric*, pp. 23–47) offers the most complete summary of residual orality in Renaissance prose and is equally suggestive about the poetry of the period. I rely heavily in my discussion of Restoration print-culture poetics on Ong's identification of oral characteristics in the earlier period, many of which, naturally, have never quite disappeared from a "literary" language that pays homage to its predecessors.

21. On changing values in rhetoric, see Croll, *Style*; Williamson, *Senecan Amble*; and Howell, *Logic and Rhetoric*.

22. Although some argue that the term *baroque* is applicable only to visual style, many use the word as a term of literary or larger cultural description. See, for instance, Warnke, *Versions of Baroque*; and Maravall, *Culture of the Baroque*.

23. There is no need to go over ground so much explored in other contexts for Congreve and his contemporaries. To mention only a few studies: Van Voris, in *Cultivated Stance*, discusses design and rigid notions of order as a response to temporal decay; Trickett, in *Honest Muse*, suggests the ways in which the moderation of "honesty" replaces the abundant metaphorics of the Renaissance.

24. Congreve, "To Sir Godfrey Kneller" (S: p. 146).

25. Those studying the oral epics of Yugoslavia discovered that poets who were able to recite works as long as Homer's and who believed that they were repeating them verbatim each time actually varied the words, the formulae, the structures, and the ordering of events considerably. See Ong, *Orality and Literacy*, pp. 59–60.

26. Congreve, *Letters*, p. 214.

27. Again, Jonson is an awkward example for any historical argument that tries to distinguish the end of the century from the beginning because, particularly in his criticism, he both anticipated so much and served as such a strong model for playwrights between the Restoration and the turn of the century.

Chapter Four

1. Eisenstein does not discuss the late-seventeenth-century desire for the reassurance of finitude and thus may overstress the modernism of the moderns' exploration of the ancients. This exploration was, in her view, an attempt "to find out what had been done in order to surpass it—to go beyond the limits prior generations had set." She recognizes the sense of the advancement of learning in the early part of the century, the "cumulative cognitive advance which called into question traditional concepts pertaining to growth and decay" (*Printing Press*, p. 291). But she does not note the sense of defeat in the face of a cumulation that did not seem to increase human wisdom. This feeling was already strong by the end of the century and was emphatic throughout the eighteenth, as Paul Fussell recognizes when he links the "immoderate love of 'humane learning' " with both the belief that "most human 'problems' cannot be solved" and "grave doubts about the probability of any moral or qualitative 'progress,' " and identifies these notions as characteristic of his eighteenth-century Augustan humanists. See his definitions of "humanist" in *Augustan Humanism*, pp. 4–10.

2. Print perpetuated as much mystical and occult material as technological material, as Eisenstein shows (*Printing Press*, pp. 272–302). Frances Yates has explored this phenomenon in detail, especially in *Giordano Bruno* and *Rosicrucian Enlightenment*. But by the late seventeenth century, the interest in distinguishing the two had become widespread and made a strong impression even on nontechnological imaginative writings.

3. See, for instance, Lord, *Heroic Mockery*. Rather than attempt a

complete reevaluation of the mock-heroic, I will only briefly indicate the connection between the growth of scholarship and the growth of the mock-heroic.

4. Doody suggests that burlesque (and later parody) may be related to the experience of civil war and may also "have been in the seventeenth century an impulse to escape the Renaissance" (*Daring Muse*, p. 50).

5. Doody (*Daring Muse*, pp. 50–54) and Weinbrot (*Formal Strain*, pp. 13–14, 22–23) discuss parody and travesty of Virgil and others during the period. Weinbrot points to the importance of print to these burlesques, whose authors often printed the original text as footnotes and specially requested that their readers look at the footnotes: "Throughout the Restoration and well into the eighteenth century, comic parodists . . . use printed parallels to enhance the burlesque" (p. 26).

6. Lionel Gossman, in *Men and Masks*, notes an analogous alteration in class relations during the seventeenth century, when physical proximity (in the business world and coffeehouses) was decreasing the gap between people (especially would-be gentlemen and their models): "In the modern world, the imitator is increasingly the rival of his model, from whom he is separated by an ever narrowing margin" (p. 255).

7. Doody (*Daring Muse*) stresses the Augustan value for the sublime (see pp. 18–20, on Longinus). See also pp. 84–118, on the Augustan poets' association with the freedom, variety, energy, and wit they found in their models.

8. Congreve's Whig politics were unwavering, even during the brief period of Tory power from 1710 to 1714, when he felt he was seriously in danger of losing his post as commissioner for licensing wines. See Congreve, *Letters*, pp. 117–21.

9. The echoes of Milton (as well as of Virgil and Dryden) in the poem are many. It was nearly impossible to write a poem about creation in the last decades of the seventeenth century without responding in some way to Milton. This was especially true for Whig poets, who must have read the political implications of Milton's epic, his refusal to accept the divine authority of the human king, as a prefiguration of their own political claims and a justification of their own revolution.

10. Again, I do not wish to imply, as Williams (*Approach to Con-*

greve) might argue, that the Christian framework is the motivating force in the poem. Rather, it serves as structural metaphor, as important as, but no more important than, say, the Muse herself, the Book of Life, the collection of epics of origin that both inform the poem's structure and are enfolded within it. Like them, God is a topos.

11. See Marc Shell, *Money*, p. 180.

12. Shell writes: "The South Sea Bubble of 1720, including the increase in popular pamphleteering and the beginning of widespread political cartooning to which the Bubble first gave rise, first directed public discussion to paper money as 'the devil in specie' and a 'nothing' pretending to be 'something' " (ibid., p. 15).

13. He changed, for instance, "Tom-tell-troth" to "Truth" in the mad scene of *Love for Love*, because "the sound and meanness of the Expression displeas'd me." See "Amendments of Mr. Collier's False and Imperfect Citations," in Congreve, *Complete Works* (Summers ed.), vol. 3, p. 187.

14. Dryden, *Works of Virgil*. This is exactly the notion which many of the romantics, in their passion for an exotica veiled in obscurity, would challenge. Hölderlin, for instance, strove for utmost literalism in his Pindar as a way of maintaining the darkness of the lyric. Benjamin later elaborated on this value for keeping the strangeness in the strange in "The Task of the Translator" (*Illuminations*, pp. 69–82).

15. Cowley, *Poems*, vol. 1, p. 155.

16. Congreve addresses the Earl of Dorset and Middlesex here, having quoted from Pliny's panegyric to the Emperor Trajan. His self-consciousness may also be due to remaining pangs over the reception of *The Double-Dealer*, whose audience was not responsive to his full adherence to classical notions of form.

17. The increasingly persistent satire of pedantry throughout the seventeenth century leads directly toward the idealization of innocence of scholarship in Gray's "mute inglorious Milton" and toward anti-academic romanticism, although the tone shifts. "From the viewpoint of romantic critics of modern culture," writes Eisenstein, "the academic historian appears to be a bloodless desiccated creature in comparison with the Renaissance Man" (*Printing Press*, p. 301).

18. On satirists' interest in narratives of dynastic usurpation and disrupted inheritance, see Seidel, *Satiric Inheritance*. Harold Love, in

his very convincing chapter on *The Double-Dealer* in *Congreve*, identifies the struggle between dynastic usurpation and preservation as the central energy of the play.

19. Le Bossu's *Treatise on the Epic Poem* (1675); Rapin's *Reflections on Aristotle's Art of Poetry* (which Thomas Rymer translated in 1674); André Dacier's translation of Aristotle's *Art of Poetry* (1692). Congreve's library had all of these (items 61, 509, and 198, respectively).

20. Lady Froth's false syntax exposes a delicious double nonsense: Cynthia has no chance of "escap[ing] the Etymology"; Lady Froth is certainly not "derived from the *Greek*" (nor is her heroic-epic), although her descendants may be, through the line of baby Sappho Froth, the identity of whose father is questionable.

21. Congreve, *Letters*, p. 159. Congreve, however, had a number of nondramatic models, as his careful distinctions between romance and novel and his identification of the work as a novel suggest. On the impact of one form of prose fiction, see Stephenson, "Congreve's 'Incognita.' " On the novel's dramatic form, see Novak, "Congreve's 'Incognita.' "

22. On the influence of Raymond's *Itinerary* (item 518 in the library) on *Incognita*, see de Beer, "Congreve's Incognita." Congreve had never been beyond the British Isles when he wrote *Incognita*, and in later life he probably never went beyond Brussels and Amsterdam. See Congreve, *Letters*, pp. 14–17, 104–5.

23. Congreve, *Letters*, pp. 158–59.

24. McKeon, *Origins*, pp. 25–128, works out in great detail and with much subtlety the early novel's multifarious ways of dealing with "Questions of Truth," despite the threat of oversimplistic determinism in the title of his introduction: "Dialectical Method in Literary History." I am largely convinced by the terms he chooses to describe the movement of narrative epistemology during the period: "romance idealism," "naive empiricism," and "extreme skepticism." His identification of *Incognita* with "extreme skepticism," while the label may force Congreve into a false position, is illuminating.

25. Congreve, *Incognita* (Brett-Smith ed.), p. 43. Hereafter all citations will appear in the text.

26. For McKeon, Congreve's use of pseudohistorical authorial intrusions that interfere with the claims to historicism is part of his identification with "extreme skepticism": "So Congreve the grave recorder of events is unmasked as Congreve the creative articulator of

plots and counterplots, disguises and discoveries. The antiromance impulse is completed by its 'antihistorical' corollary movement, which effectively punctures both the claim to historicity and the pretense to verisimilitude" (*Origins*, p. 63).

27. Stanley Fish, in *Surprised by Sin*, suggests a similar pedagogic function in *Paradise Lost*, which teaches the reader to be wary of Satan's false but compellingly authoritative rhetoric, a rhetoric partly formed by the classical revival that print made possible and partly touched by the forms of classical oration that print spread.

28. As Davis notes, Pinto's stories in *Voyages and Adventures*, translated into English in 1663, were even more wildly fictitious than Mandeville's fourteenth-century stories of the "marvales of Inde." Congreve owned Pinto (item 463) and two editions of Mandeville's *Voiage and Travaile* (items 405k and 641).

29. In "Modernity," Habermas points out that a notion of the modern exists only in terms of a notion of the past: "The word 'modern' in its Latin form 'modernus' was used for the first time in the late 5th century in order to distinguish the present, which had become officially Christian, from the Roman and pagan past. With varying content, the term 'modern' again and again expresses the consciousness of an epoch that relates itself to the past of antiquity, in order to view itself as the result of a transition from the old to the new" (p. 3).

Chapter Five

1. See Spufford, *Small Books*, on the cheap woodcuts that decorated ballads and broadsides. Although there is no adequate history of seventeenth-century prints and illustrations, the most useful general works are Bland, *History of Book Illustration*; and Hammelmann and Boase, *Book Illustration in Eighteenth-Century England*, which suggests a great deal about the preceding decades.

2. Evelyn, *Sculptura*, p. 15.

3. On the way print brought a new spatiality, see Ong, *Ramus*, especially pp. 307–14. See also Ong, *Orality and Literacy*, pp. 117–29.

4. Pepys, for example, bought as many of the printed pictures of the court ladies as he could obtain, and in the 1690's such portraits continued to sell well, with William and Mary, the heroes of the rev-

olution, among the most popular. Congreve's library contained numerous books with such portraits, most of which were originally engraved as separate prints. The frontispiece portrait of Thomas Killigrew (in *Comedies and Tragedies*, item 332 in Congreve's library) exemplifies one style, with its relaxed posture and loosely draped background; the portrait of Sir Paul Rycaut (in Rycaut's translation of Garcilasso de la Vega's *Royal Commentaries of Peru*, item 500 in the library) exemplifies the other, with its tight-lipped rigidity and lack of ornament. The only collection of prints mentioned in the library catalog is John Smith's early-eighteenth-century mezzotints (item 375); Congreve's own portrait by Kneller was engraved by both Smith and John Faber Jr., sometime after 1709.

5. British Museum, Personal and Political Satire 1414. (Hereafter, all satires from this collection will be cited as BMS.) I am indebted to the detailed descriptive catalog, Stephens (ed.), *Political and Personal Satires*.

6. On the emblem book and its relation to seventeenth-century literature, see Freeman, *English Emblem Books*; Hagstrum, *Sister Arts*, pp. 94–100; and Praz, *Studies*.

7. See Bliss, *History of Wood-Engraving*, pp. 164–78; and Spufford, *Small Books*, for discussions of such ephemera. Most woodcut artisans, too impoverished to buy new materials, would pass down the same blocks from generation to generation. It is common to see an impression of the 1620's reappearing throughout the century, usually, of course, in different guises, or even to see the same block used for different purposes several times during the year. A single image, for instance, was used in 1685 for the Duchess of Portsmouth (BMS 1132), the Distressed Mother (BMS 1147), and a ballad entitled "The Fair Maid's Choice, Who Refus'd all for a Plowman" (BMS 1144), perhaps the latter two being an ironic comment on the duchess's personal life.

8. See Congreve, *Letters*, pp. 43, 178.

9. Horace writes, in Creech's translation,

> But now our *Nobles* too are Fops and Vain,
> Neglect the Sense, but love the Painted Scene;
> Four hours are spent in Show to please the sight,
> A tedious Battle, and at last a Flight.
>
> (Horace, *Odes*, pp. 534–35)

10. If it is a truism to point out that Congreve's plays, in other ways, reflect a lack of interest in the visual, it is worth noting that there is almost no color or scene painting in the verbal texts of the plays (with the exception of *The Mourning Bride*) and that in the comedies the similes nearly all refer to social situations and configurations, rather than to objects or visual scenes. Most of Congreve's visual images are drawn from books or plays: Bellmour says, "Methinks I am the very Picture of *Montufar* in the *Hypocrites*" (*OB*, IV.ii, p. 80); the "witch ridden in her own bridle" (*DD*, IV.i, p. 167) comes from Shadwell's *Lancashire Witches*; Juno's peacock's "Ogling Tail" and Argos's "hundred Eyes" (*LL*, IV.i, p. 290) come from Ovid; the "gull'd Bassa" creeping into bed (*DD*, III.i, p. 158) comes from Rycaut's *History of the Ottoman Empire*; and so on. Congreve, *Complete Plays* (Davis ed.), gives all the sources.

11. On the greater prestige of poetry, see Salerno, "Seventeenth-Century English Literature on Painting"; and Lipking, *Ordering of the Arts*, pp. 23–37.

12. For instance, Dryden draws a parallel between words in poetry and color in painting: in poetry, "the expression is that which charms the reader, and beautifies the design"; in painting, "colouring [is] *lena sororis*; in plain English, the bawd of her sister, the design or drawing: she clothes, she dresses her up, she paints her, she makes her appear more lovely than naturally she is, she procures for the design, and makes lovers for her" (*Of Dramatic Poesy* [ed. Watson], vol. 2, p. 203). Dryden's Kneller poem similarly associates painting with debauched femininity:

> Our Arts are Sisters; though not Twins in Birth:
> For Hymns were sung in *Edens* happy Earth,
> By the first Pair; while *Eve* was yet a Saint;
> Before she fell with Pride, and learn'd to paint.
> (*Works* [ed. Hooker and Swedenberg],
> vol. 4, p. 464)

13. See Lipking, *Ordering of the Arts*, pp. 23–37, and Hagstrum, *Sister Arts*, p. 130, on the new visual sophistication of the eighteenth century.

14. It is not in the least clear what constitutes more or less representational imitations. E. H. Gombrich's argument in *Art and Illusion*—that imitations imitate ideas in the mind, not the direct physical world, and that there is no such thing as more or less represen-

tational images, but only changing societies of viewers—has been much debated. Whether or not visual representations can be understood as more closely or less closely mimetic, the eighteenth century probably saw the average seventeenth-century printed image as a crude imitation.

15. Cowley, *Poems*, p. 450.

16. Hooke, *Micrographia* (introduction).

17. Ibid.

18. The connection between scientific history and literary naturalism has been much explored in different terms, most notably by Ian Watt in *Rise of the Novel*, especially pp. 9–34, and more subtly and in more detail by McKeon throughout *Origins of the English Novel*. Marjorie Hope Nicolson has written extensively on the relation between science and poetry in *Breaking of the Circle* and *Science and Imagination*.

19. Hooke, *Micrographia* (introduction).

20. Ibid.

21. In the late nineteenth century, with the growth of photography and its extreme literal imitation, exact reproduction was even further devalued (except by the socially conscious aesthetician), for its function had been entirely assumed by a machine. And although certain elements of abstract art in the twentieth century seem founded in scientific vision (light and color taken from context, form stripped of human association, sound purified of language), and although photo-realism has also attempted to reclaim a scientific literal mimesis, on the whole the modern arts have rejected scientific literalism for an abstracted version of the humane. But it is a version Congreve would not recognize.

22. Congreve, *Letters*, p. 181.

23. A story by Chikamatsu Monzaemon (1653–1724), reported by Hozumi Ikan in "Naniwa Miyage," shows a similar revulsion to an absolutely literal notion of naturalism in the East during the period. A lady-in-waiting fell passionately in love with a lord, whom she was unable to see. She had a wooden statue of him carved, but when she saw it, it was so perfectly identical to the man she loved that she felt an immediate revulsion both for the statue and for him. "For such reason," Chikamatsu said, "in any representation . . . along with exact resemblance of the shape there will be some deviance, and after all that is why people like it. It is the same for the design of a

play . . . and since this is after all the nature of art, it is what constitutes the pleasure people take in it."

24. Congreve, *Letters*, p. 181.

25. Ibid., pp. 180–81.

26. The two late-seventeenth-century quotations that Johnson's *Dictionary* gives to elucidate the primary meaning of the word *figure* ("the form of any thing as terminated by the outline") both emphasize the representational nature of the word and its abstraction of the physical: "Men find green clay that is soft as long as it is in the water, so that one may print on it all kind of *figures*, and give it what shape one pleases" (Robert Boyle); and *"Figures* are properly modifications of bodies; for pure space is not any where terminated, nor can be: whether there be or be not body in it, it is uniformly continued" (John Locke). For Congreve, the word is even more precisely identified with engravings, and the description "with Figures" is used in every entry for an illustrated book in his library catalog.

27. Congreve, *Letters*, p. 159.

Chapter Six

1. Congreve, *Letters*, p. 159.

2. Ong writes: "Words are made out of units (types) which pre-exist as units before the words which they will constitute. Print suggests that words are things far more than writing ever did" (*Orality and Literacy*, p. 118). George Steiner identifies the simultaneous materiality and immateriality of oral language when he writes: "It is knowledge older than Plato that language has both material and immaterial aspects, that there is a speech-system that is markedly physical and one that is not." He identifies the anatomical and neurophysiological functions involved in oral language as physical (material) and suggests that propositions (written or not) are immaterial in their instability and contingency. There "is a constant movement towards immateriality, a process of metamorphosis from the phonetic into the spiritual." The sense of dissolution brought about by the excesses of print might be seen as connected to the movement from the physicality of the phonetic to the immateriality of the spiritual (*After Babel*, pp. 124–28).

3. The *res et verba* problem and notions of linguistic instability during the period have been explored in great detail for both the seventeenth and early eighteenth centuries. For a traditional summary,

see Howell, *"Res et Verba."* Hans Aarsleff's *Study of Language* has much useful material on Locke. Foucault (*Order of Things,* especially pp. 78–124) discusses a more problematic breakdown of notions of representation: "From an extreme point of view, one might say that language in the Classical era does not exist. But that it functions; its whole existence is located in its representative role, is limited precisely to that role and finally exhausts it" (p. 79). Studies of the problem of Restoration "wit," a subdivision of the *res et verba* problem, continue to multiply. Fujimura's *Restoration Comedy* has called forth such responses as Alan Roper's "Language and Action"; Charles H. Hinnant's "Wit, Propriety, and Style"; and R. A. Foakes's "Wit and Convention."

4. Several have written on this notion of the writing of the self in the eighteenth-century novel, for instance in Timothy Reiss's "Crusoe Rights His Story" in his *Discourse of Modernism,* pp. 294–327. On the textual universe of Clarissa, see Castle's *Clarissa's Ciphers*; and Warner's *Reading Clarissa.* Richard Kroll's "Discourse and Power" points out the importance of the reflexivity in Sir Wilfull Witwoud's "I am Sir Wilfull Witwoud, so I write myself" (IV.i, p. 449).

5. These comments carry echoes of Locke's suggestion that at birth the mind is "white Paper, void of all Characters, without any Ideas" (*Essay,* p. 104 [book 2, ch. 1]).

6. I have found useful, here, Kroll's lecture "Hieroglyphs and the Aetiology of Language," which argues that the period confronted such anxiety with a pictorialist explanation of the origin of language, whereby the hieroglyph stood for the inalienable "thing" for which the semiological system of written language was still an approximation. Linguistic and religious skepticism were interestingly tied to each other during the period, especially through Epicureanism. (The Epicurean notion of a world made of distinct and randomly floating particles, analogous to Leibniz's monads, must have suggested to poetic imaginations the randomness of meaningless linguistic particles.) Some of the connections between religious skepticism and Epicureanism are touched on in the literature about Congreve's religious status. On Epicureanism and libertinism in the comedy, see Underwood, *Etherege,* pp. 41–45.

7. See especially Bacon's "Art of Elocution or Tradition" in *The Advancement of Learning* (1605; book 2), in *Works,* vol. 3, pp. 399–413; chs. 5 and 13 in Hobbes's *Human Nature* (1650), and chs. 4–7

in the *Leviathan* (1651); Arnauld's *Port-Royal Grammar* (1660) and *Port-Royal Logic* (1662); and Wilkins's *Essay towards a Real Character and a Philosophical Language* (1668).

8. On the history of this complaint, which goes back to Plato, see Barish, *Antitheatrical Prejudice*; and Fraser, *War Against Poetry*.

9. I do not take such characters as Bellmour and Careless to be exemplary for Congreve or even to convey versions of his own attitudes, but to reflect, in some degree, larger cultural concerns.

10. See Foucault, *Order of Things*, pp. 17–46; and Curtius, *European Literature*, pp. 302–47, for discussions of the Renaissance world as inscription.

11. The identification of the male desire for potency with the desire for linguistic fixity in the coinage "phallogocentrism" suggests a matrix of language, sex, and power that the late seventeenth century would have understood quite well.

12. Watt, *Rise of the Novel*, pp. 27–30, describes the way that disturbance over the representational nature of language encouraged certain kinds of efforts for a plain-style naturalism. Such "naturalism" led to the novel, he argues (making the dubious claim that "the function of language is much more largely referential in the novel than in other literary forms," p. 30). Although Derrida, in an antihistoricism typical of late-romantic rhetorical theory of the past two decades, allows the notion of "logocentrism" a historical nonspecificity, locating it in a floating and eternal matrix of the relation between the Word and power, it might be linked much more tangibly to this period's insistence on fixity as a source of power. Foucault suggests as much when he identifies 1657 as the year in which "natural history" is born by means of the recognition of the gap between words and things, and by means of the assertion of representation that takes place in that gap: "Natural history finds its locus in the gap that is now opened up between things and words. . . . Things and words, distinct from one another . . . communicate in a representation" (*Order of Things*, pp. 128–30). (One need not, of course, accept a precise year to accept the general historical argument.)

13. This longing for linguistic primitivism is transformed in the eighteenth and nineteenth centuries into a fascination with the origin of languages and historical etymology, and in the twentieth into the conjunction of developmental psychology and linguistics in the search for "pre- or extra-linguistic thought." On the search for a pure

language, see Steiner, *After Babel*, pp. 110–235, in which Steiner describes, among other things, his own search for a mother tongue.

14. Thomas Sprat, *History of the Royal Society*, p. 42. Quoted in Howell, *"Res et Verba,"* p. 140.

15. Although, in the thirteenth century, John of Garland made a word list that he called *Dictionarius*, the word *dictionary* in the sense we use it was not common until the late seventeenth century, with the publication of such dictionaries as César-Pierre Richelet's *Dictionnaire françois* (1680) and Antoine Furetière's *Dictionnaire universel* (1690), and later Nathan Bailey's *Universal Etymological English Dictionary* (1721). Numerous language dictionaries and several historical dictionaries were produced in the last decades of the seventeenth century.

16. Hobbes, *Leviathan*, pp. 21–22 (part 1, ch. 4).

17. Ibid., p. 22.

18. Locke, *The Conduct of the Understanding* (section 29), in *Locke Reader*, pp. 163–64. These ideas are more fully spelled out in book 3 of *An Essay Concerning Human Understanding*.

19. Butler, in "The Elephant in the Moon," accused the Royal Society of a policy exactly opposite to the one it claimed. The assembly:

> Resolved to give Truth no regard. . . .
> That 'twas more noble to create
> Things like Truth, out of strong conceit.
> (*Poetical Works*, vol. 2, p. 117)

Swift later satirized the desire for a pure language in which words equal things in his description of the Grand Academy of Lagado, where academicians communicate by carrying about sacks full of objects and holding up the things they wish to indicate.

20. Wycherley, *Country Wife*, p. 40 (II.i).

21. Ibid., p. 11 (I.i).

22. Ibid., p. 46 (II.i).

23. Etherege, *Man of Mode*, p. 127 (V.ii).

24. Ibid., p. 34 (II.i).

25. Collier, *Short View* (preface).

26. Etherege, *Man of Mode*, p. 135 (V.ii).

27. Wycherley, *Country Wife*, p. 10 (I.i).

28. Ibid., p. 49 (III.i).

29. Etherege, *Man of Mode*, p. 133 (V.ii).

30. Ibid., p. 94 (IV.i).

31. The relationship between *Le Misanthrope* and *The Plain Dealer* has been much discussed. Norman Holland, *First Modern Comedies*, p. 97, gives a concise survey of the discussion.

32. This distinction sets up the central dichotomy for Fujimura's discussion (*Restoration Comedy*) and becomes a focal point for discussions about wit in the comedies.

33. See, for instance, Fujimura, *Restoration Comedy*, pp. 165–96.

34. See Love, *Congreve*, pp. 39–59, for an interesting discussion of the connection between this modification of wit and such concerns as security for family dynasty against the threat of usurpation by the outsider.

35. For Henri Bergson, such flexible response and refusal of the mechanical are essential to refusing the role of comic dupe: "The attitudes, gestures, and movements of the human body are laughable exactly to the extent that this body makes us think of a simple mechanism" (Bergson, *Œuvres*, p. 401; my translation).

36. The recurrent debate about sentimentalism in the comedy of the 1690's is often confused by a failure to recognize the strong ties of sentimentalism to the empiricist valuation of the sensory and thus, in an odd alliance, to philosophical libertinism, which had its own sententious sentences. On sentimentalism, see, for instance, Parnell's "Sentimental Mask" and Leech's "Congreve and Century's End." On empiricism and libertinism, see Underwood, *Etherege*, p. 16.

37. Williams, *Approach to Congreve*, pp. 169–75, gives an interesting reading of this scene as Christian trial, in which Valentine's renunciation reaps him heavenly rewards.

38. The pleasure lies partly in our being led to expect one of Millamant's usual disjunctive disavowals. The simplicity of "I love him" and the way in which "violently" clashes with the lack of violence in the previous words come as a surprise. "Violently" is itself mimetic of the violent relief of laughter, that laughter which responds to the fact that our power has overcome danger, exactly the laughter this produces. This is closely akin to Hobbes's laughter, that "*sudden glory* arising from some sudden *conception* of some *eminency* in ourselves, by *comparison* with the *infirmity* of others, or with our own formerly" (*Human Nature*, in *English Works*, vol. 4, p. 46).

39. In Kroll's "Discourse and Power," he carefully delineates the

epistemological role of gesture for Congreve, emphasizing its importance as a form of discourse. I am not in fundamental disagreement
here with Kroll, but my stress is different. The importance of gesture
is self-evident in the theater; my purpose is rather to show the limitations, for Congreve, of an epistemology and semiotics of pure gesture in a world grown reliant, as a result of print, on written language
as a primary, not a supplementary, conveyor of meaning.

40. Congreve, *Letters*, p. 178. In 1706, too, Congreve wrote to
Joseph Keally of a "revolution" in the playhouses, which designed
"to have plays only at the Hay-Market, and operas only at Covent
Garden." He felt that the design was "right to restore acting," adding
that "the houses are misapplied, which time may change" (*Letters*,
p. 43).

41. See also the discussion of this in Holland, *Ornament*, p. 131.

42. The sense of the ever-present obscenity of the body is, of
course, important to late-seventeenth- and eighteenth-century literature as a whole, although it is often approached more with fascination than with revulsion. As Bernard Autriche puts it, commenting
on Marivaux, "There is something inherently obscene in the fact of
existence" ("Marivaux," p. 39; my translation). In *Dialogical Imagination*, Bakhtin connects the carnivalesque privileging of the lower
half of the body with the novel and novelistic narrative. But it belongs
much more directly to the theater, of which carnival and the Feast of
Fools are prototypes.

43. Congreve removed much of the "smut" from such passages for
the 1710 edition of his *Works*. Perhaps he was responding not only
to changing times but also to the sense that whereas such vulgar physical explicitness is appropriate to the incarnations of the stage it is
inappropriate to print and to the reading edition he intended the
Works to be.

44. The late seventeenth century would have understood well
Nietzsche's notion that only humans can be bestial, though the prob-
lem was more complicated than any simple definition would suggest.
On the "theriophily" of the sixteenth and seventeenth centuries, see
Miner, *Dryden's Poetry*, pp. 154–55.

45. Graham Greene shows an understanding of the preoccupation
in his choice of the title *Lord Rochester's Monkey* for his biography of
Rochester. Monkeys embody the period's physicality and interest in
mimesis; further, they capture the late-seventeenth-century sense of

the comic, with its touch of narcissism and self-hatred. Greene reproduces a portrait of Rochester (attributed to Jacob Huysmans), which shows Rochester crowning a monkey with a laurel wreath: both poets and monkeys are imitators of life. He also reproduces a 1681 portrait of Thomas Killigrew (p. 68), who, dressed in a jester's costume, sits beside a monkey whose posture is identical to Killigrew's, a portrait that suggests the period's identification of monkeys with the gestural nature of theatrical imitation.

46. Congreve, *Letters*, p. 178.

47. Peter Stallybrass and Allon White, in *Politics and Poetics*, pp. 84–100, remark on the way that Dryden's chastisement of unruly audiences was a way of cleansing the theater of the grotesque, even if Dryden himself made use of farce. In support of the idea that this cleansing process is tied to a growing notion that plays are better read and not seen, Stallybrass and White quote James Wright's *The Humours and Conversations of the Town* (1693): "Thô a Play be a generous Diversion, yet 'tis better to read than to see, unless one cou'd see it without these Inconveniences" (p. 93). Perhaps Congreve's move toward the text can be seen as a struggle against the "mortifying" recognition of his animal nature.

48. In his prologue to *Love for Love*, Congreve claimed that he was offering "Humour, which for chearful Friends we got," but plot "for the thinking Party" (p. 213). Many have suspected that, to satisfy an audience that could not appreciate the finer speeches and plot structure of *The Double Dealer*, Congreve played up the farcical nature both of the Sailor Ben scenes in *Love for Love* and of the Sir Wilfull Witwoud scenes in *The Way of the World* (in particular, the drunk scene in act 3, scene 1, in which Witwoud calls Petulant "as mute as a Fish" [p. 453], another association of farce with muteness).

49. Etherege, *Man of Mode*, pp. 55–57 (III.i).

50. Kroll, "Discourse and Power," pp. 733, 742–44, shows how blushing becomes an important form of signification in the play, and Lady Wishfort tries to re-create her past physical nature in her verbal delineations of her own supposed blushes.

51. This recalls Hooke's comment on print as an instrument that aids the fallible human memory, as the microscope aids the fallible human eye. Recognition of the body's vulnerability causes one to seek external assistance for that vulnerability, and that assistance increasingly comes in the form of the machine.

52. *Clarissa* offers the most obvious examples and the most dizzying plunges toward increasingly removed scenes. Much has been written on prose's appropriation of the theatrical. See, for instance, Kinkead-Weeks, *Samuel Richardson*; and Ketcham, *Transparent Designs*.

53. In "George Eliot," Doody notes the origin of the *style indirect libre* in the late-eighteenth-century novel.

54. See *London Stage*, vol. 4 (part 3, *1729–1747*), pp. cxx–cxxi; vol. 6 (part 4, *1747–1776*), pp. cxlv–clii; and vol. 9 (part 5, *1776–1800*), pp. lxvii–lxxii, lxxxi–lxxxviii.

55. Quoted in *London Stage*, vol. 2 (part 2, *1700–1729*), p. cix. For more on spectacle, see pp. cviii–cxi.

56. Quoted in *London Stage*, vol. 6 (part 4, *1747–1776*), p. cxiii.

57. The phrase itself is an interesting commentary on the alteration in the notion of the "live," just as our "televised live" means that the machines that convey the images to our machines had no further temporal intermediary.

Chapter Seven

1. See Curtius, *European Literature*, pp. 302–47, on "The Book as Symbol." Curtius traces the "metaphorics of the book" and offers many examples of the way in which the imagery of the Book of Nature expanded during the late Middle Ages and Renaissance. I am indebted to him for some of the examples that follow.

2. Ong writes: "Writing is often regarded at first as an instrument of secret and magic power. . . . Traces of this early attitude toward writing can still show etymologically: the Middle English 'grammarye' or grammar, referring to book-learning, came to mean occult or magical lore, and through one Scottish dialectical form has emerged in our present English vocabulary as 'glamor' (spell-casting power)" (*Orality and Literacy*, p. 93). Curtius shows how sacred-book and writing metaphors emerge from the sacred books of antiquity: "Here, thousands of years before our era, writing and the book have a sacred character, are in the hands of a priestly caste, and become the medium of religious ideas. . . . Writing itself is felt to be a mystery and the scribe is accorded particular dignity" (*European Literature*, p. 304). Curtius's examples of sacred-book metaphors grow particularly dense for the Renaissance, but he gives almost no examples after the mid-seventeenth century, despite the fact that he seems to date

the end of the book's sacred character to the late eighteenth century: "To be sure, many examples of writing imagery could be found in the succeeding centuries. But it no longer possesses a unique, a felt, a conscious 'life-relationship,' could no longer possess it after the Enlightenment shattered the authority of the book and the Technological Age changed all the relations of life" (p. 347).

3. If one contrasts Thomas Browne and Diderot, for example, it is easy to see the secularization and commercialization of the Book of Nature. Browne writes, "Thus there are two books from whence I collect my divinity. Besides that written one of God, another of his servant, nature, that universal and publick manuscript, that lies expansed unto the eyes of all" (*Religio Medici* [part I, section 16], in *Sir Thomas Browne's Works*, vol. 2, p. 341). Diderot writes: "[What is truly important] is not in the book printed at Marc-Michel Rey's or elsewhere; it is in the book of the world. . . . Listen to a blasphemy: La Bruyère, La Rochefoucauld are utterly common, flat books when compared with those who practice their tricks, subtleties, politics, profound arguments, during a single market day" (quoted in Curtius, *European Literature*, p. 324; my translation). The Book of Life, for Diderot, is no longer God's book, but that of human (public) interaction, and his notion of blasphemy itself has been secularized. Hobbes's sense, in 1651, that the state can no longer be the body natural but must become the body artificial might be connected to the shift from the natural book to the artificial book.

4. Quoted in Curtius, *European Literature*, p. 303.

5. Mincing later identifies the book as *"Messalinas's Poems"* (*WW*, V.i, p. 474), which, as Davis (Congreve, *Complete Plays*) and Bonamy Dobrée (Congreve, *Comedies*, p. 436) suggest, probably means "miscellany poems." Davis writes: *"The Collection of Miscellany Poems by Mr. Brown*, which had just appeared in 1699, would have spoiled the sacredness of any oath" (p. 474). The identification with Messalina, whose lust was immortalized in Dryden's *Juvenal*, serves the same function.

6. Satire of Puritan textualism can be seen most clearly in the names of Puritan characters in plays throughout the century, for instance in Congreve's own Spintext.

7. It is interesting to note that the decline of the topos is in part due to the general decline in oral effects. The whole notion of topoi is an oral one (although it was much used in writing), in that the topoi

provided speakers with ready subjects and tropes. The stress on the topoi in courses of rhetoric was much on the wane by the end of the seventeenth century, and the debasement of the world-as-book figure may be connected to this general devaluation of the commonplaces. See Ong, "Oral Residue," in his *Rhetoric*, pp. 35–38, 47, for the orality and later decline of the places.

8. Curtius, *European Literature*, p. 324, cites Jan Swammerdam (1637–80) and his investigations of the anatomy of insects with a microscope, which were published in 1737 under the title *Biblia Naturae*. Scientific investigation and Christianity, of course, were not in any way irreconcilable, and many scientists—for instance, Thomas Burnet, Robert Boyle, and Newton—still held to the older imagery of God's sacred book. But such imagery and the concomitant conception of an utterly mysterious nature were waning by the century's end.

9. Some of this is already explicit in Rabelais, or in Montaigne, who writes: "The hundredth commentator passes it on to his successor in a thornier and more crabbed state than that in which the first discovered it. . . . We do nothing but write comments on one another. The whole world is swarming with commentaries" ("On Experience" [book 3, ch. 13], in *Essays*, pp. 347–49).

10. Congreve's one use of the book as a metaphor for the divine is Osmyn's description in *The Mourning Bride* of his father's "pure Thoughts," which wafted to heaven and "There, in / The Book of Prescience, he beheld this Day" (III.i, p. 353). It is possible to find the metaphor later, although by the nineteenth century it is used infrequently.

11. The nature and art relation of the Renaissance and seventeenth century has been worked out in great detail, for instance by Tayler, *Nature and Art*. The role this relation plays in late-seventeenth-century drama has also been discussed extensively, for instance in Birdsall, *Wild Civility*; Norman Holland, *First Modern Comedies*, especially chs. 6 and 12; and such individual studies as Kreutz, "Who's Holding the Mirror?," pp. 79–88. I am most interested here not in summarizing the problem for Congreve, but in exploring the relation of the topos to print.

12. Montaigne, "To the Reader," in *Essays*, p. 25.

13. Jonson, "To the memory of my beloued, the AUTHOR Mr. William Shakespeare," *Ben Jonson*, vol. 8, p. 392.

14. Cowley, "The Muse," in *Poems*, p. 14.

15. Dryden, *Works* (ed. Hooker and Swedenberg), vol. 2, p. 59.

16. Eisenstein writes, "Self-Consciousness or a somewhat artificial effort at naturalness was one by-product of 'learning by reading.' An alertness to the fallacies of print-made abstractions was another" (*Printing Press*, p. 151).

17. This is the first definition given for the noun in Johnson's *Dictionary*.

18. Locke, *Essay*, p. 495 (book 3, ch. 10).

19. Congreve, *Letters*, p. 216.

20. Dedication to *The Way of the World*, p. 390. For Fielding, who would later appropriate Congreve's idea of affectation and identify it as the source of the true "ridiculous" (in the preface to *Joseph Andrews*), affectation went beyond wit. It extended once more, as it had before the 1690's, to a wide variety of behavioral and gestural expressions, which Fielding identified with Italian caricature and was able to describe in theatrical detail. Molière (Congreve's most obvious model), in his satire of the *précieuses* and the *femmes savantes* of seventeenth-century France, became as interested in satire of verbal pretension as he was in satire of religious and social pretension and of various kinds of ignorance (perhaps for some of the same reasons that encouraged Congreve's similar interest).

21. *The Old Batchelour*, it might be argued, is nearly as much a satire of Belinda's and Sir Joseph Wittoll's affectations as it is a warning for vulnerable old bachelors. *The Double-Dealer* stresses the relation between Maskwell's masked speech and the pedantry of Lady Froth and Brisk. In the context of Valentine's book-lined room, *Love for Love* uses the verbal affectations of Scandal and Tattle as mirrors for each other. *The Way of the World* investigates Witwoud's witty affectations and Petulant's laconicism, measuring Millamant's frivolity and Mirabell's sententiousness against the verbal attitudes of the "false wits."

22. Actors are themselves disguised, and the characters they play traditionally double that disguise. Disguise is Orestes' weapon, Pentheus's downfall. In the New Comedy, it is the gods' and mortals' principal vehicle of trickery. Shakespeare's Iago and Edmund work their evil through disguise. Hamlet, Rosalind, Portia, Edgar, Hermione, and Duke Vincentio try to reestablish harmony through disguise. Tartuffe's disguise nearly permits him to snatch up the fortunes

of a family. Philinte recognizes the necessity of disguise in a civilized world. In Shakespeare and Jonson (for instance, in *As You Like It* or *Volpone*), there is often a separation between the successful characters, who are masters at disguise, and the unsuccessful characters, who are less capable of disguise. This separation is even more strongly marked in the plays of the decades preceding Congreve. In Etherege's *Man of Mode*, Harriet never ceases to disguise her feelings, while Mrs. Loveit fails to disguise hers. In Behn's *The Rover*, Hellena is successful in her disguises, while Angellica Bianca, as a naked courtesan, is also naked in her feelings for Wilmore. In Wycherley's *Plain Dealer*, Fidelia's success lies partly in her ability to remain disguised as a boy, while Olivia's and Manly's shame lies in their repeated unmasking. In Otway's *Venice Preserved*, Jaffeir's final failure at disguise leads to the defeat of the plot and the final disaster.

23. The identification of theater and the mask hardly needs substantiation, considering the use of masks in theater from Greece to the present. It is interesting to note, however, that masks largely disappear on the eighteenth- and nineteenth-century stage, when prose fiction has most impact on the drama.

24. In *The Double-Dealer*, such words are particularly frequent: Mellefont "would have no room for serious design" (I.i, p. 129), but for Maskwell, "Opportunity, accomplish'd my Design" (I.i, p. 136). To Lady Touchwood, the flattery of Lady Plyant is "a trifling design," but Maskwell tells her that it will "gain us leasure to lay a stronger Plot" for which he "shall not want Contrivance" (II.i, p. 138), to mention just a few instances. In *Love for Love*, Mrs. Foresight interrupts Scandal's "Design" (III.i, p. 269) and asks Scandal, "You don't think, that you are ever like to succeed in your design upon me?" He, however, "will erect a Scheme" (III.i, p. 271). (The sexual connotations suggest a union between art and nature, between technical construction and the phallus.)

25. This is, of course, a cliché of the age. Pope, several decades later, would formulate the idea quite precisely, although his stress is more on nature, as it would be increasingly in the eighteenth century: "Those Rules of old *discover'd*, not *devis'd*, / Are *Nature* still, but *Nature Methodiz'd*" ("Essay on Criticism" [ll. 88–89], in *Poems*, vol. 1, p. 249).

26. During the seventeenth century, only the satiric part, before the episode of the lions, was imitated, and the satire was heightened.

But increasingly, after the mid-eighteenth century, heroism was recognized in Don Quixote, culminating in the Romantics' reappropriation of him as the melancholy dreamer and wanderer. See Tave, *Amiable Humorist*, p. 304; and Knowles, "Cervantes and English Literature."

27. Many other dramatic characters of the period—for instance, Molière's Bélise in *Les Femmes savantes* (1672), or Vanbrugh's Lady Fancyfull in *The Provoked Wife* (1697)—inherited the same delusions from the romance.

28. See Addison, *The Spectator*, vol. 3, pp. 535–82 (nos. 411–21, June 21–July 3, 1712). Oscar Wilde's "The Decay of Lying," which even more radically inverts the order in Vivian's argument that "Nature, no less than Life, is an imitation of Art," might also be seen as a culmination of this late-seventeenth-century vision (Wilde, *Complete Works*, vol. 5, p. 46).

29. Congreve, "A Hue and Cry after Fair Amoret" (S: p. 74).

30. Vanbrugh, *Provoked Wife*, p. 63 (III.iii).

31. This is partly a technique picked up from, among others, Jonson and Shakespeare, whose Edmund in *Lear* (II.ii), for instance, pretends to pretend not to have a letter from Edgar. But it appears more insistently during the period as a focus for the self-conscious artistry of human interaction. Congreve's Brisk, for example, deliberately cries aloud his "passion" for Lady Froth in her hearing and then pretends that he is hiding it: "My Lady *Froth*! Your Ladyships most humble Servant;—The matter Madam? Nothing, Madam, nothing at all I'gad. . . . (*Aside.*) I'll seem to conceal my Passion, and that will look like Respect" (*DD*, IV.i, p. 175). According to Scandal, "The Rogue will speak aloud in the posture of a Whisper; and deny a Woman's name, while he gives you the marks of her Person: He will forswear receiving a Letter from her, and at the same time, shew you her Hand upon the Superscription: And yet perhaps he has Counterfeited the Hand too; and sworn to a truth; but he hopes not to be believed" (*LL*, I.i, p. 226).

32. Congreve shows his interest in the problem, as worked out by his predecessors, by drawing on a number of earlier works: Terence's *Self-Tormentor*; *Othello*, in which Iago speaks the truth to cover his lies; *Tartuffe*; and Wycherley's *Plain Dealer*, in which Manly's plain dealing conceals his plan to conquer Olivia.

33. Lionel Trilling, in *Sincerity and Authenticity*, pp. 1–25, artic-

ulates the powerful connection between ideas of nature and of the self. In tracing the notion of sincerity, which is intimately tied to the idea of personal identity, Trilling identifies the seventeenth century as the era in which notions of the self were most radically transformed. See also Christopher Hill (*Century of Revolution*, p. 25), who identifies individualism and introspection even more closely with the post-Restoration period.

34. Book 2, ch. 27, of *An Essay Concerning Human Understanding* is Locke's central text on personal identity. The modern discussion, of course, originates with Descartes's foundation of knowledge in consciousness. For discussions of Puritan autobiography, see Delany, *British Autobiography*, pp. 88–104; and Weintraub, *Value of the Individual*, pp. 228–60.

35. Dryden, *Works* (ed. Hooker and Swedenberg), vol. 15, p. 254 (II.i).

36. Congreve's own defensiveness about the accusation of vanity is most insistent in his dedications to *The Double-Dealer*, *Love for Love*, and *The Way of the World*. For an even more insistent example of such defensiveness in a contemporary, see Cibber's *An Apology for the Life of Colley Cibber*.

37. Miner, *Restoration Mode*, pp. 3–128, discusses the largely public nature of Restoration poetry, in contrast to the more private metaphysical mode. The earlier modes, however, seem to have less a self-consciousness about public and private than voices appropriate to each sphere. Despite Horace's traditional dichotomy between town and country, a heightened consciousness of public and private in literature may be partly attributable to print, which provides two opposing impulses: the possibility of a larger and more indefinite public, and thus of an abstract entity called "the public"; and increasing claims for the solitude congenial to writers who write and readers who read in private. The idea of a private mode is necessarily dependent on the idea of a "public" mode. Erich Auerbach, in "La Cour et la Ville," in *Scenes from the Drama of European Literature*, describes the growth of a "public" in late-seventeenth-century France. Richard Sennett, in *Fall of Public Man*, p. 16, identifies the birth of the modern opposition between public and private with the end of the seventeenth century and describes the reciprocity of the modes throughout the eighteenth century and the eventual decline of the public.

38. Locke wrote: "I find, that there is so close a connexion between

Ideas and Words; and our abstract *Ideas*, and general Words, have so constant a relation one to another, that it is impossible to speak clearly and distinctly of our Knowledge, which all consists in Propositions, without considering, first, the Nature, Use, and Signification of Language" (*Essay*, p. 401 [book 2, ch. 33]).

39. The central texts are the *Leviathan*, *An Essay Concerning Human Understanding*, and *Two Treatises of Government*.

40. Much has been written on the impact of Locke on literature, particularly in the eighteenth century. See, for instance, MacLean, *John Locke*; and Tuveson, "Locke and Sterne" and *Imagination as a Means of Grace*.

41. Locke, *Essay*, p. 335 (book 2, ch. 27).

42. I take the phrase from Peter Berger and Thomas Luckman's *Social Construction of Reality*. Berger and Luckman note the way in which the accumulation of knowledge in a society leads to specialization, and thus to new forms of the old institutionalized and "objective" social agreements that constitute reality (pp. 72–74).

43. "By its very nature," writes Eisenstein, "a reading public was not only more dispersed; it was also more atomistic and individualistic than a hearing one" (*Printing Press*, p. 132). This solitary reading had an impact on a wide range of eighteenth-century changes, from the idea of private and appropriately designated rooms in the bourgeois home, to romantic ideals of individualism and solitude, to the more careful delineation of ideas of public and private, ideas that were to result in the idea of the "public" and the founding of more public institutions (museums and libraries) and that are connected to revolutionary notions of individual liberty and the public good. Many of these issues are suggested in Eisenstein's exploratory article "Some Conjectures." On the relations among the partitioning of the household, the increasingly private experience of the theater, and notions of the self, see Tuan, *Segmented Worlds*.

44. Both Drury Lane and Covent Garden were greatly enlarged in the last two decades of the eighteenth century. Each theater held about twenty-five hundred spectators; the opera house held about three thousand. See *London Stage*, vol. 9 (part 5, *1776–1800*), p. xliii.

45. Jonathan Culler, in "Apostrophe," suggests an analogous phenomenon, the apostrophizing poet's attempt to reclaim a nature made of sentient forces.

46. The first instances of the words *incognito* or *incognita* given by

the *OED* are from the mid-seventeenth century, just after Descartes's exploration of the cogito in the *Meditations* (1641).

47. On the growth of "character roundness" and introspection in the early-eighteenth-century novel, see Watt, *Rise of the Novel*, p. 75. See also Scholes and Kellogg, *Nature of Narrative*, pp. 170–79, on distinctions between dramatic and novelistic presentations of the "inward life." On the essential necessity of literacy for the "round character," see Ong, *Orality and Literacy*, p. 152. See my discussion of Shakespeare and the problem of character in the notes to ch. 1.

48. On the relations of gardens to literature, see Malins, *English Landscaping*.

49. Congreve's literal masks in *Incognita* can be seen as analogous, for instance, to Fielding's metaphoric masks in his novels. Despite strong ties to the literate, Congreve is in this respect still attached to the masked theater, but by midcentury, the literal mask disappears.

50. The mask is similar to language in this sense, and the pleasure of the theater is akin to the "pleasure of the text" in that the gaps in the mask both show and conceal what we desire. (Barthes has expressed the idea most gracefully in *The Pleasure of the Text*, especially in "Edges," pp. 8–10.)

51. This self-consciousness during the period is akin to the fascination with bodily function and the similar fascination with controlling it, in such writers as Rochester, Wycherley, and Swift. In the twentieth century, ritualized masked productions such as Artaud's "theater of cruelty" suggest the desire to reproduce the tensions of an age in which the effects of cataclysm were still felt: "A public that shudders at train wrecks, that is familiar with earthquakes, plagues, revolutions, wars . . . can be affected by all these grand notions and asks only to become aware of them," wrote Artaud (*Theater and Its Double*, p. 75). He suggests elsewhere that mechanization, which has blunted response, is partly the cause of the horrors of the twentieth century and that the theater can change this by invoking again the power of its physicality through the mask.

52. "*Nature* and *Homer* were, he found, the *same*" (Pope, "Essay on Criticism" [l. 135], in *Poems*, vol. 1, p. 255).

53. Compare, for example, Pope's "Shut, shut the door, good *John*! fatigu'd I said" in the "Epistle to Arbuthnot" (*Poems*, vol. 4, p. 96 [l. 1]) with Wordsworth's "Now laugh and be gay, to the woods away! / And there, my babe, we'll live for aye" in "Her Eyes Are

Wild" (*Poetical Works*, p. 115). See "Pope," Auden's wonderful discussion that perfectly captures Pope's directness and subtly suggests Wordsworth's indirection.

54. Steele, *Conscious Lovers*, pp. 5–6.

55. See Meisel, *Shaw*, p. 435.

Conclusion

1. Congreve to Joseph Keally, July 2, 1700, in Congreve, *Letters*, p. 12.

2. Hazlitt, *View of the English Stage*, pp. 156–57.

References

Bibliographical Note

There are extensive bibliographies of historical work on printing and publishing, as well as bibliographies of theoretical work on orality, literacy, and print. I would like to mention here only a few of the works that have been most important in fortifying the historical and theoretical orientation of my study. I give specific citations wherever possible but have relied heavily on the following in my compilation of general information about publishing history: the Term Catalogues; *Stationers' Register*; Henry R. Plomer's *A Dictionary of Printers and Booksellers, 1668–1725*; Donald Wing's *Short Title Catalogue, 1641–1700*; the *Eighteenth-Century Short-Title Catalogue*; and D. F. McKenzie's "The British Book Trade, 1641–1714: A Chronology and Calendar of Documents." John Dunton's *The Life and Errors of John Dunton* and Joseph Moxon's *Mechanick Exercises On the Whole Art of Printing* are, for me, essential early sources. The principal general histories of the book trade are Frank Arthur Mumby, *Publishing and Bookselling. Part One: From the Earliest Times to 1870*; Marjorie Plant, *The English Book Trade: An Economic History of the Making and Sale of Books*; Cyprian Blagden, *The Stationers' Company: A History, 1403–1959*; and S. H. Steinberg, *Five Hundred Years of Printing*.

Much attention has been given in recent years to the revolutions that print caused in consciousness. Lucien Febvre and Henri-Jean Martin's *L'Apparition du livre*, Marshall McLuhan's *The Gutenberg Galaxy: The Making of Typographic Man*, and Elizabeth Eisenstein's *The Printing Press as an Agent of Change: Communications and Cultural Trans-*

formations in Early-Modern Europe are symptomatic of this attention. I am much indebted to them, and to Eisenstein in particular, for the formulation of many of the problems with which I deal. McLuhan's essay, which historians like Eisenstein have proven wrong in many details, has been very suggestive; the other two studies focus primarily on the initial spread of Continental printing (both concentrate heavily on the Continent in the sixteenth century). Work on print's impact on consciousness has relied heavily on studies of orality and literacy, which are numerous. The best and clearest compilation is Walter J. Ong's *Orality and Literacy: The Technologizing of the Word*, which summarizes much of the work in the following important studies (just a few of many): Milman Parry, *The Making of Homeric Verse*; Albert B. Lord, *The Singer of Tales*; and Eric A. Havelock, *Preface to Plato, The Literate Revolution in Greece and Its Cultural Consequences*, and *The Muse Learns to Write: Reflections on Orality and Literacy from Antiquity to the Present*.

Numerous less-comprehensive but equally important studies touch on Continental printing. Among the most important are Natalie Zemon Davis's "Printing and the People," "The Protestant Printing Workers of Lyons in 1551," and "Publisher Guillaume Rouillé, Businessman and Humanist"; and Robert Darnton's "The Grub Street Style of Revolution," "Reading, Writing, and Publishing in Eighteenth Century France," and *The Business of Enlightenment: A Publishing History of the Encyclopédie, 1775–1800*.

Somewhat less attention has been paid to English publishing and print culture, but there is a good deal of material, bibliographically oriented work in particular, on the eighteenth century (when English printing finally achieves some of the quality of Continental), for instance: John Feather, *The Provincial Book Trade in Eighteenth-Century England*; "The Printed Word in the Eighteenth Century," a special issue of Raymond Birn, ed., *Eighteenth-Century Studies*; several of the essays in Isabel Rivers, ed., *Books and Their Readers in Eighteenth-Century England*; Alvin B. Kernan, *Printing Technology, Letters and Samuel Johnson*; David Foxon, "Pope and the Early Eighteenth-Century Book Trade"; and in particular Terry Belanger, "Publishers and Writers in Eighteenth-Century England." Very little attention (even of a straightforward historical nature), however, has been given to print in England between 1660 and 1700. There is some historical material, for instance James Sutherland's *The Restoration Newspaper and Its*

Development, subchapters in the general histories (which reproduce each other), and biographies of individual publishers. The only works that deal with the relationship between publishing and literature during the period are D. F. McKenzie's "The London Book Trade in the Later Seventeenth Century," on which I rely heavily; and Richard W. F. Kroll's "Mise-en-Page, Biblical Criticism and Inference During the Restoration." In "The Sociology of a Text," McKenzie suggests that a greater effort might be made to join the work of bibliography, literary criticism, cultural studies, and what the French would call "sociologie du livre." Such studies as those of Eisenstein, Kernan, Kroll, and McKenzie succeed admirably here, and I have tried in my own work to achieve something of this fusion.

Works Cited

Aarsleff, Hans. *The Study of Language in England, 1780–1860.* Princeton, N.J.: Princeton University Press, 1967.

Adams, Hazard. *Critical Theory Since Plato.* New York: Harcourt Brace Jovanovich, 1971.

Addison, Joseph. *The Spectator.* Ed. Donald F. Bond. Vol. 3. Oxford: Clarendon Press, 1965.

Altick, Richard D. *The English Common Reader: A Social History of the Mass Reading Public 1800–1900.* Chicago: University of Chicago Press, 1957.

Artaud, Antonin. *The Theater and Its Double.* Trans. Mary Caroline Richards. New York: Grove, 1958.

Auden, W. H. "Pope." In *From Anne to Victoria.* Ed. Bonamy Dobrée. London: Cassell and Co., 1937. Pp. 89–107.

Auerbach, Erich. *Scenes from the Drama of European Literature.* Trans. Ralph Manheim. Minneapolis: University of Minnesota Press, 1984.

Autriche, Bernard. "Marivaux et l'idée de la profondeur." *French Studies*, 7 (1984): 37–56.

Bacon, Francis. *The Works of Francis Bacon.* Ed. James Spedding, Robert Leslie Ellis, and Douglas Denon Heath. 14 vols. London: Longman and Co. et al., 1857–74.

Bakhtin, Mikhail. *The Dialogical Imagination.* Austin: University of Texas Press, 1983.

———. *Rabelais and His World.* Trans. Hélène Iswolsky. Bloomington: Indiana University Press, 1984.

Barish, Jonas. *The Antitheatrical Prejudice*. Berkeley: University of California Press, 1981.

Baron, Hans. "The *Querelle* of the Ancients and Moderns as a Problem for Renaissance Scholarship." *Journal of the History of Ideas*, 20 (Jan. 1959): 3–22.

Barthes, Roland. *Michelet*. Trans. Richard Howard. New York: Hill and Wang, 1987.

———. *The Pleasure of the Text*. Trans. Richard Miller. New York: Hill and Wang, 1975.

Bayley, John. *Shakespeare and Tragedy*. London: Routledge and Kegan Paul, 1981.

Belanger, Terry. "Publishers and Writers in Eighteenth-Century England." In *Books and Their Readers in Eighteenth-Century England*. Ed. Isabel Rivers. Leicester: Leicester University Press, 1982. Pp. 5–25.

Benjamin, Walter. *Illuminations*. Ed. Hannah Arendt. Trans. Harry Zohn. London: Jonathan Cape, 1968.

Berger, Peter L., and Thomas Luckman. *The Social Construction of Reality*. Garden City, N.Y.: Doubleday, 1966.

Bergson, Henri. *Œuvres*. Ed. André Robinet. Paris: Presses Universitaires de France, 1970.

Birdsall, Virginia Ogden. *Wild Civility: The English Comic Spirit on the Restoration Stage*. Bloomington: Indiana University Press, 1970.

Birn, Raymond, ed. *Eighteenth-Century Studies* (special issue: "The Printed Word in the Eighteenth Century"), vol. 17, no. 4 (Summer 1984).

Blagden, Cyprian. *The Stationers' Company: A History, 1403–1959*. London: George Allen & Unwin, 1960.

Bland, David. *A History of Book Illustration*. London: Faber and Faber, 1958.

Blayney, Peter. "Shakespeare's Fight With *What* Pirates?" Typescript. 1987.

Bliss, Douglas Percy. *A History of Wood-Engraving*. London: J. M. Dent & Sons, 1928.

Bradley, A. C. *Shakespearean Tragedy*. London: Macmillan, 1904.

Bronson, Bertrand. *Facets of the Enlightenment*. Berkeley: University of California Press, 1968.

Browne, Sir Thomas. *Sir Thomas Browne's Works.* Ed. Simon Wilkin. 3 vols. London: William Pickering, 1836.

Buckingham, George Villiers, Duke of. *The Rehearsal.* London: Thomas Dring, 1672.

Butler, Samuel. *The Poetical Works of Samuel Butler.* Ed. George Gilfillan. Edinburgh: James Nichol, 1854.

Carew, Thomas. *The Poems of Thomas Carew.* Ed. Rhodes Dunlap. Oxford: Clarendon Press, 1949.

Castle, Terry. *Clarissa's Ciphers.* Ithaca, N.Y.: Cornell University Press, 1982.

Chalker, John. *The English Georgic: A Study in the Development of a Form.* Baltimore: The Johns Hopkins University Press, 1969.

Chikamatsu Monzaemon. Story reported by Hozumi Ikan. In "Naniwa Miyage," pt. 1. Trans. Earl Miner. Typescript, n.d.

Cibber, Colley. *An Apology for the Life of Colley Cibber.* London: printed for the author, 1740.

Collier, Jeremy. *A Short View of the Immorality and Profaneness of the English Stage, Together with the Sense of Antiquity upon this Argument.* London: S. Keble, R. Sare, and H. Hindmarsh, 1698.

Congleton, J. E. *Theories of Pastoral Poetry in England, 1684–1798.* Gainesville: University of Florida Press, 1952.

Congreve, William. *The Birth of the Muse.* London: Jacob Tonson, 1697.

———. *Comedies.* Ed. Bonamy Dobrée. London: Oxford University Press, 1925.

———. *The Complete Plays of William Congreve.* Ed. Herbert Davis. Chicago: University of Chicago Press, 1967.

———. *The Complete Works of William Congreve.* Ed. Montague Summers. 4 vols. London: Nonesuch Press, 1923.

———. *The Double-Dealer.* London: Jacob Tonson, 1694.

———. *Five Plays written by Mr. Congreve.* London: Henry Hills, 1710.

———. *Incognita: Or Love and Duty Reconcil'd. A Novel.* London: Peter Buck, 1692.

———. *Incognita or Love and Duty Reconcil'd.* Ed. H. F. B. Brett-Smith. Oxford: Basil Blackwell, 1922.

———. *Letters and Documents.* Ed. John C. Hodges. London: Macmillan & Co., 1964.

———. *The Library of William Congreve*. Ed. John C. Hodges. New York: New York Public Library, 1955.

———. *Love for Love*. London: Jacob Tonson, 1695.

———. *The Mourning Bride*. London: Jacob Tonson, 1697.

———. *The Old Batchelour*. London: Peter Buck, 1693.

———. *Tears of Amaryllis for Amyntas*. London: Jacob Tonson, 1703.

———. *The Way of the World*. London: Jacob Tonson, 1700.

———. *The Works of Mr. William Congreve*. 3 vols. London: Jacob Tonson, 1710.

Corman, Brian. "'The Mixed Way of Comedy': Congreve's *The Double-Dealer*." *Modern Philology*, vol. 71, no. 4 (May 1974): 356–65.

Cowley, Abraham. *Poems*. Ed. A. R. Waller. Cambridge: The University Press, 1905.

Cressy, David. *Literacy and the Social Order: Reading and Writing in Tudor and Stuart England*. Cambridge: Cambridge University Press, 1980.

Croll, Morris W. *Style, Rhetoric, and Rhythm*. Ed. J. Max Patrick and Robert O. Evans with John M. Wallace and R. J. Schoeck. Princeton, N.J.: Princeton University Press, 1966.

Culler, Jonathan. "Apostrophe." *Diacritics* (Winter 1977): 59–69.

Curtius, Ernst Robert. *European Literature and the Latin Middle Ages*. Trans. Willard Trask. Princeton, N.J.: Princeton University Press, 1973.

Daiches, David. "Presenting Shakespeare." In *Essays in the History of Publishing in Celebration of the 250th Anniversary of the House of Longman, 1724–1974*. Ed. Asa Briggs. London: Longman Group, 1974. Pp. 61–112.

Darnton, Robert. *The Business of Enlightenment: A Publishing History of the Encyclopédie, 1775–1800*. Cambridge: Belknap Press, 1979.

———. "The Grub Street Style of Revolution." *Journal of Modern History*, 40 (1968): 301–27.

———. "Reading, Writing, and Publishing in Eighteenth Century France." *Daedalus*, 100, no. 1 (1971): 214–56.

Davis, Natalie Zemon. "Printing and the People." In *Society and Culture in Early Modern France: Eight Essays*. Stanford, Calif.: Stanford University Press, 1975. Pp. 189–226.

———. "The Protestant Printing Workers of Lyons in 1551." In *As-*

pects de la propagande religieuse. Ed. Henri Meylan. Geneva: E. Droz, 1957. Pp. 247–57.

———. "Publisher Guillaume Rouillé, Businessman and Humanist." In *Editing Sixteenth-Century Texts*. Ed. R. J. Schoeck. Toronto: University of Toronto Press, 1966. Pp. 72–112.

De Beer, E. S. "Congreve's Incognita: The Source of Its Setting with a Note on Wilson's *Belphegor*." *Review of English Studies*, 8 (1932): 74–77.

Delany, Paul. *British Autobiography in the Seventeenth Century*. New York: Columbia University Press, 1969.

De Ricci, Seymour. *English Collectors of Books and Manuscripts (1530–1930) and Their Marks of Ownership*. New York: Burt Franklin, 1930.

Doody, Margaret Anne. *The Daring Muse: Augustan Poetry Reconsidered*. Cambridge: Cambridge University Press, 1985.

———. "George Eliot and the Eighteenth-Century Novel." *Nineteenth-Century Fiction*, vol. 35, no. 3 (Dec. 1980): 260–91.

Downes, John. *Roscius Anglicanus*. Ed. Judith Milhous and Robert D. Hume. London: The Society for Theatre Research, 1987.

Dryden, John. *The Dramatick Works of John Dryden, Esq; in Six Volumes*. London: Jacob Tonson, 1717.

———. *Of Dramatic Poesy and Other Critical Essays*. Ed. George Watson. 2 vols. London: J. M. Dent, 1962.

———. *The Works of John Dryden*. Ed. Edward N. Hooker and H. T. Swedenberg Jr. Berkeley: University of California Press, 1956–.

———, ed. *Examen Poeticum*. London: Jacob Tonson, 1693.

———, trans. *The Works of Virgil*. London: Jacob Tonson, 1697.

Dryden, John, et al., trans. *The Satires of Decimus Junius Juvenalis . . . Together with the Satires of Aulus Persius Flaccus*. London: Jacob Tonson, 1693.

Dunton, John. *The Life and Errors of John Dunton*. London: S. Mathus, 1705.

Eaves, T. C. Duncan, and Ben D. Kimpel. "The Text of Congreve's *Love for Love*." *The Library*, vol. 30, no. 4 (Dec. 1975): 334–36.

Eighteenth-Century Short-Title Catalogue. Microfilm. British Library (in progress).

Eisenstein, Elizabeth. *The Printing Press as an Agent of Change: Communications and Cultural Transformations in Early-Modern Europe*. 2 vols. Cambridge: Cambridge University Press, 1979.

————. "Some Conjectures about the Impact of Printing on Western Society and Thought: A Preliminary Report." *The Journal of Modern History*, vol. 4, no. 1 (Mar. 1968): 1–56.

Ellehauge, Martin. *English Restoration Drama: Its Relation to Past English and Past and Contemporary French Drama*. Folcroft, Pa.: Folcroft Press, 1970.

Emerson, Oliver Farrar. "John Dryden and a British Academy." *Proceedings of the British Academy*, 10 (1921): 45–58.

Etherege, George. *The Man of Mode*. Ed. W. B. Carnochan. Lincoln: University of Nebraska Press, 1965.

Evelyn, John. *Diary and Correspondence of John Evelyn, F.R.S.* Ed. William Bray. London: George Routledge & Sons, 1906.

————. *Sculptura*. London: G. Beedle, T. Collins, and J. Crook, 1662.

Feather, John. *The Provincial Book Trade in Eighteenth-Century England*. Cambridge: Cambridge University Press, 1985.

Febvre, Lucien, and Henri-Jean Martin. *L'Apparition du livre*. Paris: Albin Michel, 1958. Trans. as *The Coming of the Book: The Impact of Printing, 1450–1800*. Ed. Geoffrey Nowell-Smith and David Wootton. Trans. David Gerard. London: NLB, 1976.

The Female Wits: or, the Triumvirate of Poets at Rehearsal. London, 1704.

Fish, Stanley. *Surprised by Sin*. London: Macmillan, 1967.

Foakes, R. A. "Wit and Convention in Congreve's Comedies." In *William Congreve*. Ed. Brian Morris. London: Benn, 1972.

Folkenflik, Robert. "Patronage and the Poet-Hero." *Huntington Library Quarterly*, vol. 28, no. 4 (Autumn 1985): 363–77.

Foucault, Michel. *The Order of Things*. London: Tavistock Publications, 1970.

Foxon, David. "Pope and the Early Eighteenth-Century Book Trade." Typescript. British Library, 1975.

Fraser, Russell. *The War Against Poetry*. Princeton, N.J.: Princeton University Press, 1970.

Freeman, Rosemary. *English Emblem Books*. London: Chatto and Windus, 1948.

Freer, Coburn. *The Poetics of Jacobean Drama*. Baltimore: Johns Hopkins University Press, 1981.

Fujimura, Thomas H. *The Restoration Comedy of Wit*. Princeton, N.J.: Princeton University Press, 1952.

Fussell, Paul. *The Rhetorical World of Augustan Humanism*. Oxford: Clarendon Press, 1965.

Gethin, Lady Grace. *Misery Virtues Whet-stone. Reliquiae Gethinianae*. London: D. Edwards for the author, 1699.

Gildon, Charles, ed. *Miscellany Poems Upon Several Occasions*. London: Peter Buck, 1692.

——. *A New Miscellany of Original Poems*. London: Peter Buck and George Strahan, 1701.

Goldman, Michael. *Acting and Action in Shakespearean Tragedy*. Princeton, N.J.: Princeton University Press, 1985.

Gombrich, E. H. *Art and Illusion*. Princeton, N.J.: Princeton University Press, 1960.

Gossman, Lionel. *Men and Masks*. Baltimore: The Johns Hopkins University Press, 1963.

Granville, George. *Heroick Love*. London: F. Saunders, H. Playford, and B. Tooke, 1698.

Greene, Graham. *Lord Rochester's Monkey*. New York: Viking, 1974.

Habermas, Jürgen. "Modernity—An Incomplete Project." In *The Anti-Aesthetic: Essays on Postmodern Culture*. Ed. Hal Foster. Port Townsend, Wash.: Bay Press, 1983.

Hagstrum, Jean H. *The Sister Arts*. Chicago: University of Chicago Press, 1958.

Hammelmann, Hanns, and T. S. R. Boase. *Book Illustration in Eighteenth-Century England*. New Haven, Conn.: Yale University Press, 1975.

Harris, Michael. "Moses Pitt and Insolvency in the London Booktrade in the Late-Seventeenth Century." In *Economics of the British Booktrade, 1605–1939*. Ed. Michael Harris and Robin Myers. Cambridge: Chadwyck-Healey, 1985. Pp. 176–208.

Havelock, Eric A. *The Literate Revolution in Greece and Its Cultural Consequences*. Princeton, N.J.: Princeton University Press, 1982.

——. *The Muse Learns to Write: Reflections on Orality and Literacy from Antiquity to the Present*. New Haven, Conn.: Yale University Press, 1986.

——. "The Oral Composition of Greek Drama." In *The Literate Revolution in Greece and Its Cultural Consequences*. Princeton, N.J.: Princeton University Press, 1982. Pp. 261–313.

——. *Preface to Plato*. Cambridge: Belknap Press, 1963.

Hazlitt, William. *A View of the English Stage*. Oxford: Oxford University Press, n.d.

Hepburn, James. *The Author's Empty Purse and the Rise of the Literary Agent*. London: Oxford University Press, 1968.

Hill, Christopher. *The Century of Revolution*. New York: Norton, 1961.

Hills, Henry Sr. Last Will and Testament. P.C.C., 6 Dyke, PROB 11, 398, P.R.O., Chancery Lane.

Hinnant, Charles H. "Wit, Propriety, and Style in *The Way of the World*." *Studies in English Literature*, 17 (1977): 373–86.

Hobbes, Thomas. *The English Works of Thomas Hobbes*. Ed. Sir William Molesworth. 11 vols. London: John Bohn, 1839–45.

———. *Leviathan Or the Matter, Forme and Power of a Commonwealth*. Ed. Michael Oakeshott. Oxford: Basil Blackwell, n.d.

Hodges, John C. *William Congreve, The Man: A Biography from New Sources*. New York: Modern Language Association, 1941.

Holdengräber, Paul. "'A Visible History of Art': The Forms and Preoccupations of the Early Museum." *Studies in Eighteenth-Century Culture*, 17 (1987): 107–17.

Holland, Norman. *The First Modern Comedies*. Cambridge, Mass.: Harvard University Press, 1959.

Holland, Peter. *The Ornament of Action: Text and Performance in Restoration Comedy*. Cambridge: Cambridge University Press, 1979.

Hollander, John. *The Figure of Echo: A Mode of Allusion in Milton and After*. Berkeley: University of California Press, 1981.

Hooke, Robert. *Micrographia*. London: Jo. Martin and Ja. Allestry, 1665.

Horace. *The Odes, Satyrs, and Epistles of Horace*. Trans. Thomas Creech. London: Jacob Tonson, 1684.

Howell, A. C. "*Res et Verba*: Words and Things." *English Literary History*, 13 (1946): 131–42.

Howell, Wilbur Samuel. *Logic and Rhetoric in England, 1500–1700*. Princeton, N.J.: Princeton University Press, 1956.

Hume, Robert D. *The Development of English Drama in the Late Seventeenth Century*. Oxford: Clarendon Press, 1976.

Johnson, Samuel. *A Dictionary of the English Language*. 2 vols. London: J. and P. Knapton, 1755.

Jones, Richard Foster. *Ancients and Moderns: A Study of the Rise of the*

Scientific Movement in Seventeenth-Century England. 2d ed. St. Louis, Mo.: Washington University Studies, 1961.

Jonson, Ben. *Ben Jonson*. Ed. C. H. Herford, Percy Simpson, and Evelyn Simpson. Vol. 8. Oxford: Clarendon Press, 1947.

Kernan, Alvin B. *The Imaginary Library*. Princeton, N.J.: Princeton University Press, 1982.

————. *Printing Technology, Letters and Samuel Johnson*. Princeton, N.J.: Princeton University Press, 1987.

Ketcham, Michael G. *Transparent Designs: Reading, Performance, and Form in the Spectator Papers*. Athens: University of Georgia Press, 1985.

Killigrew, Thomas. *Comedies and Tragedies*. London: Henry Herringman, 1664.

Kinkead-Weeks, Mark. *Samuel Richardson, Dramatic Novelist*. Ithaca, N.Y.: Cornell University Press, 1973.

Knowles, Edwin B. "Cervantes and English Literature." In *Cervantes Across the Centuries*. Ed. Angel Flores and M. J. Benardete. New York: Dryden Press, 1947.

Kreutz, Irving. "Who's Holding the Mirror?" *Comparative Drama*, vol. 4, no. 2 (Summer 1970): 79–88.

Kroll, Richard W. F. "Discourse and Power in *The Way of the World*." *English Literary History* (Winter 1986): 727–58.

————. "Hieroglyphs and the Aetiology of Language in Neoclassic Discourse." Typescript of lecture delivered at the North East American Society for Eighteenth-Century Studies Conference, Sept. 1985.

————. "Mise-en-Page, Biblical Criticism and Inference During the Restoration." *Studies in Eighteenth-Century Culture*, 16 (1986): 3–40.

Laqueur, Thomas. "The Cultural Origins of Popular Literacy in England, 1550–1850." *Oxford Review of Education*, 2 (1976).

Leech, Clifford. "Congreve and the Century's End." *Philological Quarterly*, 41 (1962): 275–93.

Levin, Harry. *The Myth of the Golden Age in the Renaissance*. Bloomington: Indiana University Press, 1969.

Levine, Joseph M. *Humanism and History: Origins of Modern English Historiography*. Ithaca, N.Y.: Cornell University Press, 1987.

Lintott, Bernard, ed. *Miscellaneous Poems and Translations by Several Hands*. London, 1714.

Lipking, Lawrence. *The Ordering of the Arts in Eighteenth-Century England*. Princeton, N.J.: Princeton University Press, 1970.

Locke, John. *An Essay Concerning Human Understanding*. Ed. Peter H. Nidditch. Oxford: Clarendon Press, 1975.

——. *The Locke Reader*. Ed. John W. Yolton. Cambridge: Cambridge University Press, 1977.

The London Stage, 1660–1800: A Calendar of Plays. Ed. Emmett L. Avery et al. 12 vols., 6 pts. Carbondale: Southern Illinois University Press, 1960–79.

Lord, Albert B. *The Singer of Tales*. Harvard Studies in Comparative Literature, 24. Cambridge, Mass.: Harvard University Press, 1960.

Lord, George DeForest. *Heroic Mockery*. Newark: University of Delaware Press, 1977.

Love, Harold. *Congreve*. Totowa, N.J.: Rowman and Littlefield, 1975.

Low, Anthony. *The Georgic Revolution*. Princeton, N.J.: Princeton University Press, 1985.

Lyons, Patrick, ed. *Congreve: Comedies*. London: Macmillan, 1982.

McKenzie, D. F. "The British Book Trade, 1641–1714: A Chronology and Calendar of Documents." Typescript. British Library, n.d.

——. *The Cambridge University Press, 1696–1712: A Bibliographical Study*. 2 vols. Cambridge: Cambridge University Press, 1966.

——. "The London Book Trade in the Later Seventeenth Century" (Sandars Lectures, Cambridge, 1976). Typescript. British Library, 1976.

——. "The Sociology of a Text." *The Library*, 6th series, vol. 6, no. 4 (1984): 333–65.

——. "Typography and Meaning: The Case of William Congreve," *Wolfenbütteler Schriften zur Geschichte des Buchwesens*, 4 (1980): 81–125.

——. "When Congreve Made a Scene," *Transactions of the Cambridge Bibliographical Society*, 7 (1979): 338–42.

——, ed. *Stationers' Company Apprentices, 1641–1700*. Oxford: Oxford Bibliographical Society, 1974.

——, ed. *Stationers' Company Apprentices, 1701–1800*. Oxford: Oxford Bibliographical Society, 1978.

McKeon, Michael. *The Origins of the English Novel, 1600–1740*. Baltimore: Johns Hopkins University Press, 1987.

MacLean, Kenneth. *John Locke and English Literature of the Eighteenth Century*. New Haven, Conn.: Yale University Press, 1936.

McLuhan, Marshall. *The Gutenberg Galaxy: The Making of Typographic Man*. London: Routledge and Kegan Paul, 1962.

Malins, Edward. *English Landscaping and Literature, 1660–1840*. Oxford: Oxford University Press, 1966.

Manley, Delariviere. *The Royal Mischief*. London: R. Bentley, F. Saunders, and J. Knapton, 1696.

Mann, David D. "Congreve's Revisions of *The Mourning Bride*." *The Papers of the Bibliographical Society of America*, vol. 69, no. 4 (4th quarter, 1975): 526–46.

Maravall, José Antonio. *Culture of the Baroque: Analysis of a Historical Structure*. Trans. Terry Cochran. Minneapolis: University of Minnesota Press, 1986.

Meisel, Martin. *Shaw and the Nineteenth-Century Theater*. Princeton, N.J.: Princeton University Press, 1963.

Milton, John. *Complete Poems and Major Prose*. Ed. Merritt Y. Hughes. Indianapolis, Ind.: The Odyssey Press, 1957.

Miner, Earl. *Dryden's Poetry*. Bloomington: Indiana University Press, 1967.

————. *The Restoration Mode from Milton to Dryden*. Princeton, N.J.: Princeton University Press, 1974.

Molière. *Œuvres complètes*. Ed. Maurice Rat. 2 vols. Pléiade Edition. Paris: Gallimard, 1956.

Montaigne, Michel de. *Essays*. Trans. J. M. Cohen. New York: Penguin, 1958.

The Mourning Poets: Or, an Account of the Poems on the Death of the Queen. In a Letter to a Friend. London: J. Whitlock, 1695.

Moxon, Joseph. *Mechanick Exercises On the Whole Art of Printing*. London: Joseph Moxon, 1677–83.

Mumby, Frank Arthur. *Publishing and Bookselling. Part One: From the Earliest Times to 1870*. 5th ed. London: Jonathan Cape, 1974.

Nicolson, Marjorie Hope. *The Breaking of the Circle: Studies in the Effect of the "New Science" on Seventeenth-Century Poetry*. Rev. ed. New York: Columbia University Press, 1960.

————. *Science and Imagination*. Ithaca, N.Y.: Cornell University Press, 1956.

Novak, Maximilian E. "Congreve's 'Incognita' and the Art of the Novella." *Criticism*, vol. 11, no. 4 (Fall 1969): 329–42.

————. *William Congreve*. New York: Twayne, 1971.

Oldham, John. *The Works of Mr. John Oldham*. 2 vols. London: D. Brown, B. and S. Tooke, etc., 1722.

Oldmixon, John. *The Grove; or, Love's Paradice.* London: Richard Parker, 1700.

Ong, Walter J. *Orality and Literacy: The Technologizing of the Word.* London: Methuen, 1982.

———. *Ramus, Method, and the Decay of Dialogue.* Cambridge, Mass.: Harvard University Press, 1958.

———. *Rhetoric, Romance, and Technology.* Ithaca, N.Y.: Cornell University Press, 1971.

Osborn, James M. *John Dryden: Some Biographical Facts and Problems.* Rev. ed. Gainesville: University of Florida Press, 1965.

Parnell, Paul. "The Sentimental Mask." *PMLA*, 78 (1963): 529–35.

Parry, Milman. *The Making of Homeric Verse.* Ed. Adam Parry. Oxford: Clarendon Press, 1971.

Pfeiffer, Rudolph. *History of Classical Scholarship from 1300 to 1850.* Oxford: Clarendon Press, 1976.

Plant, Marjorie. *The English Book Trade: An Economic History of the Making and Sale of Books.* 3d ed. London: George Allen & Unwin, 1974.

Plomer, Henry R. *A Dictionary of Printers and Booksellers, 1668–1725.* Oxford: Oxford University Press, 1922.

Pope, Alexander. *The Poems of Alexander Pope.* Ed. John Butt. Twickenham Edition. 11 vols. London: Methuen, 1939–69.

Praz, Mario. *Studies in Seventeenth-Century Imagery.* 2d ed. Rome: Edizioni di Storia e Letteratura, 1964.

Reiss, Timothy J. *The Discourse of Modernism.* Ithaca, N.Y.: Cornell University Press, 1982.

Reynolds, L. D., and N. G. Wilson. *Scribes and Scholars: A Guide to the Transmission of Greek and Latin Literature.* 2d ed. Oxford: Clarendon Press, 1974.

Rivers, Isabel, ed. *Books and Their Readers in Eighteenth-Century England.* Leicester: Leicester University Press, 1982.

Roper, Alan. "Language and Action in *The Way of the World, Love's Last Shift*, and *The Relapse.*" *English Literary History*, 40 (1973): 44–69.

Rothstein, Eric. *Restoration and Eighteenth-Century Poetry, 1660–1780.* Boston: Routledge and Kegan Paul, 1981.

Rycaut, Sir Paul, trans. Garcilasso de la Vega, *Royal Commentaries of Peru.* London: C. Wilkinson, 1688.

Rymer, Thomas. Preface to René Rapin, *Reflections on Aristotle's Treatise of Poesie.* Trans. Rymer. London: H. Herringman, 1674.

Salerno, Luigi. "Seventeenth-Century English Literature on Painting." *Journal of the Warburg and Courtauld Institutes*, 14 (1951): 234–58.

Saunders, J. W. *The Profession of English Letters*. London: Routledge and Kegan Paul, 1964.

Scholes, Robert, and Robert Kellogg. *The Nature of Narrative*. London: Oxford University Press, 1966.

Scouten, Arthur H., and Robert D. Hume, " 'Restoration Comedy' and Its Audiences, 1660–1776." *Yearbook of English Studies*, 10 (1980): 45–69.

Seidel, Michael. *Satiric Inheritance: Rabelais to Sterne*. Princeton, N.J.: Princeton University Press, 1979.

Sennett, Richard. *The Fall of Public Man*. New York: Knopf, 1977.

Shakespeare, William. *As You Like It*. Ed. Agnes Latham. Arden Edition. London: Methuen, 1975.

———. *King Richard II*. Ed. Peter Ure. Arden Edition. New York: Methuen, 1961.

Shell, Marc. *Money, Language, and Thought*. Berkeley: University of California Press, 1982.

Simpson, Percy. *Proof-Reading in the Sixteenth, Seventeenth and Eighteenth Centuries*. London: Oxford University Press, 1935.

Sorel, Charles. *Le Berger extravagant*. Rouen: I. Berthelin, 1639.

Southerne, Thomas. *The Fatal Marriage: Or, The Innocent Adultery*. London: Jacob Tonson, 1694.

Spence, Joseph. *Observations, Anecdotes, and Characters of Books and Men*. Ed. James M. Osborn. 2 vols. Oxford: Clarendon Press, 1966.

Sprat, Thomas. *The History of the Royal Society*. London: J. Martyn and J. Allestry, 1667.

Spufford, Margaret. *Small Books and Pleasant Histories*. London: Methuen, 1981.

Stallybrass, Peter, and Allon White. *The Politics and Poetics of Transgression*. Ithaca, N.Y.: Cornell University Press, 1986.

Steele, Sir Richard. *The Conscious Lovers*. Ed. Shirley Strum Kenny. Lincoln: University of Nebraska Press, 1968.

Steinberg, S. H. *Five Hundred Years of Printing*. Middlesex: Penguin Books, 1955.

Steiner, George. *After Babel: Aspects of Language and Translation*. London: Oxford University Press, 1975.

Stephens, F. G., ed. *Political and Personal Satires*. Vols. 1–2. London: British Museum, 1870–73.

Stephenson, Peter S. "Congreve's 'Incognita': The Popular Spanish Novella Form Burlesqued." *Studies in Short Fiction*, vol. 9, no. 4 (Fall 1972): 333–42.

Stone, Lawrence. "Literacy and Education in England 1640–1900." *Past and Present*, 42 (1969): 69–139.

Suckling, John. *Aglaura*. London: Humphrey Mosely, 1658.

Sutherland, James. *English Literature of the Late Seventeenth Century*. Oxford: Clarendon Press, 1969.

———. *The Restoration Newspaper and Its Development*. Cambridge: Cambridge University Press, 1986.

Swift, Jonathan. *The Prose Works of Jonathan Swift*. Ed. Herbert Davis. 14 vols. Oxford: Basil Blackwell, 1948–68.

Tave, Stuart M. *The Amiable Humorist*. Chicago: University of Chicago Press, 1960.

Tayler, Edward W. *Nature and Art in Renaissance Literature*. New York: Columbia University Press, 1964.

Tompkins, Jane P. "The Reader in History." In *Reader-Response: From Formalism to Post-Structuralism*. Ed. Tompkins. Baltimore: Johns Hopkins University Press, 1980. Pp. 201–32.

Treadwell, J. M. "Congreve, Tonson, and Rowe's 'Reconcilement.'" *Notes and Queries*, 22 (June 1975): 265–69.

Trickett, Rachel. *The Honest Muse: A Study in Augustan Verse*. Oxford: Clarendon Press, 1967.

Trilling, Lionel. *Sincerity and Authenticity*. Cambridge, Mass.: Harvard University Press, 1971.

Tuan, Yi-Fu. *Segmented Worlds and Self*. Minneapolis: University of Minnesota Press, 1982.

Tuveson, Ernest. *The Imagination as a Means of Grace: Locke and the Aesthetics of Romanticism*. Berkeley: University of California Press, 1960.

———. "Locke and Sterne." In *English Literature and British Philosophy*. Ed. S. P. Rosenbaum. Chicago: University of Chicago Press, 1971. Pp. 86–108.

Underwood, Dale. *Etherege and the Seventeenth-Century Comedy of Manners*. Hamden, Conn.: Archon Books, 1969.

Vanbrugh, Sir John. *The Provoked Wife*. Ed. Curt A. Zimansky. Lincoln: University of Nebraska Press, 1969.

Van Voris, W. H. *The Cultivated Stance: The Design of Congreve's Plays*. Dublin: The Dolmen Press, 1965.

Velz, John W. " 'Pirate Hills' and the Quartos of *Julius Caesar.*" *The Papers of the Bibliographical Society of America*, vol. 63, 3d quarter (1969): 177–93.

A view of part of the many Traiterous . . . Actions of H[enry] H[ills] senior, sometimes Printer to Cromwel, to the Commonwealth, to the anabaptist congregation. London, 1684.

Wagstaffe, William. *Some Memoirs of the Life of Abel, Toby's Uncle.* London: T. Warner, 1726.

Waith, Eugene M. "Aristophanes, Plautus, Terence, and the Refinement of English Comedy." *Studies in the Literary Imagination*, vol. 10, no. 1 (Spring 1977): 91–108.

Ward, Edward. *Sot's Paradise.* London, 1698.

Warner, William B. *Reading Clarissa: The Struggles of Interpretation.* New Haven, Conn.: Yale University Press, 1979.

Warnke, Frank. *Versions of Baroque: European Literature in the Seventeenth Century.* New Haven, Conn.: Yale University Press, 1972.

Watt, Ian. *The Rise of the Novel.* Berkeley: University of California Press, 1957.

Weinbrot, Howard D. *Augustus Caesar in "Augustan" England.* Princeton, N.J.: Princeton University Press, 1978.

————. *The Formal Strain: Studies in Augustan Imitation and Satire.* Chicago: University of Chicago Press, 1969.

Weintraub, Karl Joachim. *The Value of the Individual.* Chicago: University of Chicago Press, 1978.

Whitney, Lois. *Primitivism and the Idea of Progress in English Popular Literature of the Eighteenth Century.* Baltimore: The Johns Hopkins Press, 1934.

Wilde, Oscar. *The Complete Works of Oscar Wilde.* Ed. Edgar Saltus. Vol. 5. Garden City, N.Y.: Doubleday, 1923.

Williams, Aubrey L. *An Approach to Congreve.* New Haven, Conn.: Yale University Press, 1979.

Williams, Raymond. *Keywords: A Vocabulary of Culture and Society.* Rev. ed. New York: Oxford University Press, 1985.

Williamson, George. *The Senecan Amble: A Study in Prose from Bacon to Collier.* London: Faber, 1951.

Wimsatt, William K. *The Portraits of Alexander Pope.* New Haven, Conn.: Yale University Press, 1965.

Wing, Donald. *Short Title Catalogue, 1641–1700.* New York: Modern Language Association, 1972.

Winn, James Anderson. *John Dryden and His World*. New Haven, Conn.: Yale University Press, 1987.

————. "On Pope, Printers, and Publishers." *Eighteenth-Century Life*, vol. 6, n.s. 2/3 (Jan. and May 1981): 92–102.

Winstanley, William. *The Lives of the Most Famous English Poets*. London: Samuel Manship, 1687.

Wordsworth, William. *The Poetical Works of Wordsworth*. Ed. Thomas Hutchinson. Rev. by Ernest de Selincourt. London: Oxford University Press, 1959.

Wotton, William. *Reflections Upon Ancient and Modern Learning*. 2d ed. London: Peter Buck, 1697.

Wycherley, William. *The Country Wife*. Ed. Thomas H. Fujimura. Lincoln: University of Nebraska Press, 1965.

Yates, Frances. *Giordano Bruno and the Hermetic Tradition*. London: Routledge and Kegan Paul, 1964.

————. *The Rosicrucian Enlightenment*. London: Routledge and Kegan Paul, 1972.

Index

In this index an "f" after a number indicates a separate reference on the next page, and an "ff" indicates separate references on the next two pages. A continuous discussion over two or more pages is indicated by a span of page numbers, e.g., "pp. 57–58." *Passim* is used for a cluster of references in close but not consecutive sequence.

Library of Congress Cataloging-in-Publication Data

Peters, Julie Stone.
   Congreve, the drama, and the printed word / Julie Stone Peters.
      p.   cm.
   Includes bibliographical references (p.   )
   ISBN 0-8047-1751-6 (alk. paper) :
      1. Congreve, William, 1670–1729—Knowledge—Book arts
and sciences.   2. Congreve, William, 1670–1729—Publishers.
3. Drama—Publishing—England—History—17th century.
4. Printing—England—History—17th century.   5. Theater—
England—History—17th century.   I. Title.
PR3368.B58P4   1990
822'.4—dc20   89-26167
                                                      CIP

   ∞ This book is printed on acid-free paper